# TRIAL BY BASKETBALL

## THE LIFE AND
## TIMES OF
# TEX
# WINTER

# TRIAL BY BASKETBALL

## THE LIFE AND TIMES OF
# TEX WINTER

BY
MARK BENDER

FOREWORD BY
PHIL JACKSON

ADDAX
PUBLISHING
G R O U P

Lenexa, Kansas

Nelson Elliott
Managing Editor

Judy Widener
Editor

Randy Breeden
Art Direction/Design

Laura Bolter
Dust Jacket Design

Photos courtesy Tex Winter and as noted

Published by Addax Publishing Group, Inc.

Copyright © 2000 American Biography, L.L.C.

A work of American Biography, L.L.C.

For information address:

Addax Publishing Group, Inc.

8643 Hauser Drive, Suite 235, Lenexa, KS 66215

ISBN: 1-886110-90-5

Printed in the U.S.A.

1 3 5 7 9 10 8 6 4 2

ATTENTION: SCHOOLS AND BUSINESSES

Addax Publishing Group, Inc. books are available at quantity discounts with bulk purchase for education, business, or sales promotional use. For information, please write to: Special Sales Department, Addax Publishing Group, 8643 Hauser Drive,

Suite 235, Lenexa, KS 66215

# DEDICATED TO COACH DON J. ODLE

Who coached the Taylor University Trojan basketball team for decades and co-founded, with Marion Crawley, Taylor Basketball Camp—where I spent the summers of my youth learning the game.

Don was a tremendous innovator, motivator and communicator. I still remember his jokes. His camp, founded in Upland Indiana in the late 1950s, became a model for myriads of sports camps that have sprouted around the country. He made the game fun. At the end of his clinics he would shoot the basketball through the old Maytag Gym rafters with amazing accuracy, gracefully arcing the ball with his powerful wrists.

Don Odle, like Tex, realized early on that besides being a great game, basketball is also a venue for character-building.

Thanks, Coach.

M. B.

# TABLE OF CONTENTS

Dedication .................................................................5

Acknowledgments ......................................................9

Foreword ...............................................................13

Prologue ...............................................................17

Chapter One: Trifles ................................................27

Chapter Two: Things Were Worse in California ...............35

Chapter Three: Spring is Here, Winter Must Go ..............53

Chapter Four: The Triangle .......................................73

Chapter Five: Traveling Violations ..............................91

Chapter Six: Traveling Violations, The Sequel .............109

Chapter Seven: Tex Winter, Consultant......................125

Chapter Eight: Calves to Bulls ................................155

Chapter Nine: Easy as 1-2-3 ...................................171

Chapter Ten: Flying Without Michael.........................187

Chapter Eleven: Return of the Jedi ...........................201

Chapter Twelve: Send in the Clowns .........................219

Chapter Thirteen: Forgotten Championship .................241

Chapter Fourteen: Mud on the Horns ........................251

Chapter Fifteen: Last Tango in Utah .........................269

Chapter Sixteen: Escape to L.A. ...............................281

Epilogue ...............................................................299

# ACKNOWLEDGMENTS

Heartfelt thanks to Tex and Nancy Winter for letting me undertake this project, and for their fearlessness in allowing me to candidly portray their lives. I also appreciate their patience as I worked to get the facts straight and their assistance in finding materials from which I could work. Any errors made are my own.

I am grateful to the staff and brain trust of American Biography for support throughout the effort: President Bill Hart for his vision, direction and undaunted courage in the face of the many adversities the project faced; General Counsel Nick Winter who edited, advised and inspired; Jeff Givens, Bill Lawson, Steve Newell, S. Townley Meyer and Myra Sturm, for their insights and ready assistance.

Thanks to Brian Winter for his research and exegesis on the triangle and Tom Bender for his work with the text and title. Bob Snodgrass and Nelson Elliott at the Addax Publishing Group were a pleasure to work with.

Also helpful were Anthony R. Crawford, Associate Professor and Chair of the Morse Department of Special Collections for the Kansas State University Libraries and assistant Sarah Coddington.

President Jimmy Carter's *The Virtues of Aging* and James Hillman's *The Soul's Code: In Search of Character and Calling* were helpful backdrops in evaluating the life of Tex Winter.

Discussions of free-throw shooting were augmented by references to Ted St. Martin's *The Art of Shooting Baskets* and *Free Throw: Seven Steps to Success at the Free Throw Line* by Dr. Tom Amberry with Phillip Reed.

David Smale's *The Ahearn Tradition* and *The Purple Pinnacle* were tremendous resources on Kansas State athletics and James C. Carey's *Kansas State University: The Quest for Identity* was helpful in understanding the institution that Tex Winter continues to root for to this day.

The late Wilt Chamberlain's *A View from Above*, *Who's Running the Asylum*, and *Wilt: Just Like Any Other 7-Foot Black Millionaire Who Lives Next Door* with David Shaw were helpful in appreciating this superb athlete and his accomplishments.

*They Call Me "The Big E"* by Elvin Hayes and Bill Gilbert was an interesting story that included Tex's time with the Houston Rockets as was *A Rocket at Heart* by Rudy Tomjanovich with Robert Falkoff.

Dale Brown's *LSU Basketball Organizational Handbook* was helpful in understanding the LSU basketball program at the time Tex assisted there, as was his book with Don Yaeger, *Tiger in the Lion's Den*. *Fighting Tigers Basketball* by Joe Hunter and Joe Planas was also helpful.

Big college games were chronicled by Blair Kerkhoff in *A Century of Jayhawk Triumphs* and in *Fifty Years of the Final Four* by Billy Packer with Roland Lazenby. *The Complete Book of the Olympics* by David Wallechinsky and *Chronicle of the Olympics* by Dorling Kindersley were valuable resources.

Roland Lazenby's incomparable *Blood on the Horns* was a gold mine of information into the Chicago Bulls and is a must-read for anyone seeking to understand the agonies and ecstasies of the Bulls dynasty. His *Bull Run!* is a fascinating chronicle of the Bulls epic 1995-96 season.

A number of books focusing on the career of Michael Jordan were also helpful: *Taking to the Air* by Jim Naughton, Sam Smith's entertaining and insightful *The Jordan Rules*, Bob Greene's *Rebound: The Odyssey of Michael Jordan*, David Halberstam's *Playing for Keeps*, and Michael Jordan's own *For the Love of the Game*, edited by Mark Vancil. Melissa

Isaacson's *Transition Game* was a great record of the Bulls performance during Jordan's baseball hiatus.

Phil Jackson's *Maverick* with Charles Rosen and *Sacred Hoops* with Hugh Delehanty were helpful in understanding the life and philosophies of a man Tex Winter loves and admires.

Dennis Rodman's *Bad as I Wanna Be* with Tim Keown and his *Walk on the Wild Side* with Michael Silver were fun reads that revealed the character who enlivened Tex's life for three seasons.

Terry Pluto's *Falling From Grace: Can Pro Basketball be Saved?* gave insights into issues confronting the game and Nelson George's *Elevating the Game: Black Men and Basketball* superbly detailed the contributions of black athletes. Similarly, Ralph Hickok's *A Who's Who of Sports Champions*, Dave Anderson's *The Story of Basketball*, and the 24th edition of the *Complete Handbook of Pro Basketball* were full of useful facts and details.

And of course *The Triple-Post Offense* by Fred "Tex" Winter.

I want to acknowledge the work of numerous writers and reporters who cover the sport, including Nancy Armour, Terry Armour, Lacy Banks, Skip Bayless, Howard Beck, Zack Burgess, Kevin Ding, David DuPree, Mark Heisler, Melissa Isaacson, John Jackson, Mark Janssen, Kim Kawakami, Bernie Linicome, Bill Mahoney, Eric Matuszewski, Jim McCormick, Fred Mitchell, Roman Modrowski, David Leon Moore, Mike Nadel, Michael O'Shea, Kent Pulliam, Steve Rosenbloom, Rich Sambol, Chris Shendan, Sam Smith, Phil Taylor and others.

I made use of a variety of publications, including *Sports Illustrated*, *Hoop Magazine*, *Time*, *Newsweek*, *The Sporting News*, *ESPN Magazine*, *Chicago Tribune*, *Chicago Sun-Times*, *Orange County Register*, *Los Angeles Times*, *Kansas City Star*, *USA Today*, *Manhattan Mercury*, *Seattle Times*, *The Oregonian*, *Press-Telegram*, *Daily Forty-Niner* and *The New York Times*.

# FOREWORD

It was with great anticipation that I met Fred "Tex" Winter in 1987, while I was interviewing for the assistant coaching job with the Bulls. I had seen "Coach" on TV, coaching college ball and on the bench with the Houston Rockets in his abbreviated stint in the NBA. I was curious because Bulls General Manager Jerry Krause swore by the character of this man, Tex Winter. I had been interviewed two years previously by the Bulls but hadn't been hired. Krause had hired Tex immediately and told me Tex was going to be the advisor to the coaching staff — in effect, the coach's coach. Jerry told me about going to Kansas State as a young scout, sitting in the stands and watching this man coach good — but not great — talent to winning seasons in a very tough conference. Tex had a concept about how the game should be played.

Two years later and not a lot had happened to the Bulls, except they had changed head coaches, with Doug Collins taking Stan Albeck's position. They still were placing eighth in the division, playing three games in the first round of the playoffs and going home for the summer, but with the young Michael Jordan, they were a very exciting team to watch. The assistant coaching position I was to fill was that of the scout — the leg man. It required traveling the NBA, watching teams play and writing reports. I would be paired with Johnny Bach, another coach of great repute, the defensive scout for the team.

During the interview, Tex Winter hadn't said much as the coaching staff talked basketball. He waited until I was into the work year to build a relationship with me. At the insistence of Krause, he gave me a copy of his book, *The Triple Post Offense*. I was informed by Krause that Tex would be teaching the summer league players. During my first summer, I would be his assistant and learn "the offense."

After coaching in the minor leagues for four years, I spent my first year in the pros learning all about the NBA and the styles of game in the league. So I was curious and determined to figure out the historical element to the style of play coaches used. Tex and Johnny Bach would sit in the office with me and discuss the styles of game and how they evolved. It was an education because they had come from two different places in America — New York City and Los Angeles — as high school players. Both had been in the service during World War II, then played ball in college. They had seen the transformation of basketball from a set-shot game to the athletic ballet the present game had become. Tex, however, had a philosophy of basketball — a style he insisted of how the game should look and be played, yet he never put down any other style of play. Tex was a basketball sage.

During the next two summers, I received the hands-on experience coaching with Tex. He had the best build-up drills for incorporating the simplest skill into the most sophisticated offense in basketball. He insisted on the details and made the players mind their business, yet he wasn't overbearing or oppressive as a coach. It was two years of the best basketball education I could have received. In 1989 when the Bulls made me the head coach, I was willing to bet the world we could win an NBA championship using the triangle offense. Little did I imagine we would win six NBA titles, but the offense wouldn't have mattered if Tex hadn't used his skill as a practice coach to build in the drills necessary to execute the offense. He was the best skill coach.

Our relationship has flourished over the nine years we were in Chicago together and now in L.A. with the Lakers. I consider him a vital part of my ability to coach. He sits beside me during the games and writes down each possession for each team. A game doesn't go much farther than a couple of minutes before he and I are discussing what's happening to the team. There isn't a person on the floor who isn't above the ire of Tex's criticism. If they are hurting the team's effort, he won't hesitate to let them or me know. The number of times he asked me to remove Michael Jordan from the game because he was hurting the ability of the team to play ball together is incalculable. It may seem unsound, but his reasoning was always in the best interest of how the team was moving the ball or playing together. Our arguments have become almost historical and hysterical, but we have argued with the best humor and greatest respect for each other.

I value Tex as a teacher and a mentor, but his value as a person of good character is even more important. His respect and loyalty are unparalleled. I thank God and my lucky nature for the opportunity I've had to work with this man for the past decade. With his help, I expect to win another title with the Los Angeles Lakers.

Phil Jackson

*Tex has a twin sister down in Texas. Her name is Mona. They're as different as night and day, except for one thing — they will tell you the unvarnished truth.*

— Nancy Winter, November, 1998

# PROLOGUE

Nancy Winter is making omelettes, at the same time filling me in on life with Tex. There is a lot to tell. The Winters recently celebrated their golden wedding anniversary. They've been married as long as Tex has been coaching basketball.

I can hear Tex in another conversation off to my left — "Plan A is everybody back, Plan B is Michael, Plan C is Michael and Scottie, Plan D is … it's hard to plan … I'm anxious to get started."

It is mid-November 1998 and the NBA lockout has delayed the start of the season. At a time in life when most men are anxious to take a nap, Fred "Tex" Winter is anxious to leave his expansive new house in the Chicago suburb of Deerfield and begin flying around the country on a schedule not his own. Anxious to teach young millionaires the fundamentals of basketball, anxious for the rantings of hostile crowds and the tough questions from a media possessed with the Chicago Bulls. Anxious to get started.

He is shorter than expected. I could guard this guy. He's looks like any of the 50-somethings I hold these days at the Fort Leavenworth gym. Except he's 76. He is handsome and relaxed, with a thick head of silver-gray hair, cut in Perry Como style.

Michael Jordan's two volume set, *For the Love of the Game*, sits prominently on a display case, a full face portrait of Michael, looking angelic, on the cover. Tex picks it up and drops it, bouncing it on the hardwood floor, crushing a corner, tearing the cardboard case. It is an awkward moment, but it doesn't phase the Coach. There is no damage assessment.

"I'm not overly impressed with Michael Jordan," he says. "Impressed, but not overly impressed. There are still parts of his game that need work — fundamentals. He's gotten better, but he can get better still, though he's certainly the best ever to play the game."

Remington sculptures adorn the great room, symbols of his western past. "I don't much care for this one," he says in passing. A cowboy lies prostrate on the ground, a bronco rearing over him.

A Bulls championship banner hangs in the foyer. There are two more underneath. And the others? A nice problem to have. What to do with the banners.

I have known my share of coaches. Guys that blew-up under the strain, guys that could win them all except the big one, guys that never won anything. Guys that won the big games early in their careers, and could never do it again. Guys that are now stockbrokers and insurance salesmen.

The best coaches have a physical presence that can make you do what you thought you couldn't do because of their belief in you; others can keep you from doing what you could have done with their disdain.

I love coaches. I love the idea of coaches. Where else in society do we have this concept? What greater compliment than to call someone "Coach."

At last we find a basketball. A red and black one, Bulls colors. I ask Tex about hand placement for the jump shot. Should the ball touch the fat of the right hand? "No," he says and demonstrates, the ball resting on his thick, powerful fingers, with air between the ball and the palm of the hand. Noting my disappointment at his response he adds — "But then Scottie Pippen holds it down on the hand and he's had some success that way."

Tex takes out a copy of Naismith's original basketball rules, tied scroll-like with a red ribbon. "Many of them still apply," he notes. "You still can't strike the ball with your fist."

"No running with the ball either," I add.

"Naismith would turn over in his grave if he saw how we were applying that rule today," says Tex. "Players are palming the ball and routinely taking an extra step to the basket. It makes it tough on the defender, but I suppose it's fun to watch."

We move to the great room, and Tex begins channel surfing, searching for the score of the Kansas State-Missouri football game. "I'm still a K-State fan," he says, "it will always be home to me." And well it should be. Winter spent 15 seasons at State, winning eight conference championships and building the best regular season record of any coach in conference history. Leading the Wildcats to four top-ten rankings, Winter was UPI Coach of the Year there in 1958, and was the only coach or player in K-State history to be associated with all four of their Final Four appearances.

We happen onto a sports history basketball game. The 1971-72 Lakers with Wilt Chamberlain and Jerry West are playing the Milwaukee Bucks with Kareem Abdul-Jabbar and Oscar Robertson. Wilt throws up two pitiful free throw attempts.

"Wilt was the most physically imposing player of his era," Tex opines, "like Shaquille O'Neal can be. He precipitated rule changes. I was on the coaches' board when he was in college at Kansas. When he was a freshman he could get a running start from the top of the circle, take off at the free-throw line and dunk the free throw. They had an out of bounds play where they would in-bound the ball by passing it up over the backboard. Wilt would catch it above the rim and dunk it down. I told the board 'I don't know what you guys are doing, but when he comes to my gym I'm putting chicken wire above the backboard.' Wilt still called me 'that little coach at Kansas State who tried to legislate me out of the game.' "

West passes lamely across the middle. The pass is intercepted.

The players look skinny, anemic. We surf for football scores, passing a hockey game. "I don't understand hockey," says Tex, moving on quickly.

West commits another turnover. "He's having a bad game," I venture.

"He's one of the very best," Tex corrects. "He could play with today's players, if he put on weight. Every player you see out there would have benefited from weight training."

West dribbles to the right baseline and in one silky motion pivots and buries a jump shot. A work of art, the coach and I exchange glances. It is as if West were responding to his accolade.

"Milwaukee is running the triangle," says Tex. "Right there, that was a guard squeeze. This must be '72. The Lakers are riding a 33-game win streak. Larry Costello is coaching the Bucks. He and Del Harris asked me to meet them at a hotel room. I was at Northwestern. They were after more teamwork, and we talked about the triangle. See that? That's a wing quickie."

No, I do not see that. I do see Oscar Robertson glide through a maze of players and arch a jump shot high over everyone. What he did to get there is a mystery to me.

"Oscar made the game look easy, he was probably the most efficient player to ever play the game. The first time I watched him I thought he was loafing. We played him while he was at Cincinnati in the '58 Midwest Regional Finals — what *Sports Illustrated* called the 'game of the year.' Oscar drove the lane with a second left in regulation and Boozer was charged with a block — though it looked like a charge to me. He hit the first free throw and walked around celebrating and missed the second. Then we beat 'em in overtime."

Jabbar blocks a Chamberlain shot attempt.

"I think we played Wilt the week before the Cincinnati game with Robertson. It might have been the Big Seven Championship — the last college game Wilt played. We put a man in front of him and a man behind and hoped they wouldn't hit their outside shots. They didn't and we won."

Bill Sharman is coaching the Lakers. "Played with him in college." Tex recalls, " I was a senior and he was a freshmen. Nice guy — and you could see he was going to be a great player."

Is there anyone Tex Winter doesn't know?

"That's Richie Powers reffing, he was absolutely the very best."

Hap Hairston takes out Jabbar under the basket and a fight erupts. It passes without comment.

"That's a weak-side sneak. It's better to name plays or sequences rather than number them. It creates a nomenclature that improves communication and imaging. Coaches should have a syllabus, a system of plays, and a philosophy. That's why the triangle has stuck to me, because I wrote the book. Your scouts have to understand the system too, so they can find players that fit. Paxson and Kerr are perfect examples for our team. As spot-up shooters, they fit our system because they provided Michael a credible scoring option he could count on."

Milwaukee wins the game, ending the Lakers win streak.

"That was good tape," says Tex. "I gotta get that tape."


Tex routinely drove Phil Jackson to home games. He insists on driving by Phil's house, as if to confirm what he has tried to deny. The Jacksons have moved. There's a "For Sale" sign on the front lawn and handouts are available. They've lowered the asking price.

Tex drives his big Oldsmobile hard through the neighborhood curves, then slows on a long straightaway "where the deer are." He drives like he lives, hard at times, but always with a certain conservatism, easing to stops, conserving fuel. Stopping at a red light his eyes continue ranging right and left, like a guard leading a fast break or a fighter pilot looking for trouble.

"The Olds is a company car," he says. "They give us a new one every 5,000 miles." He says it as though he can hardly believe his good fortune. "It's a great car, but the engineers kind of screwed up the ergonomics. They've got the light switch next to the gas door release."

Nancy is an able co-pilot. "Gas?"

"Yes, topped off yesterday."

We are headed for Jimmy's Char House, though neither Tex or Nancy are sure where it is or whether Harry Caray ever owned it. By his own admission Tex never played baseball and knows little about the game or the personalities associated with it. Tex spies a passerby and asks directions.

"Right here," Nancy commands suddenly. Tex instantly reacts right and in the same instant brings the vehicle back, correctly identifying Nancy's right as a short dead-end into a construction site.

"Pretty smooth, Coach," I offer, thankful to be alive.

"I could land on a carrier today if I had to, especially the big ones."

"Tex was a naval aviator during the war," Nancy explains.

I dismount the vehicle while Tex looks for a place to park. "The name is Winter, Tex Winter of the Chicago Bulls," I whisper to the maitre'd. "He'll be here in a couple minutes." The maitre'd does a double take. I'm not sure he believes me.

Tex's arrival creates a stir and way is made at the bar. A round of cheer appears. Tex passes his championship ring around. A young woman befriends him. Soon she is deep into his space, massaging him. "This is so cool … so incredible … I can't believe … I don't get this lockout … please explain it to me."

And then Tex is explaining "It's simple …" Nancy is just now noticing that the woman is all over Tex.

"Did ya hear anything?" he asks of Joe Blow, as if Joe Blow just returned from a back room session with David Stern. Another round appears. Not just for Tex but for all of us. Mine is a double vodka. I try to remember the last time a stranger bought me a drink. I try to forget the four years of misery down the road at Wheaton College, where drinking was verboten, where I struggled unsuccessfully in college athletics. I deserve this double. Here's to you, dear Wheaton.

For those of us who labor in anonymity it is difficult to imagine the buzz that accompanies Tex Winter in Chicago. It's not the frantic, disruptive gotta-get-an-autograph frenzy of a Michael Jordan sighting, but a friendly and respectful admiration that is altogether pleasing; an embrace.

Our table is ready. The one in the back, where the mob would sit if they were with us tonight. Tex and I sit with our backs to the corner. The masses beam appreciatively. It's a big night in this little corner of Chicago. "Sat right next to Tex Winter last night at Char's," they will say, and Mom will tell junior, "I tried on the ring!"

In the '60s my dad would take members of the New York Yankees to church on Sunday mornings in Chicago. It was impossible to slip in quietly. It was like a little bit of Jesus had returned. An otherworldly glow enveloped our pew; people just had to look. Attendance would spike for weeks afterward.

The maitre'd appears and is giving Tex his business card. I fight successfully for the tab, it is half of what it should be. "If you ever want to bring Michael ..." Tex cuts him off, "If I ever see him again ..."

It is close to midnight now. Tex and Nancy have retired for the evening. Nick Winter, Tex's nephew, and I are sifting through size 13 and a half shoeboxes, Michael Jordan's, in search of treasure. The TV drones irrelevantly in the background.

Jimmy and Rosalynn Carter are on *Hardball* and Chris Matthews is drooling all over them. Carter has a new book out, *The Virtues of Aging*. According to Carter a man his age, 74, has a life expectancy of 15 more years.

In a box marked "old glasses" we find old glasses. The boxes themselves are worth a fortune, after all they're Michael's, and he breaks out a new pair of shoes for each game. The litany of clipped articles grows strange —

"How does Michael Fly?"

"The Progression of the Pole Vault Record."

Martin Luther King's "I Have a Dream" speech.

"Remembering a Pioneer Black Coach — Will Robinson."

"Should Athletes be Expected to Act as Role Models?"

"Cocaine — Its Effect on the Brain."

There's an April 1990 article entitled, "Phil Jackson, Then and Now." It has two pictures of Jackson. In one he's posting up as a Knick, reaching out to the ball, a look of crazed ecstasy on his bearded face. I have seen that face somewhere — Charles Manson. The second is Coach Phil in tie and jacket, left hand in pocket, the right arm pointing directly at something on the floor. Again the look is otherworldly, strange.

There's a large manilla envelope. The words "Youthful Secrets" is written directly over the name of Brad Sellers. In the upper right hand corner are the words — "Clippings on Doug Firing!" In the envelope are clippings on the Doug Collins' firing — I was hoping for youthful secrets.

In a box of its own, a color cut-out of an NBA Championship trophy.


The Winters have had dreams in the new house. "The red rock," says Tex. "I dream about a giant red rock near Wellington, Texas, that my dad would drive us by. I'd cry every time we passed it, sure it would fall on us. I see that rock in my dreams."

"I dream about our players being gone," Nancy says. "I'm at the United Center and we're playing the Pacers and Michael and Scottie aren't there. Tex is saying he can make it work but it looks like the Alamo down there. The scary part, where it just gets too surreal is when Bird starts celebrating, that's when I wake-up. It's horrible."

"The foul on Pippen in '94," said Tex, "that's the worst nightmare … no … Jeff Simons' shot in the tournament game at K-State. It goes in. It literally goes in, rolls around and spins back out. There's no way it can come out but it always does. I've dreamt about that many times."

It's 2:30 a.m. at the Winter home and I have dreamt some kind of nightmarish metaphor for the start of a season — or a book. Going through Tex's shoeboxes must have thrown me into information overload; I am realizing, straight through to my subconscious, what it takes for a player to take on an NBA season, what it will mean to take on the life of Tex Winter. In the dream, Michael and Dennis are branded in a fraternity rite, each clutching a basketball and taking the pain. Then it is my turn. I wrap my arms around the ball and hold on. The branding iron sears my shoulder; I am being honored with the Omega scar. I hold my scream until the iron is ground into one of serifs, then can take it no longer. "We got it," someone says.

Awake now and shaken, I return to the shoeboxes.

*Great events hang by a thread. The able man turns everything to profit, neglects nothing that may give him one chance more; the man of less ability by overlooking just one thing, spoils the whole.*

— Napoleon Bonaparte

*I came here with the physical skills. To some degree, I was built with the appetite to enhance them as I got older and as I played the game. The mental skills come with the education of the game. I learned them from Coach Smith or from the coaching staffs I've been associated with, Tex Winter being the most important because he probably criticized my game more than anybody. To me, that's a plus and a driving force.*

— Michael Jordan, in his retirement remarks at the United Center, January 13, 1999

# CHAPTER ONE
# TRIFLES

Mona Frances Winter was born to Ernest and Theo Winter February 25, 1922, in Wellington, Texas. Fifteen minutes later the doctor informed Theo she had another one on the way. "No, no, no," she responded. She gave the second child, a boy, to the doctor, who offered to keep the child. Later, Theo asked for him back; it was a misunderstanding, she said. They named him Morice Fredrick Winter. It was only after the family migrated to California 14 years later to escape the Dust Bowl that he would become known as "Tex."

"Michael's giving defense a lick and a promise," Tex said to Phil Jackson. Maybe it was understandable, with Jordan carrying so much of the load in Game Six. Scottie Pippen was a mere shadow of his former self with intense back pain and Ron Harper was struggling with a stomach illness. But it was Tex's job to point out what he saw to Phil. The two were good that way, sharing and deciphering information. They both knew Michael was rationing his energy, hoping to keep the Bulls in the ballgame, hoping to have something left at crunch time.

It is the second time around with the Utah Jazz in the battle for the 1998 NBA title, and NBA history teaches that last year's runner-up will be back to win the championship — and the Jazz — are favored. Utah wins Game One on John Stockton's heroics — a last-second shot in overtime.

The triangle works perfectly in the first half of Game Two, but Tex watches helplessly as the team abandons it in the second half, barely hanging on to win. Game Three is all Bulls — the biggest rout in NBA history. However, before Game Four, Dennis Rodman misses practice to appear on *Wrestlemania* and is fined $10,000. Despite the distraction, Rodman hits two decisive free throws at the end of the game and the Bulls win to go up 3-1.

The Bulls lose Game Five at the United Center and must travel to Salt Lake City's Delta Center for Game Six. It's the second loudest arena Tex has experienced in his 50-plus years of coaching — the loudest being Ahearn Fieldhouse where he coached the Kansas State Wildcats. "The crowd wouldn't let you lose," he often said of the frenzy created in those years. The Bulls were bucking that same sensation in Salt Lake City.

The Bulls trailed at halftime, 42-37. That was OK, thought Tex, they were still in it. Utah had failed to capitalize on numerous opportunities to put the game away. If they could just stay close. Get it down to the trifles, where the Bulls always seemed to have the advantage. "Everything turns on a trifle," Tex liked to say. He had dedicated himself to preparing a team for the tri- fles, teaching them to pivot on trifles, to expect and capitalize on them.

Pippen gamely returned in the second half. Though unable to perform to his usual standard, he was an effective decoy in the offensive scheme. The Jazz failed to put the game away, carrying only a five-point lead into the fourth quarter. The Bulls pulled even with five minutes to play, the tide of history moving inexorably to their side.

The players were tiring — all of them. It took a 76-year-old man to point it out to Phil Jackson, noting the change in Jordan as he began missing jump shots, "Look, he can't get any elevation in his shot; his legs are gone." Winter, Jackson and Jordan knew what that meant — it was time to go inside. Inside, where the fouls are, where the big boys wait to pun- ish; where anything can happen.

With three minutes left, Jackson gave Michael his cue, "To the basket." Jordan responded affirmatively, driving to the basket, hitting both free throws after being fouled. He drove again a minute later, was hacked by John Stockton and hit two more free throws to tie the game. Stockton buried a three-pointer with 41.9 seconds to move the score to 86-83.

Tex drew up a play for Jordan in the ensuing timeout. They were asking a lot of Jordan; they were asking a lot of Tex. Jordan appeared to have found his second wind and Winter felt Michael had earned the chance to continue carrying the team. Besides, there was none better than Michael Jordan at the end of a game. Changing horses now would be over-coaching, maybe even stupid. Tex fought the urge to be cute and drew up a play that cleared the right side for Jordan. Jordan took Bryon Russell one-on-one to the right side, driving all the way to the basket, laying it high off the glass and in. The Bulls trailed, 86-85, with 37 seconds remaining in the game.

"I never played basketball in Lubbock," Tex recalled. "Maybe just shot at a makeshift basket. Marbles was my game — bull's eye and cat's eye. My running buddy was a black kid named Rufus from across the tracks and we would team up. We played both sides of the tracks successfully, both of us accumulating large sacks of the other kids' marbles. But when the 8:00 whistle blew, we knew to scramble to our separate side of the tracks. There was a curfew in those days. That always bothered me — especially when that whistle blew and Rufus had to high tail it across the tracks."

Stockton brought the ball casually downcourt as the clock wound down. Time for a trifle, Tex thought. Stockton passed the ball to Malone with 11 seconds left on the shot clock; 26 seconds left in the game. Jordan sneaked in behind Malone, delicately extended himself and stole the ball. There were 18 seconds left as Jordan started upcourt with the ball, the Bulls out of timeouts. It was just as well, Tex thought, to attack before the defense had time to set a strategy. That was what the triangle offense was all about anyway, the ability to read the defense and take whatever was given.

The crowd grew strangely quiet at the ominous turn of events. So much can happen in those last few seconds, during which reputations are enhanced or tarnished.

Utah left Bryon Russell alone on Michael Jordan. In the reflection of a timeout they might have opted to double-team him, might have been able to draw the crowd back into the game, perhaps turn the tide. Stockton made a vague move at Jordan, then headed left to pick up

Steve Kerr on the right side. There was no way Kerr could be left unguarded with a clear look at the basket. Kukoc stayed left, posing another scoring threat. Rodman wisely abandoned his position high in the post and cut sharply toward the basket. He would be well-positioned if a rebound were required.

At eight seconds, Russell made a wild swipe at the ball. Jordan deftly avoided the attack and made a move of his own toward the basket. Russell, having already been burned by Jordan in that direction, overreacted to cut Jordan off. It was too late. In perfect control, Jordan had squared up to shoot, leaving Russell sprawling to recover.

The unpredictability of basketball attracts people to it. Shots fall, or they roll out. Basketball empires can rise and fall on a single shot. Teams — coaches, players, systems and franchises — are validated by winning and sometimes winning comes down to a single shot. Often overlooked are the actions that put teams in position for the shot. For the Utah Jazz, it was 13 years of Stockton and Malone and 10 years under head coach Jerry Sloan. Ironically, a former Bulls player and coach, Sloan's number was retired by the Bulls, his jersey hoisted high in Chicago's United Center. Jerry Sloan's Jazz had been to the conference finals five times, winning over 50 games nine times. They are typically the best shooting team in the NBA with a machine-like offense whose only gig is that it is rather predictable. While the Bulls have won five NBA championships and are about to make it six, the Jazz failed in their previous attempt — and are about to fail again.

> *"Since a single point determines the game, you've got to get as many little things going as you can. It boils down to precision. Fundamentals. I've spent my coaching career with this emphasis. Today's player brings more talent to the equation, but it doesn't change the fact that success and failure will often hinge on the little things that come with fundamentals."*

The Bulls, too, have had their share of disappointments — indeed, failures. Seven times during the 13-year Tex Winter era, they have failed to reach the NBA Finals. For years, the Detroit Pistons stymied them. Then there was the Hugh Hollins phantom call on Scottie Pippen that ended the 1994 season and Jordan's ill-fated drive to the basket against Orlando in 1995. Play the game of basketball long enough and you'll have your share of heartbreaks. But playing the game long enough is the most complete teacher.

Winning alone had kept the Chicago Bulls together. As Michael Jordan executed the team's final shot of the season, victory was the only thing that could validate the traveling menagerie that had become the Chicago Bulls. "Winning covers a multitude of sins; losing magnifies them," Tex liked to say. He was right.

A win, if the basketball gods smiled on Jordan's offering now rotating toward its target, would bathe the whole insane process — the crazy, unpredictable riot that was the 1997-98 season — in the healing balm of success. If he missed, the series would go to a seventh game, the pressure would intensify and the chance of losing the whole thing would be close to 50-50.

Fifty-fifty that the cadaver of the Chicago Bulls would be picked over like a dead man, who, with all the talent and success in the world, began hanging out with strange individuals, acting erratically and whose life ended in a violent death. Oh, the signs were all there, they would say of the Bulls. We could see it coming — the egos, the overconfidence, the infighting, the good guys Stockton and Malone gaining on them. All the effort would be lost. Not really lost, just the perception of being lost — the hours of practice, planning, plotting and dealing with it all. All that would be lost.

Tex knew better. He was still around at age 76. There was no way you could stay in the game of basketball if your value system was based on winning and losing. No way. The pain of losing is too great, too unpredictable, too violent. Even the most ardent fans can cope with the win-lose system, because no matter how involved they become, they can always walk away. At the end of the day, it's not their effort that matters, it's somebody else's. Not so for coaches and players. The wins and losses stick to them, both as part of the objective numbers that make up their resumé and part of the emotional chemistry that makes up their lives.

"I don't let losing get to me," says Tex. A host of family and friends will attest to the remarkable fact that Tex Winter is the same man after a win as a loss. It is a simple statement, but is almost as remarkable as saying, "I don't let gravity get to me."

Tex Winter is in it for the love of the game. He just loves basketball. Fortunately for him and the game, Tex is blessed with a peculiar intellect that has allowed him to understand the game as few have. His understanding transcends winning and losing, seeing into the very essence of the game itself.

Tex Winter is a basketball systems man. He is capable of breaking the game down to its fundamental components and then piecing it back together in a whole new way, such that few students of the game can understand. That's why Tex is still at the highest level of basketball. Quite simply, the world champion Chicago Bulls need him — and are willing to employ him well beyond retirement age for the benefit he brings.

Just as Winter is a systems man, Phil Jackson is a master psychologist. Phil motivates the people — the parts — that Tex melds into a basketball machine. Jackson and Winter are a good match: Tex is enough psychologist to complement Phil's genius and Phil is technically competent enough to appreciate Tex's approach to the game. Tex is the perfect assistant. A coach with his experience has seen and done just about everything — had his ego inflated and stomped on, realized the limitations and drawbacks to fame and success while keeping his ego in check. Tex is more than happy to contribute, but is not overly concerned with who gets the credit. Head coaches are generally appreciative of assistants who are more concerned with assisting than with taking their job.

Tex's dad, Ernest, was a mechanic. Though his father was a successful farmer, Ernest had gotten a bellyful of farming. Times were tough in the early '30s, but he stayed with his trade, even though they were often forced to move when the rent came due.

The culture of the era was to work hard and drink hard. Children were expected to contribute. Tex became a proficient rabbit hunter, sometimes roasting them up in the hills with the other children.

Ernest made moonshine in a wash tub. Pure alcohol. Poison. Men got crazy on the stuff and Tex's dad was no exception. "One time, dad was drinking. He said he was going to drive us off a cliff into the river. There was a road that ran right off into the Red River, so he could have done it. I was in the rumble seat of the Chevy and he was picking up speed heading for the river. When we got to the point of no return, I screamed as loud as I could and he slammed on the brakes. I was sure we were all gonna die. He made life interesting."

An era ends with Jordan's shot. The platform from which he elevates is the team, but in the end it is appropriate that he brings the ball down alone, makes his own move, defeats his own opponent and one last time wins the game. But even Jordan's magic will not be enough to put Humpty Dumpty together again. The Bulls organization, with all its complex relationships is too fragmented. It seals the sarcophagus with a win.

Jordan's shot went in. A small thing, really, and for a moment everything was OK.

For two years, the doctors told him they needed to amputate his leg at the hip, but Ernest Winter wouldn't let them. The leg had become infected, then abscessed, the result of being finned by a fish in the Gulf of Mexico. Unable to walk, he had gotten around on a mechanic's trolley board, still working when he could.

Ernest Winter died on a day the dust in the air was so thick you could barely see your hand in front of your face — right before Christmas, 1932. Morice Frederick Winter was 10 years old. He had never played basketball. No one had ever called him "Tex."

*And then the dispossessed were drawn west —
from Kansas, Oklahoma, Texas, New Mexico;
from Nevada and Arkansas — families, tribes,
dusted out, tractored out. Carloads, caravans,
homeless and hungry; twenty thousand and
fifty thousand and a hundred thousand and
two hundred thousand. They streamed over
the mountains, hungry and restless — restless
as ants, scurrying to find work to do — to lift,
to push, to pull, to pick, to cut — anything,
any burden to bear for food. The kids were
hungry. We got no place to live. Like ants scurrying for work, for food and most of all for
land.*

*We ain't foreign. Seven generations back
Americans and beyond that Irish, Scotch,
English, German. One of our folks in the
Revolution, an' they was lots of our folks in
the Civil War — both sides. Americans.*

*They were hungry and they were fierce.*

**— John Steinbeck, *The Grapes of Wrath***

CHAPTER TWO

# THINGS WERE WORSE
# IN CALIFORNIA

California used to have a certain attraction. The ocean is there; it's
the edge of a continent, the western end of the great national experiment. There has always been a reason to go there: the Spanish in search
of rich cities, the Russians for sea otter pelts, the Chinese for salmon and
sardines and people the world over in search of gold. It was the
Americans who settled, throwing off Mexican rule. Whole industries
grew up around the elusive gold strike of 1848 and the influx of 49ers
who arrived willy-nilly. The population grew twentyfold from 1848 to
1860. There was cheap land after the Civil War; free love and surfing in
the 1960s. It has only been since 1990 that California has experienced
negative population growth, with thousands from Los Angeles and
Orange Counties fleeing to Las Vegas and elsewhere.

However, to throngs of American farmers wiped out by the Depression
and drought of the 1930s, California was the logical place to go. To
return east would be to admit failure. As the new home of the movie
industry, California glittered and was less affected by drought. It also had
a great climate for agriculture.

The refugees poured in. To the already established locals they were a nui-
sance, "hillbillies," not unlike the Clampetts of *The Beverly Hillbillies* —
only without the money. They were broke, the victims of bank foreclo-
sures and failed farms. They found work scarce and the land already

taken. They found they were not welcome.

The Winters paid for space in a car headed west, following Elizabeth's lead. Tex's older sister by four years, she had married at 18 and moved to Los Angeles. She thought her mother could find work there.

It was not an easy move for Tex, who had been "loaned out" to his Uncle Ben and Aunt Minnie as a field hand. Since his father's death, Tex had spent his summers on their farm near Lubbock, where he milked cows, slopped hogs and picked cotton. Uncle Ben praised his every move, calling him a "hard worker." Tex took enormous pride in the moniker and would use the praise technique throughout his coaching career. Summers on the farm were among the happiest days of his life.

Mornings began before sunup to beat the heat. The all-day work sessions were punctuated only by Aunt Minnie's good cooking and a short midday nap on the cool linoleum floor. As the day's heat abated and the sun set over the plains of the Texas Panhandle, the makeshift family would relax in rocking chairs and watch the stars come out, straining to see the lights of Lubbock, some 35 miles north. On a bad night, Aunt Minnie would take out her glass eye; the fiery red socket made Tex pine for his mother.

Theo felt the family should be united, even if it meant moving to California. The move was quickly consummated when Uncle Ben began talk of adopting Tex.

They settled in Huntington Park, a suburb of Los Angeles near Long Beach. Theo found work in a ladies' ready-to-wear store selling to a population with little disposable income. Tex could walk to the Grand Central Market, where he fortunately found work as a boxboy, shuttling vegetables in his apron and collecting discarded boxes for a nearby bakery. It was work normally reserved for men with families. Watermelon sold for a half-cent a pound and Tex worked a six-hour shift that paid in leftover vegetables. It kept the family alive.

They subsisted on two meals a day, consisting largely of oatmeal, peanut butter sandwiches, chipped beef and cream gravy. "We used to take a can of evaporated milk and dilute it with four cans of water so it would go as far as possible. The vegetables I was allowed to carry home from the market were important to us. They helped vary the cream gravy and chipped beef routine."

Tex felt the stress of responsibility for the first time. Ernie remained in Texas to finish high school where he was a football star, making Tex the man of the house. Ernie had assumed a central role in Tex's life after the death of their father, demanding Tex make something of himself. They were close, though their relationship was complex.

For example, Ernie had coached Tex in an 880-yard race, urging him to hold back at the beginning of the race and let the other boys burn themselves out. Tex had finished first among 50 boys, getting his second wind just as Ernie told him he would, edging out several boys at the tape and breaking the county record. There was just one problem — he had also bested Ernie's time in his previous race among the older boys. That was taking success a bit too far. Ernie sulked for days over the incident and for the first time in his life, Tex felt the flush of pride in an athletic accomplishment.

Now he missed Texas, the rabbit hunting and his extended family and friends. The California kids said he talked funny and dubbed him "Tex" — not a compliment in those days. He felt the sting of prejudice; he felt poor and rejected by the other kids. School was harder, too. As far as Tex was concerned, things were worse.

As the financial situation stabilized for the Winter family, Tex had time to be a kid again. He began playing sports, discovering that despite his small size, he could more than hold his own with the California locals. Nearby Gage Avenue Park was open night and day. It was where Tex Winter first played basketball.

Tex wasn't the best player on the playground, but he was quick and could jump. In time, he picked up skills that earned him the respect of the other kids. Besides, he liked the game.

He also liked the new gym at Huntington Park High School. The old gym was destroyed in the earthquake of 1933, one of the worst quakes in southern California history. The community replaced it with a modern facility that sported three full basketball courts.

"I was enthralled with the gym," Tex recalled. "It was paradise to me, especially compared to the Texas Dust Bowl I was used to. I spent a lot of time there."

As a sophomore, Tex was 5'7" and weighed 125. He played in the Huntington Park Southern League, an exponent league based on age, height and weight.

"My small size and inexperience made me class D out of A,B,C, D — the bottom, which was lucky. I became a big fish in a small pond. After a few practices, the coach, E.C. Neander, picked me out of the crowd and announced, 'This boy's got leadership,' and made me team captain. I wasn't sure how he arrived at that conclusion, but I look back on that moment as my first step toward coaching. I enjoyed being a leader."

After his team won the D League, Tex moved up to C his junior year and he was again selected captain. "We got beat by a reform school that year. One of their boys challenged the official and began swearing. 'That's kind of poor sportsmanship,' I told him. He hit me right in the mouth. I learned to pretty much keep my mouth shut on a basketball court after that."

A quieter Tex went on to again captain his team in Class B, where they captured the Southern League championship. Success gave Tex the confidence he needed to survive in the foreign land of California. His athletic prowess and natural leadership abilities helped him fit in. After a time, he found he made friends quite easily.

But for Tex Winter, playing athletics would carry risk. "Before my junior year, I had a problem with the physical. Something didn't sound right and they told me I had an enlarged heart. I was warned about overexercise and banned from distance running. I tried the high jump, broad jump and hurdles. High jump was my best, I got over six feet, but I gained weight from the inactivity of the heart condition and couldn't get up my senior year. I tried the pole vault and liked it real well. I vaulted lefthanded, jumping off the right foot."

Using a bamboo pole, Tex broke the school record his senior year. He graduated in the winter class of 1940 and attended nearby Compton Junior College, where he continued vaulting and playing basketball.

California was a hotbed of sports. Tex found himself reveling in the competition, including his match-up with Jackie Robinson, who at that time was playing basketball with Pasadena City College. "Jackie was already a renowned athlete, a tremendous football player and track star — terrific in the long jump. In basketball, he was extremely competitive. He was not fun to play against — a bit like Michael Jordan. One time he said to me, 'Winter, I'm going to kick your butt.' And he did, too."

Despite the Robinson tutorial, Tex made the all-state team and accepted a scholarship to Oregon State. Friends Don Cecil and Bob Howard from Long Beach City College were going to OSU and they put in a good word for Tex, whom they had frequently played against. Coach Slats Gill accepted Tex on their recommendation. "He probably didn't want to lose Cecil or Howard," Tex said of the situation.

Tex found playing for Gill to be difficult. "He was a great coach, but old school. Very intense. He would stand there 15 minutes chain-smoking cigarettes while you sat with your head in your hands reflecting on the upcoming game. He tensed me up."

Tex also found himself with less playing time, as guards Lew Beck and Don Durdan garnered most of the minutes. Beck and Durdan were all-conference players, known even today as two of the best athletes in Oregon State history. "In retrospect, it was a great learning experience. I came thinking I was a world-beater but found it wasn't so. Gill taught me to be a role player, to come off the bench and contribute. I grew up a lot and learned discipline. Beck and Durdan reminded me there were players out there better than I was."

Oregon State also provided the meeting ground for Tex Winter and one Nancy Bohnenkamp, who had her eye on Tex well before they actually met. She had seen him in a group and asked a girlfriend his name. "That's Don Cecil," was the reply.

Cecil, of course, was Tex's buddy from California and quite the local heart throb.

"Then I went to a basketball game and I saw him again," said Nancy. "A dream man — jumping, hustling for the ball and scoring. 'You must mean Don Cecil,' I was told."

"The next time I saw him, he and some fellows stood beneath a window in our sorority house, serenading us. I still cry when I think of the song, 'From One Love To Another.' Tex's voice was the one I was listening to. He could really sing. One of the girls said that the guy leading the song was Don Cecil."

"Don was leading the song," Tex recalled. "I was just moving my mouth in the background."

---

**"It's funny. I've never really been sure who it was Nancy was initially attracted to. The story varies every time she tells it. The amazing thing is that we've stayed together all these years. It's not easy being a coach's wife."**

---

Neither Tex nor Nancy are exactly sure to what degree Don Cecil and Tex Winter were juxtaposed in Nancy's mind, but whatever the mix-up, "It was probably to my advantage," admitted Tex.

It was at a baseball game that Nancy finally discovered the mix-up. "Don Cecil was pitching," she recalled, "and I thought, 'If that's Don Cecil pitching, then who is that other guy?' "

The other guy was Tex Winter. Not one for baseball, Tex was pole vaulting that spring with the track team. He would later vault to the Pacific Coast Conference championship.

"I told Lew Beck to tell Tex I would sure like to go to the spring dance with him," said Nancy.

But there was no response from Tex. "I was a little ashamed because I didn't have much. I didn't have money or fancy clothes like most of the other students and Nancy came from a well-to-do family. Her father was a successful businessman and was very influential in La Grande, Oregon."

So Nancy took the initiative and called. "I did it on a dare from my roommate. In those days that was pretty bold, but Tex was someone I wanted to meet — so I guess I was bold. He came over right away and we hit it off. Later he told me I was 'awful skinny, but prettier than I thought you'd be.' Tex always had a way with words. He didn't spend a nickel — because he didn't have a nickel. He didn't have anything but the clothes on his back. We'd just go for long walks together."

As World War II escalated, Tex and Nancy joined the Navy. Tex followed his brother Ernie into the Naval Air Corps and Nancy joined the WAVES, hoping to be stationed near Tex. They wound up at opposite ends of the country, she in Seattle, Washington, and Tex in Florida. They would not see each other for nearly three years. Ernie got the worst of it, flying repeated missions in the thick of the Pacific air war. His plane was hit on three different occasions, forcing him to make dangerous carrier landings.

Tex received pilot training in the Naval Aviation V5 program during the war — it took him 24 months to get his wings, a very long time during World War II. Ernie earned his in just six months.

Tex earned a reputation as an athlete, both in basketball and as a pole vaulter. But each phase of his training was delayed as he competed on various teams. As part of the V5 training program, he attended Monmouth College in Illinois and Marquette University in Milwaukee. Tex became a favorite at Marquette — his spirited team play and the contacts he developed would later lead to a coaching position there.

Eventually qualifying as a fighter pilot, Winter flew FM2 Wildcats and was part of a replacement group heading for the Pacific. But again, fate intervened. A telegram arrived from the Department of the Navy: "Ernest Winter is Missing in Action and is presumed dead."

Though mounting war casualties prepared everyone for the worst, the Winters were devastated. "My mother took it particularly hard," Tex recalled. "I kept up hope for awhile, but slowly accepted his loss."

Two and a half months after Ernie's plane went down and the Navy presumed him dead, an Air Force Tech Sergeant showed up in Lubbock asking about the family of Ernie Winter. He brought with him a box. In the box was the head and hide of a Bengal tiger. He said a downed pilot he met in China asked him to deliver it to his family in Lubbock. Ernie Winter was alive!

Ernie's F6F Hellcat had been hit by antiaircraft fire as he strafed a Japanese airfield on the island of Formosa. Too low to deploy his parachute, he crash-landed in the Strait of Formosa. With his plane sinking, Ernie worked furiously to free himself from the cockpit. No use. The cockpit cover was jammed shut. Pilot procedures called for the pilot to wedge open the cockpit before a crash landing in water, but there hadn't been time. Now Ernie was trapped as his plane slowly took on water and began sinking. He started praying. With the plane under 40 feet of water, the cockpit opened, either because the water depressurized the cockpit or by divine intervention, or both. Whatever the reason, Ernie would always feel it was the hand of God that opened that cockpit. He would not be ashamed to tell others he became a believer that day in the Strait of Formosa.

Ernie Winter broke the surface of the water alongside a Chinese fishing boat. He startled the fishermen, who mistook him for Japanese and began to attack him with knives. But Ernie knew just enough Chinese to tell them he was American. In an area heavily patrolled by the Japanese, the fishermen hid him under their fish and made for Mainland China.

Ernie was fortunate to be taken to an area of China that fiercely resisted Japanese rule and had developed an underground to assist downed American pilots. The area included a contingency landing site for Doolittle's raiders of *Thirty Seconds over Tokyo* fame. Ernie was given a local militia uniform. He teamed up with a Chinese engineering student who spoke English and went by the name of "Joe Ma." Hiding Ernie's 6'2" frame was not an easy task — his hands and arms extended well beyond the sleeves of his new uniform. But the cost of failure at the hands of the Japanese would be deadly for all involved.

Joe and Ernie began a two-and-a-half month trek across China. Ernie carried a carbine given to him by the Chinese. One day, they encountered a Bengal tiger. Ever the hunter, Ernie shot the tiger when it confronted them in the mountains. Inside the tiger they found human remains — the tiger had been terrorizing the local village for some time.

Hence the tiger sent home in a box. Their journey ended when they linked up with Chiang Kai-shek's forces and Ernie was flown over the hump to India.

As a result of their shared experience, Joe and Ernie became friends. The silk from Ernie's parachute was used in the wedding gown for Joe's bride. Joe eventually came to America where Ernie assisted him in gaining a scholarship at Texas Tech. He went on to a successful career with IBM, developing a personal computer years before IBM execs were ready to listen. He later taught engineering at the University of California at Santa Clara.

Ernie was taken off carrier duty and assigned as an instructor at the Navy's Escape and Evasion Course. He was one of only 180 Americans to escape from Japanese-held territory during the war.

As soon as the two brothers could take leave, they headed north to Seattle. Tex wanted Ernie to meet Nancy. The two had kept up correspondence during their separation. Ernie was impressed, repeatedly telling Tex, "You should marry that girl."

But there was a war to finish and Tex returned to training, eventually earning his wings as a carrier fighter pilot in the FM2 Wildcat. He stayed competitive to the last, trying hard to record the final landing on the Sable, a converted cruiser that served as a carrier at Glenview Air Base on Lake Michigan.

"It was down to me and one other guy, jockeying to be last. I figured I'd come in fast and high and take a wave off, then I could swing around, let the other guy land and be last. I was getting 'too high, too fast' flags as planned, but then he unexpectedly waved me in. You had to do what the flagman signaled. It was a hard landing."

The war over, Tex discovered he would not be the first discharged. Selected as a test pilot, Tex and seven others were given the hazardous duty of testing experimental aircraft. "The Navy told us we were the best, but we were really guinea pigs," Tex said of the experience. Four pilots died during the training, including a buddy Tex was following when he suddenly dropped out of the sky. A shaken Tex Winter flew back to base.

Promoted to ensign, Tex was assigned to Corpus Christi, Texas, as a flight instructor. His job was to check ride-commissioned officers trying to qualify for their wings. "I was Santa Claus. It was kind of political. I only gave one failure the whole time. The guy I failed told me I'd live to regret the day. 'I'm sorry I saved your life,' I told him."

Corpus Christi also afforded Tex the opportunity to play basketball. While there, he met a coach who would establish the foundation of his approach to the game. Sam Barry coached the Main Station team at Corpus Christi. Tex played for an outlying field. Tex's game impressed Barry, who in peacetime coached the USC Trojans. Barry liked the way Tex played against Ralph Vaughn, a pre-war All-American at USC. "For some reason, I always played my best games against Main Base," Tex recalled, "probably because they were Main Station and we weren't."

Whatever the reason, Tex's play so impressed Barry that he recruited Tex for USC. "He didn't have to work too hard. I had already been recruited as a pole vaulter. I had talked to Slats Gill about returning to Oregon State, but when I found out Beck and Durdan were already back from the war, I knew he didn't need another guard. The last thing I wanted was to chase those two around with Coach Gill taking notes."

The problem of Tex and Nancy's separation was solved when the two were married July 11, 1946. They set up their home in a Quonset hut near the USC campus. It was a humble beginning. Tex constructed a wall across the single room, thus separating the kitchen from the bedroom.

---

**"Nancy says Steve Kerr reminds her of how I used to play — except that Steve's a better ball handler and shooter."**

---

Tex enjoyed playing his final year of eligibility for Sam Barry. "He was considerably more relaxed than Coach Gill. He trusted my game and I was able to respond. Of course by that time, I was a lot more mature than I had been before the war."

His maturity was put to good use, both as a player and as a mentor for an outstanding freshman guard named Bill Sharman. Sharman would go on to be an NBA All-Star and coach. "I could see he would be good. Coach Barry teamed me up with him. I was a pretty good free-throw shooter and Coach wanted me to work with Bill on that part of his game. The rest he pretty much had already." Sharman later became a better than 90 percent free-throw shooter in his NBA career.

Also on the team was Alex Hannum, a 6'7" junior who would later coach championship teams in the AAU, ABA and NBA — the only coach ever to do so. "He was tough — a competitor," said Tex. "He was also our team leader and the only height we had. Alex was just a great guy. He was a natural leader who became a great coach." Both Hannum and Bill Sharman were inducted into the Basketball Hall of Fame.

Barry ran what he called the "center-opposite offense," a motion offense he made popular in southern California at the time. Barry was a master of half-court offense schemes, employing many of the techniques Tex would later employ in his triangle offense. Barry picked up the motion offense while coaching at Iowa, probably from Doc Meanwell, who coached at Wisconsin. Barry brought the center opposite to USC.

Tex was ahead of the class, having run what came to be known as the "reverse action" while at Huntington Park High School. The reverse action was one of several systems perfected by Coach Jimmy Needles at nearby Loyola University. Needles coached Loyola to the AAU National Championship and Twentieth Century Fox to the National Amateur Championship in 1936. He was named the first coach of the U.S. Olympic basketball team. He and Sam Barry were close, gaining much through their mutual friendship.

Tex worked as a ball boy at Loyola, attending every practice and learning the offense, along with a variety of coaching techniques. There he observed the outstanding players of the day, like Phil Woolpert, who later coached Bill Russell and the University of San Francisco to NCAA Championships in 1955 and 1956. Another team member was Pete Newell, who used the motion offense in capturing the 1959 NCAA Championship as coach of the California Bears. As general manager of the San Diego Rockets, Newell would hire Tex to coach the team in 1971.

Coach Needles' reverse action called for the center to set-up away from the ball and the weak-side wing man to rub-cut off the post. Needles' reverse action and Barry's center opposite seemed similar to Tex. He would later discover that the players formed a triangle and would build on the configuration to form "the triple-post offense" or "triangle."

Barry, Needles, Woolpert and Newell are all members of the Naismith Memorial Hall of Fame in Springfield, Massachusetts. Tex was a beneficiary of their synergy. Fate placed him at the crossroads of two of the most significant basketball schools of the twentieth century and he made the most of it — learning and then mastering the art of motion basketball. His savvy and hustle earned him the "Most Inspirational" award from his Trojan teammates.

Tex was also inspirational in the pole vault, one of three vaulters named to the All-American team in 1946. His top vault of 14' 2 $^1/_2$" tied Guinn Smith of nearby University of California as the highest vault of the year. A year later, Tex would extend to 14'4". This was the era of bamboo poles and sawdust pits.

Tex frequently competed with a freshman from the University of Illinois, Bob Richards. Richards showed promise, though at the time his vaults were well below Tex's. Nancy, who attended all of Tex's meets, noticed Richards easily clearing the bar — but would knock it off with a hand or finger. She told Tex he would soon be one of the best. Her opinion proved prescient. Richards placed third in the 1948 Olympics with a vault of 13'9" — with Guinn Smith winning the Gold at 14'1". Richards would go on to win the Helsinki Olympics in 1952, soaring to 14'11", capturing the hearts of Americans and being enshrined on the cover of a Wheaties box.

Tex was not so lucky. As he prepared for the 1948 Olympic trials, he pulled stomach muscles he had first injured playing basketball. In an odd way the injury proved fortuitous, as at the time Tex was considering a track coaching position at Ventura Junior College. It was almost as if basketball were calling him back. He tried to vault through the injury, even squeezing into one of his mother's girdles for support — but to no avail.

At the AAU National Championships in Lincoln, Nebraska, Tex struggled to come to grips with his injury. While there, he agreed to meet with

Jack Gardner at the suggestion of Sam Barry. Gardner, the head basket-ball coach at Kansas State University, had traveled from Manhattan, Kansas, to offer Tex an assistant's job. Gardner played for Barry at USC and had inquired if his former coach knew of anyone who would make a good assistant. Barry gave Tex the nod. Barry was impressed with Tex's leadership style, along with his unique ability to grasp the essentials of the motion offense and visualize its future possibilities.

Gardner and Tex hit it off and although Tex thought his future lay in track and field, he agreed to take the job. He became Kansas State's first paid basketball assistant — albeit with a subsistence-level salary of only $3,000 a year.

---

**"I learned a lot from Jack Gardner. He was meticulous, organized — a master of detail."**

---

As former USC players and Barry disciples, the two men spoke a common language. Gardner ran what he called the "overload" — a motion game with interchanging positions and the USC emphasis on proper spacing. Players moved with a purpose. Offensive footwork was the foundation; constant innovation was the exciting byproduct.

Gardner was determined to build a basketball program at Kansas State. The Wildcats were 14-10 his first year after struggling to an abysmal 4-20 the previous season. In 1947-48, Tex's first year as an assistant, they blossomed to 22-6, winning the conference championship for the first time since 1919. K-State attained a national ranking for the first time and took fourth in the NCAA tournament.

Tex shared recruiting duties with Coach Gardner, who instructed him to find players with heart — even if they had less physical ability. Gardner believed players with character and mental toughness could acquire physical skills if properly coached. Gardner was developing a basketball brain trust — 21 of his players and assistants would go on to become head coaches.

Gardner was realistic about the situation. "You can't count on too many blue chippers at Kansas State. There aren't many in Kansas and it's hard to take the good ones out of another state."

Tex quickly became an excellent recruiter. He had an eye for talent and his honesty and perspectives were a big hit with parents. He put his southern California connections to good use and his down-home demeanor was much appreciated in the Kansas countryside.

Tex's first recruit was Ernie Barrett, a 6'3" guard out of Wellington, Kansas, who became an All-American at Kansas State. Barrett would later serve with distinction as the school's athletic director, playing a major role in fund raising and campus development. He is known today as "Mr. K-State," and is still considered one of Kansas State's all-time best players.

"I chose Kansas State because of Tex Winter," Barrett said. "But my high school coach was an Oklahoma State graduate and he wanted me to go there. I made several trips there and one to the University of Kansas. Tex was genuinely interested in me coming to Kansas State. He really wooed my parents."

Because freshmen weren't eligible for the varsity at that time, they focused on fundamentals. Tex was given the task of readying the freshmen for their varsity future. Ever the fundamentalist, Tex was especially adept at the challenge of grooming young talent for the challenge ahead. Since he had recruited many of the players, establishing rapport was not difficult.

In addition to Ernie Barrett, the class of '51 included Jack Stone, a 6'3" forward Tex knew from California AAU ball and Eddie Head, the "diamond in the rough" out of Los Angeles University High School. Stone had played with and against Head and encouraged K-State to offer him a scholarship. Joining these three in the next freshman class were 6'7" Dick Knostman from Wamego, Kansas; Lew Hitch, a 6'8" transfer from Stockton College in Missouri; and Jim Iverson, an all-stater from Platte, South Dakota. These players formed the nucleus of one of the greatest teams ever to play at Kansas State.

"The '50-'51 team has to be one of my favorites," Tex recalled. "I am still very close to most of those players. We thought they had the chance to go far because the team was made up of a group of guys who either started or were front-line replacements for their three years of varsity competition. We had won a couple of championships, so we thought we had the makings of an outstanding team."

On December 9, 1950, the Kansas State Wildcats took to the floor in the still-to-be-completed Ahearn Fieldhouse. Because work remained, it was doubtful whether the Wildcats' first game could be played there. The players dressed at Nichols Gym and used classrooms at the engineering building across the street for halftime.

Center Lew Hitch scored the first basket, a tip-in off a missed layup by Winter recruit Ed Head. Both players had worked on construction crews for the new facility, the largest state building in Kansas and the fifth largest basketball facility in the United States. Built from two million bricks manufactured by the state penitentiary, it accommodated 13,000 fans and would become known alternatively as "The Barn" and "The Basketball Palace." It would be the home of Kansas State basketball for the next 38 years.

The Wildcats had a team to match the vision the new fieldhouse represented. They won the Big Seven preseason tournament, defeating non-conference invitee Minnesota, 70-62. More telling, they played the entire game *without committing a single turnover.*

The Wildcats took the Big Seven Conference, compiling an 11-1 record in league play. They advanced through the NCAA Tournament, racking up impressive victories over Arizona, Brigham Young and Oklahoma State.

Unfortunately for Kansas State, star Ernie Barrett separated his shoulder in the semifinal against Oklahoma State and struggled in the final against Kentucky. He played the game unable to effectively use his right arm.

The Wildcats led throughout the first half, but hit an eight-minute dry spell at the start of the second half and Kentucky pulled away.

"I don't think there's any question we would have won if I had been healthy," said Barrett. "I still feel we had a better ball club and we would have beaten them nine out of 10 times."

It was a bitter loss for a team whose goal had been the national championship. Their final record of 24-4 earned a UPI ranking of 3rd; the AP ranked them 4th.

Their success did not go unnoticed. Marquette University, where Tex played during World War II as a Naval V5 Cadet, was looking for a basketball coach to replace Bill Chandler, who was retiring. Tex had played for Chandler and made a positive impression — so much so that Chandler recommended Tex for the job. At age 28, Tex was on his way to becoming the youngest head coach in NCAA Division I basketball.

*I hope he comes out for basketball.*

— Jayhawks coach Phog Allen, when told Wilt
  Chamberlain would attend the University of
  Kansas.

# Chapter Three
# Spring is Here, Winter Must Go

Tex's four years as an assistant provided excellent preparation for his head coaching duties at Marquette. Marquette basketball had fallen on hard times, so he had the sense of building his own program from the ground up. He enjoyed the disciplined approach to education and life the Catholic school provided, although there were occasional snafus in acclimating to the culture. For example, when a priest once asked Tex if he was going to Mass, "No," was his response, "I've already eaten."

Tex guided the team to a respectable 25-25 record during his two-year tenure, improving his first-year record of 12-14 to 13-11 in the second. The highlight came when the team won the National Catholic Invitational, serving notice that a new era of Marquette basketball had arrived.

During the summer of '52, Tex coached in Puerto Rico — the first American Division I coach to do so. He led *Leones de Ponce* to their first championship in the *Baloncesto Superior Nacional*. A long line of Division I coaches would later follow his lead, enjoying the energy of Puerto Rican basketball and establishing a fertile recruiting ground.

Nancy and son Russell accompanied Tex, the young family sharing an apartment with a widow and her son. Russell, now 18 months old, provided most of the entertainment during their stay. He was into everything, easily distracted and known for his disappearing acts. He had to be reined in constantly at the pool or beach, compelled to plunge in at the slightest opportunity. Early on, he found the loaded gun the widow kept hidden and began playing with it. The gun was then secured.

"If I turned around to talk to someone, he'd be gone," recalled Nancy. "Once we searched the entire apartment for him and he was nowhere to be found. I had to bring myself to look out the window to see if he had climbed up and fallen out. We lived on the third story, so I was petrified. I eventually found him in a tiny water closet drinking out of the toilet. I was never so glad to find a child drinking out of the toilet."

The following season, Tex took his Marquette Hilltoppers into Ahearn Fieldhouse to play Kansas State before one of their largest crowds ever. Comprised largely of sophomores playing their first year of college ball, the Hilltoppers were an excellent group of overachievers. They were sporting a four-game winning streak that included an upset victory over the nationally-ranked Minnesota Gophers. Everyone wanted to see what the upstart Winter could spring on the nationally-ranked Wildcats. It was like old home day for Tex, facing players he had recruited and coached as freshmen at K-State, with an equally talented group he had recruited for Marquette.

Tex had worked with Dick Knostman, the Wildcats' senior center who averaged 22.7 points that season. Tex taught him the hook shot. "One of the finest players I ever coached," Jack Gardner said of him and Tex concurred. Knostman had been heavily recruited by Phog Allen at the University of Kansas, but he lived just down the road from Manhattan. Tex and Jack Gardner frequently popped in to watch his high school games.

"Tex would go visit my parents in Wamego," said Knostman. "They thought he was the greatest — that's what my mother kept saying. They thought he was the salt of the earth and I agreed with them."

Marquette struggled gamely, but in the end was no match for Knostman, the nationally-ranked Kansas State Wildcats and the hometown fans at Ahearn. They fell, 88-72.

No one could have imagined that in a few short months Tex Winter would be back in Manhattan, this time as head basketball coach of the Wildcats.

◆ ◆ ◆

To everyone's surprise, Jack Gardner was leaving Kansas State. Gardner had differences with the athletic director, Moon Mullins, over fund-sharing within the athletic department. Mullins, one of the "Seven Mules" that fronted for the "Four Horsemen" of Notre Dame, was a stickler for abiding by the NCAA rules. He demanded school control of funds raised for the athletic department by the booster club. Gardner felt otherwise and was also miffed that conference regulations forbade his coaching the 1953 All-American basketball team on its coast-to-coast world series against the Harlem Globetrotters. In June, he announced he would be the new basketball coach at the University of Utah.

Gardner was a popular coach. During his seven seasons, Kansas State achieved national rankings, won three conference championships and twice traveled to the Final Four. In 1953, his final season, the Wildcats beat both Indiana and Kansas — teams that would play each other for the NCAA Championship.

Mullins recommended Tex for the head job, a choice that was also favored by a majority of the athletic committee. The choice boiled down to Tex and Dobbie Lambert, who had replaced Tex when he left for Marquette. At one point, school president James McCain seriously considered appointing the two men as co-coaches. Mullins advised against the plan and Tex got the nod. Lambert stayed on as an assistant for a year before taking the head job at Montana State.

It was a difficult move for the Winters. Nancy had recently given birth to their second son, Chris, and she already had her hands full with Russell, now in his terrible twos. "But Tex loved moving," Nancy recalled. "He engineered the whole process, right down to squeezing the boys into an overpacked car. He's good at it."

The Winters enjoyed Milwaukee and the unique environment Marquette offered. Tex felt he had recruited two very good classes — maybe the best he had seen — and was reluctant to leave them. Jack Nagle, who inherited the job, would lead Marquette to a national ranking and would defeat Kentucky in the Mideast NCAA Regional with the nucleus of players Tex had recruited. But Tex saw Kansas State as a challenge. The pull was overwhelming.

◆  ◆  ◆

The first two years were underwhelming —spent in rebuilding mode. Most of the great players of the recent past were gone, players like "Sophomore of the Year" Gary Bergen who transferred to Utah to be with Jack Gardner. The Wildcats posted identical 11-10 records for the 1953-54 and 1954-55 seasons and lost all four conference games to their nationally-ranked nemesis, Kansas Jayhawks.

---

**"I saw Wilt play as a freshman. It was an awesome experience. I knew we were in for what could kindly be called a bit of a challenge."**

---

Tex was concerned about the bitterness of the rivalry between the two schools and as the principal speaker at a Lawrence Chamber of Commerce dinner honoring the Kansas University basketball team, he spoke out, decrying "hate campaigns between rival schools." Tex lauded several Jayhawk players for their performance during the season, but disagreed with Jayhawk coach Phog Allen on an important issue of the day. "I am opposed to the 12-foot baskets," Winter said. "It still gives the big man a better chance in the game. There also would be more congestion near the baskets and the big man would have more time to get set to grab the rebounds."

The Wildcats lacked size at the center position. Gone was scoring king Dick Knostman. With him went the national rankings and prestige the university had come to expect. Winning seasons were not going to be good enough at Kansas State. Toward the end of the '55 season, the ubiquitous signs appeared: "Spring is here — Winter must go."

But Tex Winter had been recruiting. For the 1955-56 season he added two sophomores, Roy DeWitz and Jack Parr, both of whom would achieve All-American status. DeWitz was a 6'2" guard with scoring and ball-handling skills and at 6'9", Parr had the size to be a legitimate force at center.

Parr was heavily recruited out of his Virginia high school. He heard about the wonders of Ahearn Fieldhouse while playing halfcourt with a K-State student during the summer. The student recommended him to Tex and the two hit it off. "I was really impressed with Tex," Parr recalled. "I made a decision to come to K-State largely based on Tex Winter."

Tex was a low-key recruiter. He would not violate NCAA rules to get a high-quality player, nor would he resort to high-pressure tactics. "Some of my best players were not heavily recruited," recalled Tex, "players like Hayden Abbott and Wally Frank." With 25 scholarships and freshmen ineligible for varsity competition, players had a year to adjust to college life and learn the system. Players could mature and develop their skills. Many developed into outstanding players and citizens. It was possible to build a program from the ground up under the rules of the day.

Some recruiting decisions were critical. Almost lost was future All-American Bob Boozer, who would go on to an illustrious 11-year pro career. Boozer had supposedly displayed a poor attitude during the Nebraska high school championship, causing many schools to pass him by. "My assistant, Howie Shannon and I had him standing out in the hallway a long time while we discussed whether to offer him our last scholarship," recalled Tex. "It's scary to think we almost let him get away."

Boozer was 6'6" and an angular 180 pounds at the time. Tex correctly assessed that he would grow three more inches and gain 15 to 20 pounds in two years. By his senior year, Boozer was 6'9", weighed 235 and could play any position on the court.

But Boozer was an ineligible freshman for the 1955-56 season. After getting off to a good start, the Wildcats failed their first major test of the season, losing to Kansas at home, 91-86. The Wildcats were having difficulty beating Phog Allen's University of Kansas Jayhawks.

Allen was a coaching legend. In his 39 seasons, he won 590 games against 219 losses. His Jayhawks won 22 conference championships and three national championships. They had won the conference championship four of the last six years and were NCAA champs in 1952. The visionary Phog Allen was instrumental in establishing the NCAA tournament, the National Association of Basketball Coaches and in establishing basketball as an Olympic sport.

For years, Allen's Jayhawks had played in tiny Hoch Auditorium, seating capacity 3,000. But by 1955, they had a facility designed specifically to surpass that of their rivals at K-State with a seating capacity of 17,000 and an appropriate name — Allen Fieldhouse.

After months of wrangling, the Kansas University administration agreed to overturn a rule stipulating that buildings could be named only for the deceased. The announcement was kept secret until the dedication. Allen Fieldhouse was dedicated March 1, 1955, a date specifically chosen to coincide with a scheduled home game against the Kansas State Wildcats. What better way to show off their new facility?

Tex and his Wildcats joined what is to this day the largest crowd ever to pack into Allen Fieldhouse. More than 100 returning Jayhawk basketball lettermen joined in a 40-minute tribute to Kansas University basketball.

Despite the unfavorable surroundings, the Wildcats put up a fight, pulling to within three points with 7:42 left. Then the Jayhawk jinx struck and they spurted ahead to win by 10, despite stalling out the last three minutes of the game. The Wildcats did not forget the lessons learned that day. Losing in Allen Fieldhouse was humiliating.

Now, a year later, they again faced the Jayhawks in Allen Fieldhouse in the last conference game of the season. A home loss to the Jayhawks earlier in the season made it five times in a row Allen's Jayhawks had defeated the Winter-coached Wildcats. The Wildcats clung to a one-game conference lead over Kansas — a lead they would forfeit with a loss. They had just failed to clinch the conference in a home loss to Missouri, falling 85-72.

To compound matters, it was Phog Allen's final game as a coach. He would turn 70 before next season and an obscure tenure rule was invoked, rendering him ineligible to remain on the university staff. The legendary Phog Allen was being forced into retirement. What better way to go out then another win over arch-rival K-State?

*"Human motivation is fascinating. A kid has a date the next day in Kansas City and needs to take advantage of a day off if we win. So he shoots the lights out. Pretty simple, really."*

The Wildcats seemed to be cooperating and trailed 45-37 at halftime. "There was no pep talk at the half," said Tex. "There was no lack of motivation. We just covered the changes we wanted to make in our offense."

Especially motivated was junior Fritz Schneider. K-State had declared a school holiday in the event of a victory over Kansas. At the time, it seemed a fairly safe offering. But Schneider had other ideas, "I made a date with my girl in Kansas City for tomorrow in anticipation of the day off," he said after the game.

Schneider played like a man possessed, scoring 36 points on 63 percent shooting from the field. The Wildcats came storming back, fueled by Schneider's scoring blitz and Jack Parr's 16 rebounds.

This time it was the Wildcats who used the clock, paced by junior guard Pachin Vicens who flawlessly engineered the Wildcats' slowdown game. The Wildcats prevailed, 79-68, sealing the Big Seven championship.

Phog Allen was gracious in defeat. "I'm glad Tex won," he said. "He did it without any underhanded methods. As for me, this was just another ballgame. Of course we would be happier if we won, but after more than a thousand games, you take them as they come."

It was an insight Tex would take to heart.

The Wildcats attained their first national ranking with Tex at the helm for the 1956-57 season. Bob Boozer joined Parr and DeWitz on the varsity, averaging almost 20 points a game as a sophomore.

But the big news was all out of Lawrence, where seven-foot Wilt

Chamberlain joined the Kansas Jayhawk varsity. The year before, Chamberlain led his freshman Jayhawks to a win over the varsity. He scored 52 points in his first varsity game. There were rumors that construction on the Kansas Turnpike was stepped up to accommodate the anticipated traffic into Lawrence to see Wilt play.

---

*"Wilt was a unique physical specimen with exceptional athletic ability. It wasn't just height — he had the wingspan of someone 7'5".*

---

Chamberlain was a Philadelphia native who was introduced to basketball in seventh grade. By the time he entered high school, he was 6'11"; he was 7'2" when he graduated. He led his Overbrook High School team to three public school championships and two all-city titles. More than 200 colleges and universities vied for his talents.

He opted for Kansas University, ostensibly to play for the legendary Phog Allen. But Wilt never played for Allen, who was forced into retirement the year before. Chamberlain later admitted accepting between $15,000 and $20,000 from Jayhawk boosters.

In addition to his stature and powerful build, Wilt was a superb athlete. He was conference high jump champion, ran the 100-yard dash in 10.9, triple-jumped more than 50 feet and put the shot 56 feet. He later turned down offers from professional football and boxing and eventually starred in professional volleyball after his long NBA career ended.

But it was in basketball he would make his name. He averaged 29.9 points and 18.3 rebounds per game at Kansas and was twice named All-American. He averaged 37.6 points his rookie year in the NBA and 50.4 per game in his third season. On March 2, 1962, he scored 100 points against the New York Knicks. Contrary to popular belief, the Knicks did everything in their power to hold down his scoring. Wilt later said he would have scored 150 without their tactics.

During his 14 seasons as a pro, he would lead the NBA in scoring seven times, in rebounding 11 times. He averaged over 30 points per game and became the first player to score more than 30,000 career points. In the 1967-68 season, he focused on passing out of the double-team and became the first and only center to lead the league in assists. In 1972-73 he made 72.7 percent of his field goal attempts, an NBA record. In all, he would establish 100 NBA records.

He was the man America loved to hate. He was just too big and too talented. He was confident and intimidating — he made everyone around him an underdog. As Wilt himself said, "Nobody roots for Goliath." Detesting his role as a giant, he bridled at his nicknames — "Wilt the Stilt" and "The Big Dipper," the latter coined because of his need to dip through doorways. When programs listed him at 7'3" he took issue, claiming to be only 7'1".

Basketball purists worried that team basketball was threatened by the advent of a new breed of superstar, with Wilt the embodiment of a new super player who could defeat whole teams by himself. Even before his first collegiate game, writer Jimmy Breslin published an article entitled, "Can Basketball Survive Chamberlain?" Breslin summarized the panic sweeping the basketball world, writing that, "Many basketball authorities have already conceded the next three years to Kansas." Throughout his career, the name of the game was beating Wilt Chamberlain.

Coaches coped with the phenomenon as best they could. For many, notably Adolph Rupp at Kentucky, it meant scheduling around Kansas. Of course, for Big Seven schools, avoidance was not an option. Forced to confront Wilt on the court, many chose to hold the ball. In the era before the shot clock, teams would stall their way into a low-scoring game where they had a chance to keep from being embarrassed. Scores in the 30s and 40s were often the result — with Kansas still prevailing.

Tex never used the stall technique against Wilt; he didn't feel the integrity of the game allowed it. But he did support rule changes that were largely aimed at Wilt. Tex argued for changes similar to those enacted a generation earlier when giant George Mikan ruled the roost.

One move Tex lobbied against was Wilt's "dunking free throw." As a freshman, Wilt had demonstrated that with a running start, he was capable of taking off behind the free-throw line and dunking the ball. The current rule stated that while shooting a free throw, a player could not set foot in the key before the ball hit the rim or backboard. The new rule made it clear the free throw must be shot behind the line.

Also added to the rule book was an offensive goal-tending regulation prohibiting players from touching the ball on the rim or in an imaginary cone above the basket. This kept Wilt from guiding in his teammates' shots. The lineup rule for free throws was also changed — the non-shooting team was given both positions next to the basket. Prior to Wilt, there was one player from each team next to the basket. The advantage of an offensive player with the size and ability of Wilt Chamberlain was deemed too great.

The Wildcats lost twice to Wilt and the Jayhawks during the 1956-57 season and finished second to Kansas in the Big Seven. Still, the games were close: 51-45 in Lawrence and 64-57 in Manhattan. Tex's relationship with K-State fans seemed to have solidified, as he was presented with a new '57 Chevy. His assistant, Howie Shannon, received a set of golf clubs and a laundry dryer. Recalling the Wildcats had finished second in the Big Seven, Tex quipped, "I can only wonder what the fans would have done if we had won the conference."

Kansas manhandled the Wildcats in Kansas City, 79-65, at the start of the 1957-58 campaign. The situation called for a better mousetrap.

In Lawrence, Tex double-teamed the giant with Parr and Boozer. In simple terms, the idea was to keep the ball away from Wilt and hope for a poor outside shooting performance from the Jayhawks. They got it.

The Wildcats took rebounds off Jayhawk missed shots for five fast-break layups in the first half. Wally Frank's buzzer-beating jump shot gave the Wildcats a commanding 41-28 halftime lead.

Ten seconds into the second half, Chamberlain scored from the inside to set a new tone to the ballgame. The Jayhawks knotted the score at 56 with 5:22 remaining.

The teams traded baskets. With 2:30 remaining and the score tied at 60,

Kansas State stalled for a final shot. Jack Parr missed a jumper with five seconds left and the game went to overtime.

With the seconds ticking down in the first overtime, Parr made the defensive play of his life. Kansas had gone inside to Chamberlain on what appeared to be an easy lay-in. Parr leapt straight up and cleanly rejected the shot and the buzzer sounded with the score still tied.

Both Boozer and Parr fouled out in the second overtime, but the Wildcat second team had enough juice to carry home the win, 79-75. The Wildcats went on to win the Big Seven championship and advance to the NCAA tournament. At a time when the basketball pundits were conceding the national championship to the University of Kansas, they did not even win their conference. Wilt left Kansas after the season, skipping his final year of eligibility to join the Harlem Globetrotters.

"There was a lot of hyperbole after that game," recalled Tex. "Everyone wanted to take credit for 'driving Wilt out of collegiate basketball.' The fact is, Wilt played hurt during that game and the Jayhawks came back to give us a pretty good licking later in the season. I think the college game became unfun for Wilt because the expectations were unrealistic and teams continually focused on containing him and double or triple-teaming him. We made it as tough as we could on him within the rules — and of course, we changed the rules a bit, too. He used to call me 'that little coach from K-State who doesn't like the big man.' But you had to live the Wilt Chamberlain experience to fully realize his impact on the game. He was one of the greatest athletes of all time. He changed the game — and the rules."

Having won the Big Seven championship, the Wildcats advanced to the NCAA tournament with a strong team. Rounding out the trio of Parr, Boozer and DeWitz were 6'8" forward Wally Frank and 6'3" Hayden Abbott. Boozer had taken over the scoring lead from Parr, averaging over 20 points per game and displaying the talent that would lead to his pro career.

Kansas State faced heavily favored Cincinnati in the tournament. Led by 6'5" All-American Oscar Robertson, the Bearcats were ranked #1 in the nation. Robertson was the first sophomore in history to lead the nation in scoring, a feat he would accomplish twice more, compiling a 33.8

point-per-game collegiate average. Oscar was used to winning. He led his high school basketball team to 45 straight wins and two Indiana state championships. Phog Allen called him "the greatest player of all time for a fellow his size." A future NBA MVP and Hall of Famer, he would consistently average more than 30 points as a pro and make the first-team All-Star team in each of his first nine NBA seasons.

*Sports Illustrated* called it the game of the year. Played in Allen Fieldhouse in Lawrence, K-State faithful filled the arena to pull for their underdog team. It was a venue the Wildcats were familiar with and twice in the last four seasons had pulled upsets there.

It took all they had — including some last-second help from Robertson, who sank the front-end of a one-and-one with one second remaining to tie the game, only to miss the game winner. The Wildcats won in overtime, 83-80.

After a win over a strong Hank Iba-coached Oklahoma State team, the Wildcats faced the University of Seattle and their star, senior Elgin Baylor, in the Final Four. Baylor, a junior-college transfer, had sat out a year to regain his eligibility. In many ways he was a man among boys. At the time, Baylor was four years older than Oscar Robertson. In two years' time he would set a new NBA record, scoring 71 points in a single game. A consensus All-American, Baylor averaged 31.5 points per game, combining acrobatic moves with a team game that included exceptional passing and rebounding skills. Another future Hall of Famer, Baylor would go on to a 14-year NBA career, averaging 27.4 points per game.

Seattle was too much for K-State. The Wildcats fell in the semifinals, then lost to Temple in consolation. Still, it had been an amazing season — especially for a college team that had faced perhaps three of the top five players ever to play the game in Chamberlain, Robertson and Baylor. Finishing 22-5, UPI ranked the Cats third in the nation. They would lose three of their top five scorers for the following season — and come back even stronger.

Tex was named Coach of the Year for 1958 by United Press International, a 74-42 favorite over Fred Schaus of West Virginia. He found himself much in demand at coaching clinics around the country and enjoyed the travel associated with his new status. Other schools also noticed Tex; the offers were numerous. More people saw Kansas State play basketball in the 1957-58 season than any other team in the nation — some 338,000.

Despite his success at Kansas State, the urge to roam was a strong one, even with the completion of their new house that Tex built in his spare time, three blocks from Ahearn Fieldhouse. It was hard to know what to do, which road to take. When the University of Iowa offered Tex their head job along with a substantial pay increase, he accepted. However, he called back the following morning saying he had changed his mind.

Unbeknownst to Tex, he was having a major impact on a future genera-tion of college coaches. Bill Guthridge, a K-State player on the '58, '59 and '60 conference champion squads, would later serve as an assistant at K-State before joining Dean Smith at North Carolina and eventually inheriting the head job. Howard Shannon, a Kansas State All-American in 1947, served as Tex's assistant for 11 years before taking the head job at Virginia Tech.

Gene Keady, head basketball coach at Purdue University, was a 1958 K-State grad who followed the '59 and '60 seasons while earning a mas-ter's degree at Kansas State and coaching high school basketball in nearby Beloit, Kan. "I enjoyed basketball tremendously in college, mainly because of the influence of Tex Winter," Keady said. "There was so much enthusiasm in those days at K-State and he is the reason I'm in coaching today. That was a time of excitement; you had to get to Ahearn Fieldhouse early to get good seats. They were winning big, had great play-ers and K-State was one of the three or four schools in America where basketball was at its best."

Tex recommended Keady for his first high school job, then to Hutchinson Junior College and finally as an assistant to Eddie Sutton at Arkansas. "After that, he really didn't need my recommendation," Tex noted.

Tex's accessibility at the height of his success made him lifelong friend-ships that would be central to his career. Jerry Krause was a pro baseball and basketball scout who followed Tex's development. While scouting at

Kansas State, the two became friends. They spent endless hours review-ing game films and talking basketball. Later, he would hire Tex as an assistant for the Chicago Bulls.

Another friendship Tex nurtured during this period was with Dale Brown, a high school coach from North Dakota who would later coach at Louisiana State University. He would hire Tex as a consultant.

In his book, *Tiger In a Lion's Den*, Brown listed Tex as one of the seven most respected men in his life. "Perhaps the most special trait of Tex Winter is his unselfishness," he wrote. "When I was a high school coach and he was coaching at Kansas State, I wrote him a letter. He was hot; everyone in the country wanted him. He was coach of the year. His team was in the Final Four and ranked number one in the nation. In this let-ter, I told him I wanted to come and learn basketball from him. He was fantastic. He took me to his home to eat, took me to the country club to eat, stayed up late at night, watched multitudes of films and talked to me one on one. I really learned a lot."

Tex and his Wildcats *were* hot. Despite the graduations of Parr, DeWitz and Abbott, the 1958-59 Wildcats might have been the best K-State team Tex coached. In their first four games, they defeated Purdue, Indiana, California and San Francisco. Indiana and San Francisco were recent national champions and California would actually win the title later in the season.

After a slip-up against Brigham Young in Provo, the Wildcats won 21 straight — defeating nemesis Kansas twice and sweeping the Big Eight, which had expanded to include Hank Iba's Oklahoma State. Iba, both a legend and a visionary, was on a crusade to shrink the size of the basket, noting "if the players continue to improve, in another 10 years it may be almost an accident when someone misses." However, Tex felt similarly about Iba's smaller basket and Phog Allen's 12-foot basket — it was hokum.

Especially gratifying was K-State's 82-72 victory over Kansas on the home court — a hurdle they had not overcome in Tex's five years as coach. Bob Boozer literally shot the Jayhawks out of the water, scoring 33 and hitting eight in a row in the second half. The win put the Jayhawks in the familiar company of teams that would have trouble winning in

Ahearn; it would be seven years before they won a scheduled conference game there again.

"Kansas State won a lot of ballgames because of that crowd," recalled Tex. "Many times during timeouts you couldn't hear yourself talk. All I could do was scribble a play on the floor. The crowd there never died, even in one of our lulls — the crowd would come alive and pick us up."

The Wildcats finished the regular season ranked #1 in the nation, with a 24-1 record. They sailed by DePaul in the Midwest Regionals, 102-70, the third time in the school's history they passed the century mark. They also had done it earlier in the season, defeating Missouri, 108-69, in Manhattan.

Meanwhile, Cincinnati struggled to get by Texas Christian for the right to play K-State for the Midwest championship and advance to the Final Four in Louisville. They were again led by stand-out Oscar Robertson, who won the national scoring title with 32.6 points per game.

The game was played in Lawrence and from the outset, tensions were high. It was a short trip for K-State fans, so they packed Allen Fieldhouse. Only a few seconds elapsed before a shoving match erupted between Robertson and Boozer and double fouls were assessed. Fierce action under the boards a few minutes later caused the officials to stop play while the two captains were warned about further rough play. Then a technical was assessed to keep the game under control. During a time-out, Tex marched to the Cincinnati bench and had a heated conversation with Bearcat coach George Smith, which reporters noted was "garnished with menacing fist shaking."

"I was far from impressed with their conduct," Tex said at the time. "The guys down on the bench were cussing us. They cussed our players all through the game. I don't appreciate their conduct. I don't think there's a place in sports for that kind of conduct."

Up in the stands, combat erupted between the Cincinnati cheering section and members of the press. At one point, the reporters' view of the game was obstructed by the rowdy fans.

Meanwhile, a game was going on during the chaos. Robertson's scoring was held in check and the Wildcats would garner more rebounds with fewer turnovers. It was their shooting that was killing them— only 31 percent from the field. They led at halftime, 41-39, and trailed by a single point with two minutes to go.

Then the roof fell in. The Cincinnati press stymied the Wildcats while Robertson fed his teammates for easy scores and a 10-1 run. Cincinnati prevailed, 85-75. K-State finished the season at 25-2.

It was a devastating loss for the Wildcats. Tex was uncharacteristically bitter afterward, feeling the season had ended in disaster. One minute they were competing as the #1 team in the nation; the next minute they were run off the court.

College basketball can be cruel. Teams fall by the score at tournament time in the hardwood version of Darwin's survival of the fittest. Cincinnati's success would be short-lived. They fell in round one of the Final Four to Pete Newell's California Bears. Newell employed a similar motion offense that he and Tex had picked up on the West Coast. While Cincinnati would advance to the Final Four five consecutive times, the national championship would evade their greatest player, Oscar Robertson.

All of which was small consolation to Tex Winter and his disappointed Wildcats. With Boozer graduating, the following season looked to be a struggle. It would be.


The Kansas State Wildcats were 62-15 during the Bob Boozer Chapter of the Tex Winter Era. Rounded out by Jack Parr, Wally Frank, Don Matuzak, Roy DeWitz and Hayden Abbott, the Wildcats had become a perennial national powerhouse. "Those ballplayers could play," Boozer said of his teammates.

Boozer was the #1 pick in the 1959 draft by the Cincinnati Royals. Oscar Robertson would join him there a year later as the Royals' #1 pick in the 1960 draft. The two were also teammates on the 1960 gold medal Olympic basketball team along with Jerry West, Jerry Lucas and Walt Bellamy. Boozer would play with five teams in his successful 11-year NBA career.

Meanwhile, the Wildcats struggled. They lost three of their first four games, including losses to North Carolina and North Carolina State, where they were forced to stay in the university infirmary because of racial policies. Tex was not pleased and complained to officials. "That's where you belong," said one. "Your team looked sick to me." Tex picked up a rare technical against North Carolina. "I didn't do anything," he protested at the time. "I just told him he blew the call."

## 25 — 2
**Kansas State 96, Purdue 83**
**Kansas State 82, Indiana 79**
**Kansas State 68, California 65**
**Kansas State 53, San Francisco 52**
**Brigham Young 77, Kansas State 68**
**Kansas State 69, North Carolina State 67**
**Kansas State 68, St. Joseph's (Phil) 55**
**Kansas State 69, Missouri 66**
**Kansas State 73, Oklahoma 59**
**Kansas State 67, Colorado 66**
**Kansas State 59, Iowa State 56**
**Kansas State 89, Colorado 58**
**Kansas State 90, Oklahoma 45**
**Kansas State 75, Missouri 60**
**Kansas State 78, Iowa State 55**
**Kansas State 91, South Dakota State 65**
**Kansas State 59, Nebraska 43**
**Kansas State 70, Colorado 59**
**Kansas State 82, Kansas 72**
**Kansas State 60, Oklahoma State 49**
**Kansas State 75, Oklahoma 55**
**Kansas State 62, Oklahoma State 50**
**Kansas State 87, Kansas 77**
**Kansas State 108, Missouri 69**
**Kansas State 76, Nebraska 54**
**Kansas State 102, DePaul 70**
**Cincinnati 85, Kansas State 75**

Tex was having difficulty making his own calls, particularly who would start for the 1959-60 Wildcats. Midway through the first half against conference foe Iowa State, he pulled his starters and saw an eight-point deficit erased by his sophomores. Two minutes into the second half, he again pulled his starters when they gave up five straight points to fall behind 41-36. None of the starters would play more than four minutes the rest of the game. Ironically, starter Bill Guthridge missed a 15-foot shot to win the game at the buzzer with the score knotted at 67. The Wildcats lost in overtime, 74-73.

In Lawrence, his starters stunk up the floor, taking a 47-27 deficit into the locker room at halftime. The sophomores got another chance. They were reminded of K-State comebacks against the Jayhawks — a 16-point halftime deficit in 1948, final K-State 61, Kansas 60; a 19-point deficit in 1951, game lost in overtime; an 11-point second half deficit in 1956 and a 79-68 win.

The sophomores pressed during the second half and the worm turned. In the first seven minutes, they cut the lead to 50-41, a 14-3 run. They took the lead for the first time with four minutes to go. Mike Wroblewski, the sophomore center, was on fire — scoring 18 of his 22 points in the second half. Unfortunately, it was Wroblewski's misunderstanding at the end that may have cost the Wildcats the game.

The Jayhawks called timeout trailing 62-61 with a minute and a half remaining. When they failed to score, the Wildcats recovered, needing only to run out the clock or be fouled. Instead, from the top of the circle, Wroblewski fired an airball which sailed out of bounds.

"During the timeout I told them that if Kansas scored, we would work a play for Wroblewski to shoot at the top of the circle," Tex recounted. "He must have misunderstood. He took the shot anyway."

The Wildcats lost, 64-62.

---

**"Basketball can really burst your bubble. There are moments you want to walk away from it and never come back. Somehow, I've always gotten over those moments."**

---

They would later defeat the Jayhawks at home in Ahearn, 68-57 and win their final two conference games to finish in a tie with Kansas for the conference championship.

The playoff to determine which team would advance to the NCAA tournament took place in Manhattan. "It was a barnburner," Tex said after the game.

K-State got off to a nine-point lead early in the contest, but Kansas fought back to regain the lead in the first half. The Jayhawks led by 13 midway through the second half, but the Wildcats pulled another come-from-behind to take the lead with two minutes to go. With the game knotted at 72, they stalled for the last shot of the game. It missed and the game went to overtime. With 15 seconds left in the extra period, K-State's Phil Heitmeyer made what appeared to be a game-tying layup. Instead, he was called for traveling and the Wildcats came up short, 84-82.

After two consecutive trips to the NCAA tournament, the Wildcats would be staying home. "I couldn't be prouder," Tex said of his team.

*Triangles are closed three-sided figures. There are many special kinds of triangles.*

— *The World Book Encyclopedia*, 1962 edition

# CHAPTER FOUR
# THE TRIANGLE

Camp Audubon sat vacant 10 years — but it was perfect. Nestled high in the Colorado Rockies on a lake above Boulder, it consisted of seven cabins, a lodge and a gym. Most springs Camp Audubon was still buried in 15 feet of snow, so the first mission was digging out. Then came the inevitable repairs, a task Tex enjoyed with the mechanical bent picked up from his father. It was a perfect summer basketball camp — a place for K-State players to work as counselors and a place for Tex to escape the summer coaching clinics he found increasingly demanding of his time.

It was also a place for Tex to spend time with Nancy and the boys, all of whom quite naturally took to basketball and loved to play. But Tex didn't push. The counselors treated them just like the other kids. They were afforded the opportunity to learn the fundamentals and a love for the game. Chris, the middle son, got the size. Nancy packed him off to Oregon to visit relatives one summer when he was 15 or 16. They argued about a pair of pants she bought him. They were loose-fitting and too long, as was the style. However, when he returned from Oregon, the pants were just short of his knees. He would grow 10 inches in a single year of high school, to 6'4". Also, he was pigeon-toed, "like Elgin Baylor," people told him. Chris had a good high school career, but knee injuries and surgeries hampered his performance in college.

◆　◆　◆

The 1960-61 Wildcats learned early the kind of hustle required to be competitive. In their second game of the season, they were lambasted by the Indiana Hoosiers and Walt Bellamy, 98-80. The 6'11", 245-pound Bellamy was an Olympic veteran, having played on the same squad with Boozer, Robertson, Baylor and West — players the Wildcats were well familiar with. Bellamy was averaging 20-plus points a game as the starting center for Indiana; he would average 31.6 points in his first year in the NBA and be named Rookie of the Year. His NBA career .632 field goal percentage is second only to Wilt Chamberlain.

Having lost to the Kansas Jayhawks in Lawrence, the Wildcats found themselves down 29-22 before a capacity crowd in Manhattan. Thousands more watched on a statewide television network. But the Wildcats responded with a 20-2 run that had them up 42-31 at intermission. Continued aggressive play and rebounding carried them the rest of the way. They would grab 14 more rebounds than Kansas and their star center, Wayne Hightower. The effort was anchored by junior Larry Comley and senior Cedric Price, who averaged 18 and 17 points, respectively. Ultimately, however, the bench made the difference. The box score showed that while the Jayhawks used seven players in their final meeting of the season, the Wildcats used 10 — including Dave Nelson, a lightly-regarded sophomore from Manhattan who pumped in 19 points. The 81-63 win moved K-State into a tie for the Big Eight lead, which they would eventually win with a 13-1 conference record.

As the team prepared for the NCAA Midwest Regional, Tex commented on his 1960-61 crew. "This team gives the impression it is not classy, that it plays without poise or finesse. One of the reasons we win is that we compensate with scrapping and scrambling. This is our game." They may not have looked pretty, but they finished the regular season ranked 4th in the nation by AP and UPI, with a record of 21-4.

Their win over Houston in the Midwest Regionals was costly. Third guard Warren Brown was injured, a linchpin in the team defense the Wildcats played. For the third time in four years, they would face the Cincinnati Bearcats in the regional. Tex was wary of Cincinnati, even without Oscar Robertson, who had graduated. "Now they've gone to team effort, more pattern play and have put more emphasis on defense.

They've compensated for Oscar Robertson's loss with team unity. I think that makes them tougher."

He was right. The Cincinnati Bearcats would go on to win the NCAA tournament the next two years.

The Wildcats held the lead 32 minutes. The turning point came with 11:27 remaining. That's when Cincinnati went to its dreaded full-court press. K-State's lead, once eight points, had dwindled to 47-44. During the next five minutes they would go scoreless from the field, missing 10 in a row.

"Their press bothered us," admitted Tex. "They forced us to change the tempo. They wouldn't let us move with complete freedom."

Kansas State fell, 69-64. The Bearcats would take their patented press to the NCAA Finals where they would defeat defending champion Ohio State, 70-65, in overtime.

## "The triangle moves the ball until a player gets his best shot."

Despite the heartbreaking loss, it was tremendous year for the Wildcats. Tex was widely acclaimed; he had done a great job with the assets at hand. One writer called for the Board of Regents to extend Tex a lifetime contract. Still, the season-ending loss was a bitter one. K-State President James McCain summed it up outside the locker room after the game. "It was a great season," he said, "although it doesn't seem like it to the boys in there."

By today's inclusive standards, it's hard to imagine a Division I basketball team going 22-3 and not qualifying for the NCAA tournament. But it happened to the Kansas State Wildcats and any other team that didn't win its conference in those years. The 1961-62 Wildcats went 12-2 in conference, beat Kansas twice — by 25 points on one occasion. But because they were edged out by Colorado for the conference title, the Wildcats did not qualify for the NCAAs. Tex used the time to finish writing a book, a project he'd been toying with since 1958.

For years, Tex had run a unique half-court offense which went by various names. The triple-post offense, Kansas State's Triangular Series, the sideline triangle and the triangle were all names for essentially the same strategy. Tex preferred calling it the sideline triangle; eventually, simply the triangle. But Cliff Wells used the name triple-post in a 1949 advertising brochure when Tex appeared at his Indiana basketball clinic. The name stuck. The concept was a conglomeration — based on a scheme Tex ran under Sam Barry at USC, the offense he saw Jimmy Needles teaching at Loyola in Los Angeles and his own experiments with Jack Gardner's center-in.

Tex took meticulous notes. Since he believed the basketball program was an extension of the university learning experience, practices were structured, based on written lesson plans. The plans provide a priceless history of the development of basketball over the past 50 years. On November 4, 1949, for instance, Tex taught the two-handed push shot to the K-State freshmen from 3:30 to 3:55. The plan noted that the two-hand set was "especially good from long range," and was "getting to be a lost art west of the Mississippi." Detailed instructions began with, "Hold ball in front of eyes to start shot ..."

While some aspects of the instruction reflect a game gone by, others are timeless. Tex based his teaching on three laws of learning: Readiness, which postulated the more ready a player is to engage in basketball, the better he performs; Exercise, which stated any set of neuron connections will gain strength through correct form and practice; and Effect, which asserted if a player finds satisfaction in responding in a particular way, he will tend to repeat the experience; conversely, if he finds dissatisfaction, he will tend to avoid it.

Central to the pedagogy are fundamentals — those habits that a player must perform instinctively at the right time and place in a game. Initially, a player is taught "to be relaxed" and maintain a sense of balance. "Refrain from any team offense until the players are well grounded in fundamentals," reads one notation. "A team that has a good knowledge of fundamentals can play a fair game of basketball without any plan of offense, while the best-planned offense will bog down if the players cannot execute the important fundamentals." Drills reinforce fundamentals while at the same time "provide exercise and discipline for players."

*The Triple-Post Offense* was published in 1962 by Prentice-Hall. It is an oddly structured book, beginning with a code to the hieroglyphics of the diagrams that would frighten a physicist. That structure is unfortunate, because for the less technically inclined, the book contains a wealth of basketball insight germane to players on any level. The section on shooting, for instance, combines statistical analysis with lucid descriptions of technique and sports psychology. The numbers show teams taking 68.22 shots per game from 1948 through 1961 — about 12 per game for a starter. It pays to be ready for those relatively few shots — in fact, it is the ability to come to balance quickly that is the secret to successful shooting. Shooting technique should be honed under game conditions to the maximum extent possible. A good shooter "plays and shoots with aplomb, which frees his body and mind to perform the task at hand with relaxed abandon."

Entire sections are devoted to relaxation, concentration, temperament and discipline — a preface to the world of sports psychology. Players must "realize things won't always go the way they would like and the defense is out purposely to see that they don't." A player should become "so completely absorbed in playing the game that he is unaware of anything not directly concerned with it." Discipline is the same on the court as it is in life; a bad shot is a bad shot, whether it goes in or not.

The book was written at an interesting time in basketball history. The jump shot had not yet completely replaced the one and two hand set shots; hook shots were still a major component of a player's scoring repertoire. Tex was sensitive to the slowness with which some of these changes were accepted by coaches, many of whom chose to deny the effectiveness of the jump shot, despite overwhelming evidence to the contrary. "The coach who hamstrings his players," Tex wrote, "will likely see the game pass him by."

The business of hamstringing players was an important concept which would become a central issue 30 years later when Tex successfully exported the triangle to Michael Jordan and the Chicago Bulls. It would cause the Six Principles of Sound Offense to become seven. A pragmatist, Tex admitted in the 1962 edition that "the offensive pattern is adjustable to the material available," and that emphasis on a particular series of options could be adjusted "in order that certain individual abilities and strengths might be utilized."

At the heart of the triangle is the philosophy that it makes no sense to attack a defense head-to-head when a smoothly functioning team can find and exploit the defense's weaknesses. If the defense extends to prevent one move, the players in the triangle offense instinctively adjust with cuts and passes to find a better shot. There is no play-calling because the offense essentially allows the defense to name the play. The original Six Principles anchor the concept:

1. Floor spacing of 15 feet between players creates initial operating room.

2. The defense is kept occupied both on and away from the ball. Offensive players must learn to play without the ball, because weak-side play will be important.

3. There must be defensive balance. Offensive positioning must facilitate a quick transition to defense to stymie the fast-break.

4. Similarly, the team must maintain a strong offensive rebounding position on all shots.

5. The offense exploits the defense by attacking openings created as the defense commits itself to stopping a particular option.

6. Unlike most offensive schemes where a play is called by the offense, in the triangle the defense names the play. The offense reads and then exploits what's given.

Later, during Tex's tenure with the Chicago Bulls, the principles would be revised to increase spacing to 18-20 feet and emphasize penetration to the basket with a first option to the post position. A seventh principle would also be added — "The Michael Jordan addendum" — "Provide the outstanding individual an opportunity to use his abilities. If you

CHAPTER FOUR: THE TRIANGLE

hamstring him, the offense isn't sound."

The triangle's basic setup puts three players on the same side of the floor — one near the sideline, one near the free-throw circle and one near the basket. The player with the ball can drive to the basket and shoot if that option is available, or he can pass — usually to one of the players forming the triangle. Upon passing, he can cut to the basket for a return pass or move to an unoccupied part of the court, in which case the triangle re-forms around the new ball handler and the options are repeated.

The triangle relies on spacing, ball movement and the interchangeability of positions. The center, for instance, could find himself operating from the outside or the corners as well as from the post position. Scoring is an equal opportunity proposition, with openings for all five players on the floor to score. Teamwork and a "team" mentality are essential. Players are equally involved at all times and must think on their feet. They must read the defense, much as a quarterback reads the defense in football. "The defense doesn't just stand around," Tex said of executing the triangle, "so we have to be able to read and react. It's a constant process of adjustment that leads to small advantages that can result in baskets. The triangle produces shots, but it can't make them go in."

Players can expect to go through two distinct phases in mastering the triangle. Phase one consists of simply grasping the system — a tall order for many. Phase two entails attaining a degree of comfort in executing the system. Teams that defend the triangle best will make it as difficult as possible to execute, typically by pressuring the ball and grabbing and bumping to make cutting more difficult and less precise. Success depends upon properly executing the minute details that give the offensive team an edge. Fundamentals are the groundwork; drills meld them to the offensive scheme.

There are 36 diagrammed drills in *The Triple-Post Offense*, many with variations. There are 48 diagrammed options to the offense itself, divided into four major series — the sideline triangle, guard dribble, guard inside screen and the solo cut series. Each series has both a strong and weak-side application. All 48 options are named, for example, the "dribble weave," "center rub" and "button hook." Tex never numbered the options because his offense would not call a play. "It's important to have a nomenclature," he said. "Words mean more to the human mind than numbers. I can say to a former player 'guard squeeze' and he'll know what I mean."

There are also sections on building a fast-break, attacking zone defenses and beating the press. Most of the discourse on fundamentals is located in Part II under "Developing Programs." Part III offers a wealth of insight, aptly entitled "The Coaching Profession."

Not only did the publication of *The Triple-Post Offense* expose the innermost workings of the triangle offense and the coach who mastered it, but Tex gave complimentary copies to his fellow coaches. Some weren't able to copy what they did not understand. For most, even understanding did not translate into execution. But there was no secret to the triangle. "We could see it coming," said one opposing coach, "but we couldn't do anything to stop it."

The 1962-63 season was tough. The Wildcats started 4-6, losing by a single point to Marquette, then by 14 to the defending champion Cincinnati Bearcats in Manhattan. A quadruple-overtime loss to Kansas in the Big Eight Christmas Tournament was illustrative of the season. The winning basket was scored in the final seconds of the fourth overtime by Kansas reserve player Jay Roberts, who until that moment was better known for his football accomplishments. "When I shot it, I felt real sorry," Roberts said. "I wasn't supposed to do the shooting and I didn't think I could make it. All I knew was time was running out and somebody had to throw it up."

The Jayhawks had scored on a broken play. "This one beats all," said Kansas coach Dick Harp afterward. "It's my greatest game as a coach."

It was also his last win over Kansas State. The Wildcats would dominate the Jayhawks during their two regular season games and reel off four consecutive wins over Kansas before Harp was replaced by his assistant, Ted Owens.

The Wildcats finished league play a respectable 11-3, good enough to share the conference championship with Colorado and attain a top-20 UPI ranking. Unfortunately, their two losses to the Buffaloes meant

Colorado would represent the Big Eight in the NCAA tournament.

A bright spot on the roster was Wildcat Willie Murrell, who led the team in scoring with 18.6 points per game. At 6'6", he was a devastating inside player who sported an underhand scoop and a finger roll layup, the same move that would later make George Gervin famous. He possessed a rare combination coaches dream about — he was both a tenacious rebounder and a superb shooter. Murrell played the game with abandon and an infectious smile that won him thousands of fans wherever he played. He was the only K-State player ever greeted with cheers in Kansas' Allen Fieldhouse.

Murrell would do even more during the 1963-64 season, averaging 22.3 points per game while pulling down an incredible 321 rebounds. Despite a 20-5 record, the Wildcats finished the regular season unranked in the national polls. At 12-2 in conference, they carried the Big Eight by two games, defeating Kansas twice in the process. They defeated Texas Western, 64-60, in the first round of the Midwest Regionals in Wichita. Despite their 12-game winning streak, few expected them to match-up with the 5th-ranked Wichita Shockers in their own fieldhouse with their rabid fans. Pundits saw Kansas State having trouble with Wichita State's pressing defense and fast-break offense. They made the Wildcats 15 point underdogs.

The situation was exacerbated when Murrell revealed he was too keyed up to sleep following the team's win over Texas Western. A tired Willie Murrell did not bode well for the Wildcats. Attention also focused on Tex's "lucky brown suit," which he began wearing after K-State's previous loss, 77-58, at the hands of Oklahoma State — 12 wins ago. The suit had taken on a tattered look, sported a few holes and was not Tex's best color. But it got the job done against Wichita State.

The Wildcats dominated, leading 46-33 at intermission. Late in the game, the Shockers' Dave Stallworth went on a furious scoring binge, hitting four baskets in a 90-second span. He would finish with 37 points. But the sleep-deprived Willie Murrell would answer with 28 as the Wildcats broke down Wichita's full-court pressure defense and executed the triangle to dominate the fast-breaking Shockers. Kansas State triumphed, 94-86. Only a four-minute stretch at the end of the game during which they failed to score a field goal gave them pause.

It was Tex's 200th victory as head coach of the Wildcats, a feat attained in just 11 seasons. When asked about the achievement after the game, Tex responded that he "didn't really know about it." What he did know was that he was taking another team to the Final Four in nearby Kansas City. This time, for a rematch with John Wooden's UCLA Bruins.

John R. Wooden hailed from the basketball state of Indiana. As a 5'10" guard at Purdue University, he became a three-time All-American and was selected 1932 Player of the Year by the Helms Athletic Foundation. He coached high school basketball, compiling a 218-42 record, while at the same time playing semi-professional and professional ball himself. After a stint of military service, he enjoyed immediate college coaching success at Indiana State. Wooden went to UCLA in the fall of 1948 and quickly turned a losing program into a 22-7 record.

The next dozen years were not as easy; his teams fought to excel amongst challenging regional competition. His coaching ability was seriously questioned during those years, as teams such as Pete Newell's California Bears continued winning with disciplined half-court offenses. Wooden's Indiana heritage led him to emphasize the fast-break offense and numerous forms of a full-court press. Yet teams with solid half-court schemes still had the advantage over their run-and-gun compatriots. Kansas State, for instance, went 10-6 against Indiana University during the Winter era.

But it was John Wooden's system, supplemented by a superior talent pool, that would reign supreme. Wooden's UCLA teams set records that will almost certainly not be broken — seven consecutive national championships, an 88-game win streak, 38 consecutive wins in NCAA tournament play and four seasons in which they won all 30 of their games. From 1964 to 1975, the UCLA Bruins would win the NCAA championship 10 times in 12 years.

Although Tex Winter would become an ardent admirer of John Wooden and his accomplishments — Wooden's book *They Call Me Coach* has a prominent place in Tex's library — in 1964, Tex saw Wooden as an "edge" man. Along with his image as a church deacon who didn't smoke, drink, or use profanity, Wooden was a fierce competitor, always seeking to get his team an advantage.

Case in point: before the season, the two had tangled over a scheduling issue regarding the Sunflower Classic, an annual event in which Kansas and Kansas State played visiting teams in each other's fieldhouses. USC and UCLA were the scheduled guests, until UCLA threatened to pull out because the Bruins were playing both K-State and Kansas in their home arenas. The schedule was changed to accommodate UCLA. Kansas would play UCLA in Manhattan; Kansas State would play them in Lawrence. It was USC that would play both Kansas schools in their home arenas. Wooden's strategy paid off as his Bruins swept the series, including a narrow 78-75 win over K-State, while the USC Trojans lost twice.

Now the Wildcats had another crack at the Bruins, whose record stood at 28-0. The winner would advance to the NCAA Finals. Though K-State had played them close earlier in the season, the UCLA lineup — including Walt Hazzard, Gail Goodrich and Keith Erickson — was daunting. Though without a player over 6'5", they were a supremely conditioned team. Wooden told his players, "The fast-break is my system. We'll win 50 percent of our games in the last five minutes." His prediction would prove prophetic.

It was a see-saw game, with something for everyone. K-State conspiracy theorists noted with dismay that the chairman of the NCAA Tournament Committee was sitting on the UCLA bench. UCLA led at the half, 43-41. During the second half, the Wildcats broke down the UCLA press and Wooden called it off. The triangle was yielding the Wildcats high-percentage shots. They would outshoot the Bruins from the floor, hitting 37 of 76 to UCLA's 36 of 82.

The Wildcats led by five with five minutes to go. Whereas the Wildcats had struggled down the stretch, Wooden's Bruins had made it their specialty. They received new inspiration when their cheerleaders, who had been lost en route to the arena, made their appearance at the five-minute point. It was a heartbreaking finish as the Bruins pulled away to win, 90-84. On two occasions, shots by Wildcat junior Jeff Simons went into the basket, only to spin back out. It was a sight that would reappear in Tex's dreams for years to come — one of the few haunting memories of a lifetime in the game. Ironically, the Wildcats had won the game on the floor, only to lose it at the free-throw line — hitting just 10 of 21 to ULCA's 18 of 23.

The Bruins went on to beat Duke University with ease in the final, 98-83, while the Wildcats fell to a Cazzie Russell-led Michigan team in consolation, 100-90. UCLA would go on to win the national championship in nine of the next 11 years, while Tex Winter and his K-State Wildcats would experience their first losing season the following year and never again see the Final Four.

"I've often wondered," mused Tex, "how different things might have been for both programs if we had won that game."


The question is academic, of course. Not only was Tex's approach to basketball different, so was his approach to recruiting. Tex had focused increasingly on recruiting local talent, especially as his ties to the West Coast diminished. His philosophy was to supplement a player's education with basketball experience instead of a player entering school solely to play basketball. He recruited athletes who were best for K-State instead of focusing only on basketball. The emphasis then was to coach them to play to their maximum potential. It was a pleasant thought, especially for a school hampered by location, but not one that would win national titles.

At a time when the Beach Boys extolled the virtues of California, schools like UCLA had national allure. Wooden and his assistant, Jerry Norman, pulled the top prospects from every part of the country. K-State had a more provincial philosophy which had evolved from guidance given Jack Gardner from then athletic director Mike Ahearn, "We don't have the money to recruit. You'll have to go over to the intramural games and gym classes and pick the best you can find."

The difference showed in the records. While UCLA would repeat as national champion in 1965, falter in 1966, then reel off seven consecutive national championships from 1967 to 1973, Kansas State had its first and only losing season of the Winter regime in 1965 and would finish no higher than third in the Big Eight during the next three years.

Tex carried an additional burden during those years. Ernie, his older brother, who survived three crash landings during World War II and a miraculous journey to freedom through Japanese-held China, was killed in an automobile accident in September, 1964. The loss affected Tex deeply. Losing Ernie was like losing his father all over again. In many ways Ernie had become a father to Tex, always full of advice and often the coach's harshest critic. In a losing effort against Oklahoma, Ernie locked Tex in the locker room at halftime so he could talk to the players. Ernie could be a pain, but he set high standards. Tex wondered if he had become complacent in Ernie's absence.

Despite the disappointments — including six straight losses to the Kansas Jayhawks during those years — the K-State program remained popular, with fans continuing to fill Ahearn Fieldhouse and Tex continuing to feel the support of the community. Now something of a cult figure, he was in demand as a public speaker both for his wry sense of humor and his uncanny ability to mispronounce important names. He once introduced prominent K-State alumnus, Forest Brookover, as "Trees Overbrook."

His openness with reporters made him a favorite with the press, who noted that he appeared to be the same man after victory or defeat. "I've never refused to talk to sportswriters," Tex said at the time. "They've got a tough job and I want them to know why we've won or lost."

An editorial in the *Manhattan Mercury* after the 12-13, 1965 season summed up their feelings about Tex and his character both in winning and losing. In winning, he was described as a "champion of genuine modesty" willing to "pass plaudits where he felt they were deserved." Losing brought "no alibis and furthermore, he gave candid appraisals of why things weren't going as he and we hoped, never once attempting to spare his own responsibility." Noting the importance of a winning tradition and pride in accomplishment, the *Mercury* added, "it is rarer and far more desirable to find the type of spirit that was exhibited here this year. We can attribute that to no one other than Tex Winter himself."

Despite a disappointing showing in the Midwest Regionals, the 1967-68

Wildcats were back in form. Paced by junior guard Steve Honeycutt and 7'1" senior center Nick Pino, Kansas State finished 19-9, winning the Big Eight Championship for the first time in four years. Of at least equal importance, they ended their drought against Kansas, defeating the Jayhawks twice during the season.

The season was not without its downside, not the least of which was the demise of "the lucky brown suit," worn for the last time in a 92-68 loss to the University of Nebraska, the worst Big Eight loss in Tex's career at K-State. Assistant coach Cotton Fitzsimmons recalled the occasion. "I saw the shiny bottom to his pants and told him it wouldn't last the night. Sure enough, he jumped up off the bench and seat of his pants fell right out. I said, 'Told you so.' His response was, 'If that's all we lose here, we'll be lucky.' "

In Cotton Fitzsimmons, Tex had a personality that could compete in the national recruiting wars taking place across the country. He once spent 22 straight days in Edina, Minn., recruiting Bob Zender. It was the type of effort required to get the top talent, a chore Tex found odious, but that Cotton thrived on. The two men had different skills and personalities; yet despite their personal differences, they got along well. Cotton recalled the relationship in *The Ahearn Tradition*. "He would drive me nuts. He'd call me up at 4:00 a.m. with an idea. He'd be having some kind of a dream and he'd want me to get paper and write it down. I'd say, 'C'mon Tex, there's a time to think and a time to sleep.' "

He also had this to say about the man he would succeed at Kansas State: "Tex is unique. He invented things. He thought up certain things offensively to do on the court. I never thought things up offensively. I'd steal. If I saw Lon Kruger running a play and I liked it, I'd steal it. That's what most of us do. But Tex would think up new things. He came up with the triple-post offense and people are still using it."

Tex had a number of opportunities and accolades following the '68 season. He was one of four coaches selected to coach the Olympic Basketball Trials — along with Ray Meyer of DePaul, Arad McCutchan of Evansville and John Bach of Fordham. He teamed with Phog Allen to coach the West, with stars Rick Mount and JoJo White, to a 95-88 win over the East, who boasted stars Pete Maravich and Rick Adelman. He was also named Big Eight Coach of the Year, an award he accepted during a rally in Ahearn Fieldhouse. Cotton Fitzsimmons recalled the event in *The Ahearn Tradition*. "He thanked them all for their affection. Then he politely introduced me and said, 'I'm not even sure I'm the best coach on this campus.' Does that say it for the man? If he's got an ego, it's well hidden."

Beneath the surface of success, Tex was a tired man. Bringing the program back from three years of relative mediocrity had taken its toll. He felt stale and that persistent wanderlust was beckoning.

Life at Kansas State was changing as well. The "baby boomers" had descended upon state schools nationwide, crowding campuses and stressing the system. In 1967, violence broke out between rival K-State factions at an ROTC review. Peace demonstrators were pelted with eggs and manure when they appeared with signs reading, "ROTC Trains Murderers for Vietnam" and "Education Not Indoctrination." Martin Luther King, Jr. and Robert Kennedy, both of whom spoke at K-State in the spring of '68, were assassinated within months of their visits. James C. Carey, in his book *Kansas State University: The Quest for Identity*, summed up the mood on campus. "It was as if a cyclone of unrest passed over the seasoned old University, beating against the venerable stone walls and the weary faces within, in an attempt to force acceptance of certain aspects of a changing reality. Extremists clamored to be heard, but their methods and manners turned away those conservative students and faculty who favored a more reasonable approach."

Contributing to his decision to leave was the readiness of his assistant, Cotton Fitzsimmons, to take over the program. Tex prided himself on the professional development of both his players and assistants. In fact, he had urged assistant Bill Guthridge to go to North Carolina a year earlier because he believed it was a necessary career move. K-State moved quickly to confirm Fitzsimmons as Tex's replacement, a post he would successfully fill until the pros beckoned two years later. In the words of a school official, "Never have I seen such a smooth transition between coaches."

> **"Leaving K-State was a difficult decision, hard to quantify. I think I was made to move, to try new places and experiences. Life gets stale if I don't keep moving."**

Tex accepted the head basketball job at the University of Washington in the Pacific Coast Conference. It would move the Winters closer to Nancy's family in Oregon and Tex's mom in Los Angeles. Plus, it would give Tex the opportunity to build on a moribund Washington Husky basketball program. It would also require him to match wits with conference rival John Wooden and his national champion UCLA Bruins, led by 7'2" Lew Alcindor, a player the world would come to know as Kareem Abdul-Jabbar.

*We returned home once from the worst beating any of my teams had ever suffered. I was upset and discouraged. I said to my wife, "The worst of it — seven million people saw us play that game on television." Her reply, "Well, honey, remember, 650 million Chinese didn't even know you played," somehow removed the sting.*

— Tex Winter, *The Triple-Post Offense*, 1962

## Chapter Five
# Traveling Violations

At the first public gathering during Tex's introductory visit to Seattle, Washington Husky Athletic Director Jim Owens offered effusive praise for his new basketball coach. There was plenty of hope to offer enthusiastic Husky fans. Here was a coach who had won 262 games at K-State while losing only 117, making him one of the winningest coaches in college basketball. His K-State teams won eight conference titles in 15 years, including a 14-0 conference record in 1959, when the team was 25-2 on the season and voted #1 in the nation. They qualified for the NCAA tournament six times. The Winter Wildcats won the Midwest Regional Championship twice and produced four All-Americans. Tex was named Big Eight Coach of the Year four times and was the UPI Coach of the Year in 1958. He served on four NCAA committees, including six years as Chairman of the Coaches Rules Recommendation Committee. A fellow coach called his book, *The Triple-Post Offense*, "the greatest book on basketball offense ever written."

*The Seattle Times* termed Owens' introduction "flowing and florid."

"I hope," Tex said as he rose to the podium, "I can get some of that in writing."

Despite the need for a positive approach, the situation at the University of Washington was dismal. While Tex and his Wildcats had been major

players on the national scene, the Huskies had not won a single conference championship during those same 15 years. They had six losing
seasons in eight years. Their admission requirements were among the
toughest of any state school in the nation. Last year's team was rumored
to have racial strife. The University of Washington was a football school.

On its face the move made little sense, but Washington was a fine university with much to offer. The pressure had been building at K-State
anyway, where success had come to be expected. With its weak football
program, Wildcat basketball was the best show in town. The competition
for recruiting talent had become ferocious in the Big Eight, to the point
that Tex could predict where the "good players/poor students" would
wind up.

Tex viewed the move to Washington philosophically. He thought the
change would revitalize him. He looked forward to the challenge of
building a program from scratch. Tex even considered the Washington
football program a plus because it would provide cover while his team
worked through its inevitable growing pains. "I'm no miracle man," he
told the press. "I think I've proven that on several occasions."

Although Nancy was pleased with the move because they would be
closer to her family in Oregon, the boys were less than enthusiastic. Russ
and Chris were in high school and Brian was a seventh grader; it would
be difficult for them to leave their friends. They would also lose summers
in the Rockies at Camp Audubon, Tex's K-State basketball camp. They
were reluctant to leave the house Tex built with his own hands and the
fond memories of an exciting time in their lives.

At age 46, Tex felt he was in the prime of his coaching career. He took
conditioning seriously — for himself as well as for his teams, maintain-
ing himself in top physical condition. In working with Russ on the pole
vault he had surprised himself, easily clearing the bar at 12 feet. Still,
Russ dethroned the former vaulting champion, soaring to 12'6" during
his sophomore year.

Of the three boys, Russ took most fully to the Seattle area, opting to
attend the University of Washington, then working as a stockbroker in
Seattle for several years. He eventually returned to Manhattan for graduate work in urban planning, then moved back to Seattle where he built

a career renovating and managing urban properties.

However, 7'2" Lew Alcindor was building a career of a different type. College scouts began eyeing him when he was 13 and was still growing at 6'8". More than 200 schools recruited him from New York's Power Memorial Academy, where he scored more than 2,000 points, snared over 2,000 rebounds and led the school to 53 consecutive victories.

He chose to play for John Wooden at UCLA, leading a team that thoroughly dominated the competition, winning three national championships and losing but two games in the process. Alcindor averaged 26.4 points during his college career and was a consensus All-American all three years of his eligibility.

His pro career spanned 20 years, during which he played more games, scored more points and blocked more shots than any player in the history of the game. Alcindor's 38,387 points dwarfed even the stats of Michael Jordan and Wilt Chamberlain, with whom he was often compared. Bob Cousy said, "He combines what Bill Russell and Wilt Chamberlain individually specialized in." He was a proven winner: he could score, rebound, pass, defend and block shots. His six NBA MVPs matched the six NBA championships his teams won.

At the time Tex Winter took the Husky job, Alcindor was approaching his senior year at UCLA. "Winter 'Beat' Wilt — Next Target: Lew" proclaimed a sports page headline in *The Seattle Times*. "To a coach who 'beat' Wilt Chamberlain," the article read, "Lew Alcindor does not appear invincible. It helps explain why Tex Winter, the Pride of Manhattan, was willing to abandon an apparent paradise at Kansas State for a fresh start in the nether regions of basketball at the University of Washington."

Tex was less certain about the match-up with Alcindor, especially because the Huskies lacked size at center and would be learning the triangle from the ground up. "I'm the idiot who took the job," said Tex, "knowing that Lew Alcindor is in the Pacific Eight Conference at UCLA."

The problem was not just Alcindor, but a supporting cast that included Lynn Shackelford, Curtis Rowe and Sidney Wicks — undoubtedly the finest in college basketball. Pundits argued whether John Wooden was the best coach in college basketball, but no one argued with his success — his system worked for the players he recruited. The Bruins had plenty of big game experience. They were national champs two years running, paying back Houston in the NCAA Semifinals for their lone regular season defeat the year before, then toying with North Carolina in the championship game.

Wooden used 10 players in the teams' first meeting in UCLA's Pauley Pavilion; Tex used only six. It was no surprise when the Bruins jumped out to a 5-0 lead because they were 16-0 at the time, riding a 32-game win streak that extended into the previous season and included 37 straight home games.

However, Wooden was surprised by the Huskies' audacity to respond, with George Irvine shooting and connecting at the first opportunity and 6'9" Jay Bond taking it inside on Alcindor. Wooden anticipated a ball-control offense, not an in-your-face offense from a group of upstarts. Tex posted Bond 15 feet from the basket to draw Alcindor out, running his patterned triangle offense, complete with plenty of screening and cutting guards. The triangle opened up the middle and gave forward George Irvine, a 55 percent shooter on the season, room to operate. The Huskies traded baskets with the Bruins.

After trailing 12-10, another piece of genius in the Huskies' strategy became apparent — a tenacious zone defense. "They were overplaying me," said Bruin Lynn Shackelford after the game. "They were dropping a guard back to cover our high post and putting two men on Lew. It worked really well — that's a good way to play us." The Huskies held the Bruins scoreless for six and a half minutes, to go up 20-14.

They would lead by nine before taking a 33-29 lead into halftime. It was the first time in the 48-game history of Pauley Pavilion the Bruins had walked off the floor at the half trailing an opponent.

With the score tied at 41 midway through the second half, the Bruins kicked in the after-burners, drawing on the energy of 12,563 partisan fans and a superior bench. Alcindor stepped in front of Bond, intercepting a pass and dribbling the length of the floor before dishing off to Shackelford for a layup. Alcindor then blocked a Bond shot, after which

Shackelford connected on a 20-foot jumper.

Washington's Rafael Stone, a 5'9" guard who ran Tex's spread-court triangle offense to perfection, nailed a jumper, cutting the lead to 45-43. The Bruins hit a free throw, followed by another superb play by Alcindor, who grabbed a rebound, dribbled down the sideline past the UCLA cheering section and laid the ball in. That made it 48-43, the biggest UCLA lead since their early 5-0 run. The Pavilion erupted in pandemonium.

From there, the Bruins simply capitalized on Washington mistakes and the increasing fatigue that came with their six-man rotation. The Bruins focused on stuffing the ball in to Alcindor, taking advantage of Washington's foul trouble. The Huskies fell, 62-51, but held the Bruins to their lowest point total in two years. *The Los Angeles Times* described it as UCLA's "stiffest fight of the season."

"We didn't play too well," said Wooden, "but you have to give Washington credit for that, I guess. They threw us off and had a good game plan."

Tex was unusually upset after the loss. "I thought we had a chance all the way," he said. "We had good shots in the second half that just didn't go in. If we'd have hit them, we would have won it."

He complained bitterly about the officiating. "Alcindor had three goal-tending infractions and two charging fouls that weren't called," said Tex. "I don't know if we're supposed to say those things, but I feel they need to be said."

UCLA forward Steve Patterson, who spent much of the second half feeding the ball into Alcindor, put it simply, "We're going to have to start taking them seriously now."

A week later, in Seattle, the Bruins were taking the Huskies *very* seriously.

For only the third time in their 36 consecutive wins, UCLA trailed at halftime. Tex's Huskies had done it twice in 10 days.

They hung tough until the seven-minute mark when the Bruins unknotted a 32-32 tie with several quick baskets. When George Irvine fouled out for the Huskies, UCLA raced to a 53-44 victory, employing one of their patented strong finishes. Still, the Huskies' aggressive defense and deliberate offense held the Bruins to their lowest point total in years.

---

*"A coach has to be careful what he says — and how he says it. There's nothing more unpleasant than eating your words. You don't say things that will wind up on the opposing team's bulletin board. You don't want to unnecessarily raise expectations."*

---

◆　◆　◆

"You know," Tex confided to a writer, "I'm not so sure this isn't the best team I've ever had." The Huskies had just defeated Oregon State, Tex's old stomping ground, 85-65, and the coach was basking in the glow of victory.

After finishing 13-13 the year before, the Huskies were off to an 8-0 start for the 1969-70 season, rising to #10 in the AP poll and #6 in another. "I've never had a big man like Steve Hawes," Tex volunteered. "Parr and Boozer were good, very good, but I've never had a sophomore like Hawes. And he is going to get much better."

The 6'10" Hawes was Tex's first and most important recruit for the University of Washington. "I try to be perfectly honest with the boys," he told the reporter, "but I really bore down on Hawes, who lives near Seattle. I firmly felt we needed him and that he needed us." Hawes was to be "the symbol of a new era," and his breathtaking quickness was already leading the nation in rebounds.

With the hot start and the previous year's challenges to UCLA, Tex was quickly becoming the stuff of legend in Husky country. He was proud to have attained the status of professor. However, he was less proud of his nickname, "the absent-minded professor," coined the day his socks didn't match. He brought down the house when he appeared for a game wearing one black shoe and one brown shoe. When "listening" to other speakers at banquets, it was noted, "he'll diagram plays on a napkin."

Tex's difficulties with remembering names accurately continued. The Huskies' George Irvine, at the time the second most accurate shooter in the nation, was dubbed "George Irwin," and Husky spark plug Rafael Stone was "Rafer" or at best, "Stoney." Still, his praise for the pair was uncharacteristically effusive. "Irvine is a phenomenal shooter and we're able to get him the percentage shot. Few realize how effective Stoney is at moving the club. He has an unbelievably strong wrist-snap and unloads the ball so quickly by using his peripheral vision."

But too soon, it all came crashing down. First, Stone suffered a hairline leg fracture four minutes into the team's first loss of the season. Three nights later, the Huskies lost again when Steve Hawes suffered an identical injury. "In 21 years of coaching," said Tex, "I've never had a player with a broken bone. Now two in one week. I could just go over in the corner and cry."

Ironically, the injury to Hawes came in an 80-72 loss to the University of Seattle, a rare contest between the two schools. Like most large schools at the time, Washington had long refused to schedule their smaller, crosstown rival. "When I was at Marquette," Tex explained to reporters, "the big schools didn't want to give me any games. I promised myself then that if the shoe was ever on the other foot, I wouldn't behave like that." Tex was true to his pledge, but it had cost him. "In a week's time," said *The Oregonian*, "a pleasant dream turned into a virtual nightmare."

UCLA's John Wooden remained wary. "Even if all five Washington players should break their legs," he said, "there'd still be ample reason to fear Winter."

Tex constructed a new lineup and apologized to his reserves. "You aren't playing very well," he told them, "but it's my fault you didn't have enough practice." Then he worked their tails off. They limped home playing .500 basketball to finish 17-9, no mean feat under the circumstances. Calling Tex "affable and candid," *The Sporting News* noted Tex had "won the hearts and confidence of the entire school, as well as of the players and fans." Still, given the possibilities early in the season, it had been a heartbreaking year.

Returning to Manhattan, Kan., home of the Kansas State Wildcats, was a strange sensation for Tex Winter. "I'm so emotionally up for this game, I can't believe it," he told reporters.

He took his Huskies to breakfast, then showed them films of their loss to Utah earlier in the week. Sporting gold checkered pants, gold blazer and a new purple shirt and tie, Tex attended a Kansas State booster club luncheon. It was 1970 and Tex was experimenting with the "mod" look. According to most observers, it wasn't working.

Scores of friends and alumni turned out to welcome him home. Given the floor, Tex reminisced about his past players, many of whom were in the room. Caught up in the emotion of the moment, he appeared on the verge of tears. "Let's see, I need a joke now," he stammered. "Oh, yeah, the Utah game. That was a joke."

Tex used the occasion to make revelations about himself. For instance, he didn't feel he was as extroverted as people assumed. "I think I might have been happy farming or building something," he told them. "I'm not as involved with the public as people think I am. I get a great deal of satisfaction from being alone and working things out for myself."

Tex took a friendly roasting from his past players and staff, who focused largely on his troubles with the King's English and names. For instance, there was the time he took Cotton Fitzsimmons to the publicity office for a "biological" sketch. Or the time future Hall of Famer Westley Unseld of Louisville took apart K-State in the first half. Tex was so mad, he stormed into the dressing room at halftime, kicked a wastebasket across the room and shouted, "We've got to stop that Umblad!"

The return of Tex Winter was a nostalgic event. He was the coach who guided the Wildcats to eight conference championships in 15 years — and national prominence. Moreover, he was a man who was never too busy to visit with supporters, never in such a hurry that he couldn't take time to talk. In their minds, Tex was both a gentleman and basketball genius — a rare blend. Jeff Simons, a former player opined, "I don't think I could have played anywhere else on a major college level except for

Tex. He had a tremendous way of handling players."

That night, his Huskies trailed the Wildcats by 10 points at halftime, then rallied for a 64-51 win. For K-State fans, it was deja vu all over again. Hadn't they seen that offense somewhere before?

The visit to Manhattan gave Tex pause. It wasn't exactly a mid-life crisis, but being back on the K-State campus and feeling the competitive urge to defeat a program he had spent so much of his life working to build made him wonder if he was making the right life decisions. Winning was still wonderful and losing still hurt, but the real value in the game, he reasoned, was what it taught you about yourself and what you could teach to those who wanted to learn.

Cotton Fitzsimmons, in whose able hands Tex had left the Kansas State program, had already jumped to the NBA. He told Tex the triangle would work there, that Tex might enjoy working with professional ballplayers, that he would not miss recruiting. The University of Washington, like any college campus in the early '70s, was not a user-friendly environment for a middle-aged adult. Cotton had planted the seed.

Maybe it was time to make the leap. He'd had NBA coaching offers in the past, but never given them much thought. However, like sports fans all over America, Tex was watching more NBA games on television and attending games whenever he got the chance. He noticed as well that an increasing number of college coaches were moving to the pro ranks. In addition to Cotton Fitzsimmons, Bill Fitch, Dick Motta, John McLeod and Jack Ramsay were coaching for the NBA. Cotton assured Tex he'd have more free time in the pros, that home stands afforded plenty of family time and that Tex wouldn't have the peripheral responsibilities of college coaching. Cotton confided to Tex his only regret was that "he hadn't done it sooner."

With the graduation of Irvine and Stone, the Huskies struggled through the 1970-71 season. Steve Hawes was never the player he was before the injury. With UCLA as the dominant team in the nation and well on their way to seven straight national championships, the Huskies, along with every other team in the nation, were perennial also-rans.

Which is not to say they could not challenge.

On March 1, 1971, the Huskies took the Bruins to the final buzzer. This time, the Bruins won the first half, 38-36, and expanded their lead to 10 points early in the second. But the Huskies came roaring back, taking the lead with 56 seconds remaining in the game. Henry Bibby, the Bruins' scoring leader with 21 points, fouled out. But Curtis Rowe got free inside and scored, putting the Bruins back on top with 29 seconds to play. Washington worked the ball for the last shot. With three seconds remaining, a Husky drove the lane, broke free and tried to scoop the ball for the winning basket. It bounced off the rim. UCLA rebounded. Game over. Just another close call.

The end of the season saw Tex's three-year record at Washington at 46-34. Respectable — especially considering the state of affairs he had inherited. But the record told only a small part of the story. When the NBA came calling, Tex was ready.

"I think the scene is changing," Tex told a news conference, using the vernacular of the day, "and from the standpoint of doing what you want to do, I think the advantages outweigh the disadvantages."

Tex and Nancy were elated to be in San Diego, where Tex had just been named head coach of the San Diego Rockets. They were leaving behind the rainy Pacific Northwest for America's ideal climate, a place of surf and sunshine. Tex would be close to home and San Diego afforded an ideal place for Nancy's parents to visit.

"I enjoyed Washington very much; I love the Seattle area," Tex told reporters. "I guess you could say I was a little disappointed in the fact that there are so many things a coach no longer has any control over. I'm talking about recruiting. Even the campus scene itself is changing drastically. The attitude of students, faculty and minority groups toward athletics is different than it used to be."

Things would be different in San Diego. Besides the ideal location and climate, Tex would be working for longtime friend Pete Newell, the Rockets' general manager. Newell was well-grounded in motion offense concepts, having taken the California Bears to the national championship in 1959. Newell's boys had beaten Cincinnati and Oscar Robertson after they edged out Tex's Kansas State Wildcats in the Midwest Regional.

Tex was taking over for his old USC teammate, Alex Hannum, who had left for the Denver Nuggets in the rival American Basketball Association where he was named both coach and general manager. Hannum had his problems with players and management, but at least he left a team that had been exposed to the triangle's principles. That was a plus. Hannum was also an authoritarian leader. It wouldn't hurt that the players had experienced take-charge leadership.

"Of course, I want to be totally involved in San Diego," Tex announced, "in player selection, screening of players, promotion and public relations. It's a tremendous thrill for me to be here. You can't imagine how elated I am about it."

The elation didn't last. A month later, the team was sold and the new owners moved the team to Houston. Under contract, Tex found that he had little choice but to follow the team to Houston. So much for having more control.

To the boy who thought he had permanently left Texas years ago, Houston offered the ultimate Texas payback. While the people were friendly and understanding, the weather was more stifling than Tex remembered it. It probably was — Houston is further south than Lubbock and close enough to the Gulf of Mexico to pick up the very finest in humidity. The Winters, like many new arrivals to the city, found themselves struggling with a variety of illnesses as they adjusted to the climate.

The change in climate was not their only adjustment. The Rockets' move to Houston was precipitous and they were forced to the play the San Diego schedule exactly as structured. That meant playing home games in a wide variety of venues — the Astrodome, Astrohall and Hofheinz Hall on the University of Houston campus, where they never had a chance to practice. "Home" games also included the HemisFair Arena some 200 miles away in San Antonio, along with games in Waco and El Paso.

The theory was that Rocket superstar Elvin Hayes would pack in fans from all over the state.

Hayes was a bona fide superstar. He had performed on the national stage when it counted. On Saturday night, January 20, 1968, nearly 53,000 fans jammed the Houston Astrodome to see Elvin Hayes and the University of Houston Cougars play UCLA — led by Lew Alcindor. At that time, it was the largest crowd ever to see a basketball game, both in an arena and on television, where 55 million Americans viewed the classic match-up. UCLA came in with 47 straight victories — they hadn't lost in two years — and Houston had 16 straight, their last loss coming to the Bruins in the NCAA Semifinals the year before.

The hype preceding the contest was unparalleled in basketball. If anyone could stop the Alcindor juggernaut, surely it was The Big E. Many tried, a few came close — including Tex Winter — but few beat the UCLA Bruins in those years. Houston benefited from the hometown dome and the national sympathy for underdogs. Incredibly, the game itself exceeded the hype.

The Big E was everywhere. He jousted the opening tip from Alcindor, scoring the first shot of the game with his patented turnaround jumper. When the Cougars stole the ball, Elvin made it 4-0 with a hook shot from the foul line. He was off and running, in the first half hitting 14 of 19 shots. He finished with 39 points to Alcindor's 15; garnering 15 rebounds to Alcindor's 12. With the score knotted at 69, he hit the game-winning free throws with 28 seconds remaining. When Houston's full court press delivered the ball back to Elvin, he confidently dribbled away the game's remaining seconds. The riotous crowd poured onto the floor, carrying Elvin Hayes off on their shoulders. For the rest of his life, the name Elvin Hayes would bring to mind David slaying Goliath on a basketball court. And an entire country witnessed the spectacle.

However, by the time Tex Winter took over the Rockets in 1971, there were already chinks in The Big E mystique. Though Elvin led the NBA in scoring his rookie year, there were questions concerning whether he had the size to play center and if he had even the vaguest idea what a pass was. Hannum wanted to trade him. Jack McMahon, Hannum's predecessor, told the press Elvin was the reason for his firing. His teammates resented his whopping salary and his equally astronomical demands for the basketball. The San Diego press rode him unmercifully, as did Hannum, who was determined to mold Elvin into his kind of player. Hayes, a sensitive person, labored under the strain and was by his own admission on the edge of a nervous breakdown.

The situation was exacerbated when the owners' hopes for the Big E as a drawing card in Texas fell flat. Only 4,771 showed up for the team opener at the Astrohall. The team's first game in the Astrodome drew 4,061; in Waco only 759 attended. "It was an embarrassment," said Tex of the period. "The Astrodome looks pretty empty with 4,000 people in it. I know it hurt Elvin and the owners were devastated."

Making matters worse, the team lost its first six games, bottoming out at 2-16. Losing so many games so quickly was a unique experience for Coach Tex, who found the grind of the schedule more difficult than his college experience. Playing home games all over the state of Texas didn't help. The NBA, with its shot clock and four 12-minute quarters was a different game than Tex coached in college. In addition, the players were more developed. They were bigger, stronger, could jump higher and had an altogether different mentality.

Tex was disappointed to discover how little time there was to coach fundamentals. He was shocked to find players who thought themselves "beyond fundamentals" — able to play the game using only their physical gifts. For them, fundamentals might get in the way. Tex was not easily persuaded and though he eschewed the strong-arm tactics Alex Hannum had employed, he was nonetheless persistent.

He asked Elvin Hayes to do more passing. In his book *They Call Me The Big E*, Hayes said it was like "telling a home run hitter to stop hitting homers and start bunting instead." Hayes felt the passing option cost him his quickness and his shots were blocked as a result. Tex thought Elvin would be more effective at a forward position and planned to move him there when a suitable center could be acquired. The two were often at odds. In his book, Hayes refers to Tex "Winters" — suitable payback for a coach who frequently referred to his superstar as "Alvin."

The Winter touch had more effect with Rudy Tomjanovich, the Rockets #1 draft choice in 1970. Tomjanovich rode the bench during the

Hannum period, as Hannum's retaliation for management's refusal to trade Hayes and because Hannum didn't believe Tomjanovich had what it took to play in the NBA.

But Tomjanovich fit Tex's offensive scheme — he scored 28 points in his first start and would average just under 20 points and over 11 rebounds while playing for Tex. "We were starting to do some good things under Tex," Tomjanovich noted in his book, *A Rocket at Heart*. "Tex Winter really covered more of the fundamentals." Tomjanovich would later coach the Rockets to consecutive NBA championships in 1994 and 1995. "Tex Winter came in with a sound plan," he wrote. "He believed in an offense that reacted to the defense. Through Tex, I would learn what spacing and movement of the ball can do for you."

Players came and went during Tex's first season. For example, Tex was shocked when a newly-arrived player lit up a cigarette during a halftime pow-wow. "We don't do that here," Tex warned. The player was traded before his furniture caught up with him.

Gradually, the Rockets worked themselves out of their early season disaster. They were helped by the exploits of 5'9" Calvin Murphy, who joined the team in the same draft as Tomjanovich. Murphy was a fearless speedster who could stop on a dime and loft his soft-touch jump shot over much larger men. Tex admired Murphy's work ethic; he pushed himself to the limit in practice and had amazing focus in perfecting his free-throw stroke. A future Hall of Famer, Murphy would hold a career average .892 from the free-throw line — including an NBA record 78 in a row.

After the 2-16 start, the Rockets found their groove and played the latter part of the season at 28-26, at one point winning seven of nine games. On February 23, 1972, before a Waco, Tex., crowd that at 7,621 was more than 10 times the showing of three months before, the Rockets upset the Los Angeles Lakers 115-110. These were the 69-13 Lakers, with a 33-game win streak. Despite Jerry West's 36 points and the support of teammates Wilt Chamberlain and Elgin Baylor, on that night, the Rockets proved they could compete with anybody.

◆ ◆ ◆

Looking back on the season, there was cause for optimism. The Rockets had rebounded from a nasty start and overcame the handicap of playing in seven different home arenas. "I'd like to forget the first two months of the season," Tex said in the 1972-73 Rockets program. "Once our players matured a bit and learned to play together, it made quite a difference."

On the negative side, the situation with Elvin Hayes had deteriorated. After trying to fit in with the triangle, Tex noticed his star shooting more often, losing patience with the offense. When Tex confronted him, Hayes admitted he had consciously reverted to his comfortable game style — shooting. Tex liked Elvin and appreciated the fact that, as one of the game's greatest scorers, he was an asset. He also felt Elvin didn't get enough credit as a rebounder and hard worker. It bothered him that the two were at odds. There was a coach's maxim in the NBA at the time: "Always get along with your superstar." Break the rule and someone paid the price — usually the coach.

It had been a difficult season. In college, Tex put together the schedule himself, making sure the pace was reasonable for his players. If he wanted to, he could schedule a patsy or two to give the team confidence. Not so in the pros. You played what the NBA scheduled, when they scheduled it. For the Rockets, that meant playing their San Diego schedule all over Texas. No slack.

In college, Tex was coach, general manager — and king. He recruited who he wanted and played who he wanted. In the NBA, the general manager drafts the players and makes the trades. Marquee players are expected to be on the floor, drawing crowds. The players make more money than the coaches and situations are negotiated, not dictated. In collegiate basketball, Tex had more knowledge base than anyone around him. In the pros, he may have had the game knowledge, but even the players had more NBA experience. At age 50, he found himself having to earn his spurs.

Central to the Rockets' problem was what to do with Elvin Hayes. Tex went into the off-season thinking the acquisition of a bona fide center would solve the problem, allowing him to move Hayes to forward, which Tex thought was his natural position. But the more he thought about it, the more trading Elvin made sense. He was a huge name and a proven scoring machine. His game would fit better in a pro-style offense where he would have the freedom to play his game. The Big E had not proven to be a drawing card, as management had hoped.

On June 23, 1972, the Rockets made a trade that shocked the basketball world. Elvin Hayes was swapped to the Baltimore Bullets for Jack Marin, an All-Star shooter few would put in the same class as Elvin. The Rockets played the Bullets five times during the previous season and Tex was impressed with Marin's game. Three out of the five games, Marin was the team's high scorer, connecting for 41 points in the teams' first meeting.

The Rockets probably changed too much. In addition to Marin, they traded for guard Jimmy Walker from Detroit and centers Otto Moore from Phoenix and Don Smith from Seattle. A realignment of divisions put the Rockets in the NBA's Central Division.

The 1972-73 season started out well. The players seemed to be picking up the triangle and the team was ahead of last year's mark. Then a series of calamities and questionable calls struck with a ferocity Tex had never seen in his coaching life. Teams scored on the Rockets at will. Tex was criticized for his substitution methods and had a minor uprising on his hands when several players complained they weren't playing enough. The Rockets lost 10 straight.

The end came when the Rockets played perhaps their worst game of the season, losing 130-115, to the Portland Trail Blazers, who had the second worst record in the NBA. The Rockets' president and general manager announced shortly before a televised game with the New York Knicks that Tex Winter had been relieved of his duties. The Rockets then went out and upset the Knicks to end the streak.

"Tex Too Nice, Gets Ax," read one headline. "Tex is so good-natured, warm and friendly," said his replacement and former assistant, Johnny Egan. "He didn't like to be a disciplinarian. Tex is such a fundamentalist and there are very few pros who want to go back to fundamentals. He'd get along better with younger people who would go along with his coaching."

Tex Winter prepared to leave Texas for the second time.

*There comes a time in every coach's life when he has to do battle with himself. It generally comes after losing a few games or after a bad season. After a few losses, "the wolves begin to howl." The coach becomes the target of every critic in the area. This is when it becomes necessary for him to be courageous, to take setbacks like a man — no excuses, no rationalizations or alibis, no defenses. He must not let his dignity, integrity, or character wane in the face of adversities.*

— Tex Winter, *The Triple-Post Offense*, 1962

## Chapter Six
# Traveling Violations — The Sequel

Tex scouted for the Rockets for a few months before taking the head basketball position at Northwestern University. When asked to comment on the change, Tex replied, "I didn't leave pro ball bitter. It was a broadening experience, although not necessarily an enjoyable one. I learned some things that will make me a better college coach. But I honestly like college coaching better. The teaching-learning situation is much better in colleges and I think I'm better suited to that. I think of myself as a teacher and there's just not that much opportunity for that in pro ball."

When asked if he would be a more permissive coach after his experience in the NBA, Tex responded, "I won't be freer with the players. Maybe I'll be a little more stringent with them. That's what they need. The good college coach is there to consider the total individual. I don't want to say you mold character, but you are concerned with their development as a person. They're not men yet."

Accepting the coaching position at Northwestern was not exactly a career move. Brad Snyder, the previous coach, moved on after a 5-19 effort, concluding Northwestern's excessively stringent admission standards made recruiting impossible for Big Ten competition, where the team had gone 2-12. Northwestern was the only private school in the Big Ten, a conference known for its physical play and production of pro prospects. Its enrollment of 6,600 was dwarfed by every other school in the conference. In addition, NU's admissions standards, which included a 1200 SAT composite score, effectively eliminated 90 percent of college basketball prospects.

"There are probably not many coaches that this would be a good job for," said Tex, "but it's a good job for me. I've played that other game and lived that win-at-any-cost life. Now, I've got what I really want."

Tex's record was 44 and 87 during his five-year stint, but it was an experience he measured differently from any other. "I can't base our success on the loss column," he said during his tenure. "I have to take into consideration the material we've got and try to project what I think we're capable of doing. I haven't been discouraged. We've been competitive at times and that's all I hoped for."

---

**"I enjoyed Northwestern. They had the right philosophy for the student-athlete mix. Unfortunately, we couldn't really compete with the kind of competition we faced. Losing there was tougher than I thought it would be."**

---

Tex hoped his reputation and contacts would help bring quality athletes to Northwestern. His stint in the NBA would be a plus. Northwestern's greater Chicago location also brought him back into contact with Jerry Krause, who at the time was a basketball scout. Krause was always interested in Tex's offensive strategies and Tex enjoyed Jerry's insatiable desire to learn.

The key to the Northwestern job was turning minuses into pluses. In an interview with Barry Wolff, Tex related, "The incoming freshmen know they'll have to make it academically and that's a minus to many of them. But I turn it into a plus by telling them the academic atmosphere will ultimately benefit them. A lot of people also say Northwestern has one of the poorest basketball facilities in the Big Ten, but the court itself is a good one. It cuts down on leg injuries. I also tell recruits the fact that the stands are close to the floor makes McGraw attractive."

But McGraw Hall *was* the poorest facility in the Big Ten. The entire floor was hard-packed dirt. The north bleachers were a temporary design made of steel tubing and splintered wood boards. The walls and supporting steel beams were painted with a single layer of gray paint. The lighting was inadequate. It was a fieldhouse used for all sports.

Tex arranged the purchase of Kansas State University's former basketball court. He had the Northwestern court lowered and the K-State court added on, which widened the court by 44 feet, doubling the usable space. He bought four portable goals and set up two full courts running crosswise. The court, baskets, transportation and installation cost a mere $20,000. The floor was like an old friend. "The Kansas State court has a lot of sentimental value for me," he said at the time. Coincidentally, K-State and Northwestern shared the same school colors — purple and white, as well the same team name — Wildcats.

Tex had big plans for McGraw, envisioning a sparkling, modern facility that would be one of the best all-purpose sports complexes in the Big Ten. His pencil drawings and cardboard models revealed plans to increase seating capacity from 8,000 to 12,500 and provide for four basketball courts, six tennis courts, eight volleyball courts or ten badminton courts. After the dirt floor was excavated a few inches, concrete would be poured over crushed gravel. A 220-yard track would be constructed. Tex enjoyed dabbling in architecture; he thought the 1952 structure was sound, offering a plethora of possibilities.

The reality was the $3 million price tag was beyond the school's immediate resources.

The Northwestern women's team had already had a run-in with the men's coach of a major university. The coach's jeers as the women played on "his" floor became a media event.

It was a difficult time for men's and women's athletics; programs nationwide were grappling to coexist, sharing finite facilities, trying to come to grips with women's changing role in sports and society. The Bobby Riggs-Billie Jean King tennis extravaganza was symbolic of the mentality of the time. Around the country, "women jocks" were having a tough time with "male egos."

Northwestern's women's coach Mary DiStanislao went on record as resenting the digs she and her team were subjected to. "It's just very, very hard for most of these men to feel that we belong out there on center court," she said.

She also noted that back home at Northwestern, she and Tex Winter cooperate in a flexible exchange of Northwestern's limited facilities. "Tex loves basketball," she noted. "He knows basketball and therefore he's as interested in my team as I am in his. When he was playing Illinois this week, he scouted their women's team for me. He came back, put some things on the blackboard and it will help."

In the same article that outlined her problems as a woman coach, DiStanislao applauded her professional relationship with Tex Winter. "I guess I like him so much," she concluded, "because he thinks of me as a basketball coach."


The Northwestern Wildcats beat every team in the Big Ten except Indiana during Tex's tenure with the school. Tex had dominated the Hoosiers, winning 10 of 16, while at K-State. The Wildcats also enjoyed major non-conference wins against the University of Kentucky and Oregon State — where Tex played ball before the war. But the most satisfying win of the period came against the second-ranked University of Michigan.

The high-flying Wolverines, known as "the quickest team in college basketball," were 15-1 in late January 1977 and undefeated in the Big Ten. Phil Hubbard, Steve Grote and Rickey Green anchored the team. The Wildcats staggered into the contest at 4-13. Summarizing the situation, Tex quipped, "There are a lot of teams we can beat, but they're not on our schedule."

Among others, Northwestern had lost on the road to Notre Dame,

Arizona, Arizona State and at home to Marquette. Just before the Michigan game, Northwestern lost to three Big Ten teams on the road in five days — losing by one point at Wisconsin, two at Iowa and three at Illinois. They had fallen to the Wolverines earlier in the season, 102-65.

"You could take a nationally-ranked team and not win those games," Tex said. "If Kansas and Kansas State played the schedule we do, they might not do much better. If you lose when you play well, your confidence suffers."

Michigan drew Northwestern's largest home crowd of the season, but the Wildcats were not intimidated. They ran off 10 straight points to lead 35-26 and had a six-point lead at the half. Only the stone-cold shooting of Billy McKinney gave Tex pause. It's tough to beat a team like Michigan if your shooter is off.

The 6'0" McKinney was already Northwestern's all-time leading scorer. He was also an adept ball-handler who could distribute the basketball as well as shoot it. Hailing from nearby Zion, Ill., McKinney was a Northwestern fan favorite, appropriately dubbed, "Mr. Excitement." McKinney would go on to a pro career, play nine games with the Chicago Bulls in Tex's first year as an assistant there and later work in the Bulls organization. In the four games leading up to Michigan, McKinney scored 102 points. He once lit up Notre Dame for 37. "Our Billy McKinney is as fine an open-court player as you can have," Tex said of the lad.

McKinney would not disappoint, pouring in 21 points in the second half to finish with 29, winning a personal showdown with Michigan's Rickey Green, whom he held to 15 points. "Billy is the only guy on our team with the quickness it takes to guard Green," Tex explained after the game. "I hated to give him a tough assignment like that."

When Northwestern ran off 11 straight for a 70-57 lead in the second half, Michigan Coach Johnny Orr switched to a three-guard offense. The Wolverines clawed their way back, making it 74-72. But the Wildcats didn't quit.

The Wolverines seemed poised to take over the game with a jump ball under their own basket. The ball hit a Wildcat and sailed out of bounds.

Out of nowhere came McKinney, leaping 10 feet into the crowd to bat the ball back to a teammate. McKinney landed hard, but the immediate result was a Michigan foul, two made free throws and another turn of the tide. "It was just hustle," McKinney said afterward. "I threw my life and body out there to get the ball."

Northwestern won going away, 99-87.

"We got outplayed and outshot," said Michigan coach Orr. "We tried everything and it didn't work. We thought if we ever caught them, we'd beat them. The trouble is, we never caught them."

Mighty Michigan crashed to defeat. "We weren't super high," said Tex afterward, "but we were ready. We didn't do anything tricky. Michigan is awfully quick and relies on a devastating full-court press. But we feel we can handle pressure pretty well. Their press didn't hold up. That's where the 99 points came in."

Jubilant players tossed Coach Winter into the showers during their celebration. "I've been carried off the floor lots of times," said Tex, "but this is the first time I've ever been thrown into the showers. I like it better the other way."

The dripping coach was asked to elaborate. "It was worth it, but there was one guy in there trying to drown me."

Still, the upset win was special. "I've had some sweet victories in my 30 years of coaching," said Tex, "but this one was the sweetest."


Tex went to Long Beach, Calif., in the spring of 1978 on a scouting mission, looking for players in California's junior college tournament. It was the same old story, kids with game couldn't meet Northwestern's academic requirements; the few who did were hardly interested in leaving sunny California to freeze their keisters in Chicago.

Tex was already hearing the Sirens' song when Perry Moore, Long Beach State athletic director, approached him about the head basketball job. Moore was a basketball man. Unlike many athletic directors who were football-oriented, Moore could talk the game of basketball and knew the conference well. The two men saw a wealth of possibilities. Long Beach already had a winning tradition and someone like Tex could take them to the next level, maybe even a national championship. Long Beach had the immediate problem of attracting good teams for their non-conference schedule; someone with Tex's national reputation would be a big plus. Tex took the job, thinking he had a better chance of winning games at Long Beach than at Northwestern.

Nancy was pleased. It wasn't Oregon, but it was the same coast. With the boys out on their own now, the Winters took up residence in a California bungalow near campus. Nancy's parents would stay with them during the Oregon winters because she was quite involved in their care. Long Beach, near Los Angeles, had a lot to offer — a beach on the Pacific, beautiful weather and an urban flavor with plenty of recruits nearby. And it was home, just a few miles from Huntington Park High School and Compton Junior College — Tex's old stomping grounds.

Even the normally acerbic Bobby Knight from Indiana added a blessing. "No one coaching today knows the game more at both ends of the floor. Long Beach State in no way could have hired a better basketball coach. The situation at Long Beach State will afford Tex an opportunity to develop a first-rate basketball team."

Tex's first recruit for Long Beach was a hopeful sign. Craig Hodges was a quality player and person Tex had recruited originally for Northwestern from Chicago's Forest Park High School. His coach there was Steve Fisher, who would later coach the Michigan Wolverines to an NCAA championship. However, Hodges missed the grade point average requirements for Northwestern by the slimmest of margins. He wanted to play for Tex Winter and followed him to Long Beach. Hodges would star for the 49ers and later join Tex with the Chicago Bulls. Among other achievements, Hodges would become a multiple winner of the NBA's three-point shooting competition, at one point nailing an astonishing 19 in a row.

Not all of Tex's recruiting decisions were as brilliant. In the same year Tex recruited Hodges, he turned down a skinny, 6'3" guard by the name of Jeff Hornacek. Told the kid had great basketball instincts and could score, Tex was skeptical when others told him Hornacek was too slow and was not being recruited by the big name schools. Hornacek would walk on at Iowa State and later exceed 15,000 career points in the NBA.

It wasn't long before other realities surfaced. Tex's predecessor, Dwight Jones, had been fired largely as a result of the disenchantment of the players. Jones had taken over from Lute Olsen, who had coached for a year after the personable Jerry Tarkanian. While the 49ers had been successful on the scoreboard, the program Tex took over was under a cloud — and on probation with the NCAA. Tex had been chosen over Bill Mulligan, a local legend who had played his high school ball in Long Beach. Mulligan was the favorite with the players and fans.

Tex was confident he could overcome both obstacles. His honesty was part of the reason he had been hired in the first place; that was non-negotiable. As long as you were honest, probation could be overcome. The players would come around. Coaching changes were always tough.

But the situation was worse than he originally anticipated. Some players weren't the rational, academically-inclined types he had grown accustomed to at Northwestern. These kids were headstrong — and they were angry. A number already had a relationship with non-select Bill Mulligan who was coaching in the area at Saddleback College. The players told Tex he was too old. They questioned his credentials. What they didn't know could fill a gym and they were sure they were right. The list of grievances with the University, the selection process and life itself was staggering. Tex wondered what he had gotten himself into. He would say later of those years, "It looked a lot better from the outside looking in, than from the inside looking out."

Long Beach State had tasted success on the cheap during previous years. They had won the Pacific Coast Athletic Conference championship eight of the last nine years and been to the NCAA tournament in five of those years. Expectations were high.

At first it seemed the team could meet them. The 49ers won their first eight games, rising to #11 in a national poll. However, a series of injuries and a schedule of Tex's own making — Duke, North Carolina State, Kansas State, Cincinnati and Texas — brought them crashing to earth. They finished the season 16-12.

The probation lasted four years and nearly killed the program. Despite

Tex's impeccable honesty — not a single infraction was found on his watch — the Long Beach State administration dabbled in every activity, insisting the NCAA be consulted on even the most mundane matters. Tex felt himself functioning as a cog in a paranoid, bureaucratic wheel.

Recruiting for Long Beach was difficult. Not only did the school labor under the shadow of NCAA probation, but the Long Beach Arena, where games were played, was in an advanced state of decay. Jim McCormick of the local *Press-Telegram* described it during those years as "a civic disgrace … parking akin to driving through New York City, the lighting in the arena would have to be improved to be termed 'dark,' and the majority of the ceiling tiles which haven't fallen are badly stained."

Other schools in the conference had the same weather as Long Beach, as well as better facilities and the absence of NCAA probation. Parity had come to the PCAA and Tex Winter had arrived just in time to absorb the blows. No longer could Long Beach expect to dominate their conference rivals. Tex labored through his five years with the school with the available talent, compiling a respectable record of 78-69. But it was never enough for his critics, who for the most part wanted Long Beach to counter the run-and-gun tactics of opponents with more of the same.

---

**"Long Beach State looked a lot better from the outside looking in, than from the inside looking out."**

---

◆ ◆ ◆

With a vociferous group of hooligans sitting behind the bench wearing bags over their heads and heckling the team's efforts, home games became a nightmare. Bill Mahoney of the *Daily Forty-Niner* suggested Tex "should have a Plexiglas shield behind him like those at hockey rinks … to protect him from the verbal abuse hurled his way." Home attendance dropped to fewer than 2,000 a game. The team actually welcomed going on the road — at least they knew who the enemy was. They were the only team in the conference to hold a winning record at Fresno State's Selland Arena over the five-year span.

For the 1982-83 season, former 49er player Ed Ratleff joined Tex's staff, reportedly being groomed as his successor. Ratleff was a Long Beach State All-American during the Tarkanian years and was a well-known figure on campus. Tex liked Ed, but he was miffed because Ratleff had been made an assistant without Tex's input. It was symptomatic of the administration's Politburo approach to management. When decisions rolled down from the top, you were expected to accept them without comment and you could usually read a lot into those decisions.

At a time when he struggled to manage the juggernaut of 49er basketball, Tex Winter's esteem was never higher with his peers, who recognized his unique contributions to the game and his uncompromising integrity. He served as president of the National Association of Basketball Coaches, heading the Board of Directors consisting of coaching greats Dean Smith, Bobby Knight, Eddie Sutton, John Thompson, Jud Heathcote and others. The position gave Tex a forum for expressing his concerns about the direction of college basketball.

Having witnessed the poverty from which many of his players came, he was increasingly concerned about the limited assistance available to them. NCAA room and board rates did not cover the cost of living off-campus and the book stipend was unnecessarily stingy — about half of the required amount. Student-athletes were often left in the lurch over holidays — they typically didn't have the money to return home and weren't allowed to stay in the dorms.

Worse yet, they were prohibited from working during the school year. For Tex, who had grown up working his way through everything, this seemed downright un-American. It also seemed strange that a coach couldn't lend a helping hand. "If an English teacher takes a student home for dinner, he's a humanitarian," Tex said. "If a basketball coach does the same, he's a crook."

Tex found the system hypocritical, with the players suffering. He thought it encouraged coaches to cheat, not out of self-interest, but to help their players cope with an untenable situation. The NCAA overfocused on little stuff; they were out of touch with the realities players faced. When the rules weren't realistic, even honest coaches would cheat to do what they thought was right. Once the cheating started, where would it end?

The real cheating was already out of hand. The NCAA was uncovering illegal gifts, including cars and bribes of up to $10,000. Tex, under pressure to recruit from the local area, found it impossible to compete with unscrupulous programs that enticed players with illegal gifts. He had been losing players to rival programs for some time.

When Digger Phelps, the highly visible coach at Notre Dame reported evidence of recruiting violations, Tex followed suit. It was time to clean up the game. "We encourage coaches, when they feel there is evidence of or suspicion of recruiting violations, to report it to the NCAA," Tex told *The New York Times*. "When a coach feels he is being disadvantaged in a recruiting situation, it is for his protection and for the protection of the game of basketball and it should be reported."

Tex saw college basketball was poised to spin out of control, so he used his position as president of the NABC to attempt to restore sanity. He urged his fellow coaches to take responsibility as stewards of the game, not just to take what they could from it. He worried about the mass exodus of coaches from the college ranks, citing a 90 percent turnover rate in the 1970s. The average tenure of a college coach was five years, Tex noted with alarm. Though coaches were making more money, they were also being fired or quitting at a much greater rate. He saw coaches working harder and enjoying it less, feeling tremendous pressure to win at all costs. This pressure cooker situation created an atmosphere of frustration and desperation.

He saw a reward system giving windfalls for making the NCAA Final 48, with coaches being judged largely on their ability to get to the postseason tournament. With schools being challenged to fund well-rounded programs for both men and women, they were placed in the unenviable position of either winning the money through NCAA tournaments — or cutting budgets and hence, programs.

Tex recommended expanding the tournament to include more teams and finding a more equitable means of dividing the money. Both concepts would be adopted in later years. As it was, the numbers dictated that only a few schools could advance to the really big money. The system made the rich richer and the poor poorer.

Long Beach State, recognized as a pillar of honesty in the Winter era, had clearly become poorer and was operating in the red. It was unrealistic for the school to think it could compete against the best Division I had to offer. Not only did it lack a financial base, there was a lack of commitment within the school itself. Compared to its conference rivals, Long Beach was a second-class operation, constantly watching the nickels and dimes. PCAA rivals UC Irvine and Cal State Fullerton had more Long Beach players than Long Beach State. The probation image hurt Long Beach; it no longer held a preeminent position in the league. In the 1982-83 season, Nevada-Las Vegas had its best record ever, surpassing the record Jerry Tarkanian, the UNLV coach, had accomplished during his time at Long Beach. Cal State Fullerton had its best team ever, Utah State won 20 games and Fresno State had the best two-year record in the league. It was a tough time to coach at Long Beach.

*"Pressure is an insidious thing. Sometimes it builds without your knowing it, and blows when you least expect it and are least able to control it. The consequences for a single act can be enormous. And sometimes your actions are misinterpreted by fans and the media. The character you've spent a lifetime developing can be tarnished by a single rash act."*

Abandoned by boosters and fans, the 49ers labored in a dilapidated arena. It was next to impossible to recruit top local players. At 60, Coach Winter was considered old and rumors about his imminent retirement were spreading — some of which he started himself. It was difficult to recruit for a coach who might not be there.

Tex found himself increasingly at odds with Long Beach State President Stephen Horn. Tex's outspoken remarks on the treatment of his players alienated the administrator who seemed fixated on the bureaucratic aspects of probation. The two never clicked; Tex never felt supported and Horn seemed to want Tex silenced. The relationship was further strained as the situation deteriorated under the glare of unrealistic expectations.

Many of the pressures Tex feared for his fellow coaches, he began to see in himself. He still knew he could coach, that he was a better coach than he had been as a younger man. He still loved the game of basketball and the young men who played it. It was the peripheral stuff that was out of control and it was wearing on him.

The cauldron of discontent boiled over in the last two minutes of a game against Jerry Tarkanian's Nevada-Las Vegas Rebels. With the 49ers trailing, Long Beach's Reggie Payne intentionally fouled UNLV's Eldridge Hudson. A shoving match erupted and with Hudson holding Payne, UNLV's 6'10" 240-pound center, Paul Brozovich, began pummeling the defenseless 49er player. When officials failed to intervene, Tex joined the fray, separating the players and pinning the out of control Brozovich to the scorer's table, where he proceeded to slap some sense into him. "I went down with the intent to separate Payne and Hudson," Tex said to reporters, "but then I reacted when I saw what was happening. It was my reaction when I saw this guy hit Reggie in the face with three hard blows. I'd have been less of a man if I hadn't gone to his defense."

Reports of the incident varied. Eldridge Hudson, for whom the incident marked his third fight of the season, blamed the referees and said his teammate, Brozovich, should not have hit Payne. *The Los Angeles Times* chastised Tex's involvement. UNLV Coach Jerry Tarkanian defended Tex. "I've known Tex a long time. He's great for college basketball. I've never known Tex to do anything out of line. I think he was just trying to settle everyone down."

It was nice to have a fellow coach come to his defense, especially in an emotional situation. But the incident was one more ugly symptom of a situation out of control. Something was wrong. It was time to take stock.

As the season wound down, Tex kept his gutsy 49ers in games they should have been blown out of, employing a stifling zone defense and exhorting his team to stick with the triangle. Despite a freshman center and diminutive forwards, they beat highly-ranked Texas Christian by 18 and turned back Danny Ainge and Brigham Young on the BYU home court. They were clearly a better road team, giving Fresno State a basketball clinic at Fresno's Selland Arena before a hostile crowd.

They drew the heavily-favored #2 seed, Cal State Fullerton, in the PCAA Tournament. In a brilliantly coached game at the Los Angeles Forum that saw many Long Beach boosters leave at halftime, the 49ers rallied for a 61-59 win. Their season ended in a loss to the eventual champion, UNLV, in a hard-fought 67-64 contest.

Tex resigned. The university called it "retirement" and asked Tex to stay on in an advisory role.

The interlude gave Tex an opportunity to examine his priorities in light of the new realities of college basketball. He knew he could coach and he still loved the game. He loved teaching and seeing the results of the triangle against more talented teams. Tex questioned whether he had the drive it took to recruit and the patience and diplomacy to cope with the ignorance of boosters and administrators.

The pressure to produce winners at any cost had changed the coaching profession. No longer were coaches teachers and mentors; increasingly they were becoming entrepreneurs — in it for big bucks, notoriety and recognition. Very few coaches were under long-term contracts or faculty tenure. Recruiting had become the name of the game. Moreover, the temptation to cheat was often too strong for an entrepreneurial coach to resist.

Was there any place in the game for a teacher?

> *The time may never come when coaches can be placed in the same category as members of the academic faculty.*
>
> **— Tex Winter, *The Triple-Post Offense*, 1962**

# CHAPTER SEVEN
# TEX WINTER, CONSULTANT

D ale Brown was a high school coach from Minot, N.D., with an insatiable drive to master the game of basketball. His quest took him to numerous college gymnasiums in search of the holy grail. He discovered it in the 1950s on the floor of Kansas State during practices conducted by Tex Winter. He witnessed a rare synthesis of theory and practice — every action contributing to the philosophic whole. Dale took notes. He asked questions. The two became friends.

Dale Brown rose to the top of the college profession, becoming head coach of the Louisiana State University Tigers, building a program that terrorized the Southeastern Conference, dominated the legendary Kentucky Wildcats and rose to national ranking. When an assistant position opened in the spring of 1983, he had 250 qualified applicants. He wanted Tex Winter.

Brown offered Tex a deal he couldn't refuse — all coaching, no recruiting and more money to work nine months than he made at Long Beach State in a year. He would be a consultant, not an assistant — mentoring Dale, teaching team fundamentals and working with players one-on-one. "By Gumbo, It's Tex Winter at LSU," read a sports headline in *The Los Angeles Times*. Leaving a basketball program that had finished $40,000 in the red, Tex joined a program that was $1.2 million in the *black*, with 13 television appearances. The 14,236 seat Assembly Center, nicknamed the "Deaf-Dome," was usually filled to capacity. It was a superior environment for home games to LBSU, where the team preferred to play on the road.

Dale Brown was elated to work with his former mentor, calling him "the Rembrandt of basketball," and "one of the greatest coaches who's ever coached the game of basketball." Brown compared him to UCLA's John Wooden, North Carolina's Dean Smith and Indiana's Bobby Knight. Calling it a "huge day for LSU basketball," Brown predicted LSU players would "fall in love with Tex Winter because of his exceptional knowledge, teaching ability and for the kind of person he is." He outlined Tex's consulting duties as coaching, private drills with individual players and scouting.

Tex was pleased with the arrangement. He had always liked Dale and the two had maintained contact over the years. Tex said at the time, "This is an ideal situation for me because the thing I love to do is teach — work with the young players on the court and develop their skills. At this point in my career, I'm not that excited about all the things that go with being a head coach. I'd just as soon be in the background, spending my time working with young men and helping Dale any way I can. It's really what I was looking for. I would not have taken another job as a head coach."

---

**"Always be nice to people on your way up, you may see them again on your way down."**

---

Initially, Tex found it odd not being the head man, but he kept his ego in check, fitting the niche Dale carved for him. Tex didn't miss recruiting or the promotional activities inherent in the head job — areas in which Dale excelled. He also noted Brown's superb organizational skills and his ability to effectively delegate. He found Brown to be secure in himself and more than generous in sharing the limelight and the credit, frequently inviting Tex to press conferences and directing questions his way.

Brown once said the following in response to a question about his "consultant." "Bear Bryant once told me, 'Hell, it isn't me. I've been smart enough to hire people at least as smart as I am or smarter.' You can find a 'yes' man in any hole. You need a creative, intelligent, successful individual to continue to improve and progress in our situation."

Tex enjoyed the perks that went with his special status of "Professor of Basketball." He gained 10 pounds savoring Cajun cuisine and he appreciated the chartered flights for away games. His office was down the hall from Coach Brown's, so they enjoyed frequent basketball and strategy discussions. Tex scouted opposing teams with an eagle eye, warning Dale of an opponent's strengths and advising how to exploit weaknesses. It was a basketball dream come true.

LSU took full advantage of Tex's teaching ability, setting up individual tutoring sessions during the day. Tex scheduled meetings with players in the mornings and held one-on-one sessions in the afternoon. Most of the players met with him for 45-minute periods once or twice a week. Some came out every day for instruction.

"We're unique in that we have a guy with the experience and ability to work one-on-one with people," said Brown. "First of all, most coaches don't have the desire to do it. Most coaches don't have the knowledge to do it. And most coaches don't have the time to do it. Well, he has all of them."

Tex enjoyed every minute he spent on the court, frequently handling the basketball like the old point guard he had been in an earlier incarnation, dribbling the ball from side to side, constantly studying the movements of the players while getting into the flow himself. Minus a few gray hairs and the 10 extra pounds, he might have been any of the LSU players out on the court.

"We work with each player on weak points and their overall game," said Tex. "There are fundamental skills you often don't have time for when you're working in the team concept with 14 or 15 guys in practice. It's unique that we're approaching it this way. Some of the players have benefited from it greatly, particularly some of the freshmen and sophomores, because they're still pretty young and in the learning process."

Brown was pleased with the improvements he saw in his players and the teaching concepts Tex installed. "If another program does it, I don't know about it," he said. "And if they do it, they don't have a man like him doing it. It will pay dividends, particularly later this season and next year."

Nikita Wilson was Tex's prize pupil. After a disappointing freshman season, he progressed into an outstanding power forward under Tex's tutelage. Early in his sophomore season, he was already second on the team in scoring with over 15 points per game and pulling down almost six rebounds per game. Fans noted Wilson hardly looked like the same player. He was much smoother and more confident with the basketball and he had learned to put some arc in his shot — shots that were now falling.

"I think the individual drills, particularly his footwork in the post have helped him get over hurrying himself," Tex said modestly. Tex also concentrated on footwork with the Tiger centers, showing them they could get places more quickly if they moved the proper way. Tex was an excellent big man coach and he found the LSU centers to be quick learners.

Coach Brown found the team running the offense better than they had the year before at tournament time. The entire skill level of the team was lifted and assist numbers demonstrated they were effectively passing the basketball. "I think it's partly due to fundamentals being called to their attention," said Tex. "Coach Brown is very thorough in presenting what he wants them to do in practice. So it just becomes a question of getting out and doing it."

The LSU Tigers were definitely getting it done during Tex Winter's two-year tenure with Dale Brown, compiling a 37-21 record, winning an SEC Championship and advancing to the NCAA tournament in both seasons. Tex might have been inclined to stay on had he not heard from another old friend who had risen to a position of power and influence. In his second day as general manager of the Chicago Bulls, it was Jerry Krause on the line.

A hoop still hangs on the old garage where Tex Winter first shot a basketball—in Wellington, Texas.

Tex's dad, Ernest Winter. "He made life interesting."

"Things were worse in California," Tex said after moving from Texas. He worked for leftover vegetables during the Depression.

Tex (left) and brother Ernie, with their mom, Theo.

Tex clears the bar for Compton Junior College in Los Angeles, 1941.

Ernie (left) was shot down three times in WWII; Tex played basketball and pole vaulted for the Navy.

The men of VF6 Flight 353, U.S. Naval Air Station, Sanford, Florida, in 1945. Tex is second from the left, standing.

**Tex played basketball while in the Navy, 1943-44.**

**Tex and Nancy Bohnenkamp are married in July, 1946. But did she have the right guy?**

Tex vaulted at USC in 1946 and planned to coach high school track and field.

Kansas State glory days in the late fifties. 2nd row from left: Roy DeWitz, Don Matuszak, Hayden Abbott. First row from left: Bob Boozer, Tex, Jack Parr.

Christmas circa 1961. Brian points a cocked toy pistol at brother Chris, as Russell looks on in amusement. Tex and Nancy show the first inkling of parental concern about Santa's surprise.

You're Invited
To FOLLOW THE WILDCATS
In 1965-66

It took 15 copies of Tex's book, *The Triple-Post Offense*, to put him on an equal plane with Kansas State's seven-foot center, Nick Pino.

THE NEW LOOK!

"TEX" WINTER NEW HUSKY COACH

1968-69 HUSKY
BASKETBALL
UNIVERSITY OF WASHINGTON

Tex left Kansas State to coach the Washington Huskies, and looked forward to coaching against John Wooden and UCLA.

**Michael Jordan looks on as Tex makes a point.** *(Photo by David Markwiese)*

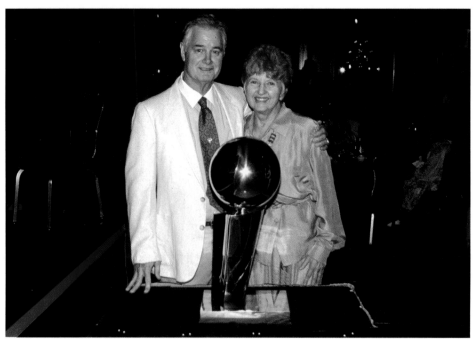

**Tex and Nancy with the Bulls first NBA Championship trophy, 1991.** *(Photo by Bill Smith)*

Tex and Nancy celebrate the first Chicago Bulls three-peat in 1993.

Tex receives his third NBA Championship ring from Commissioner David Stern. Bulls announcer John Kerr looks on. *(Photo by Bill Smith)*

Tex and his running buddy, Dennis Rodman. Waiting for a plane. *(Photo by Bill Smith)*

When the first lady asked about the challenges of a half-century of coaching Tex replied—"It's easy, kinda like being President of the United States." *(Photo by White House photographer)*

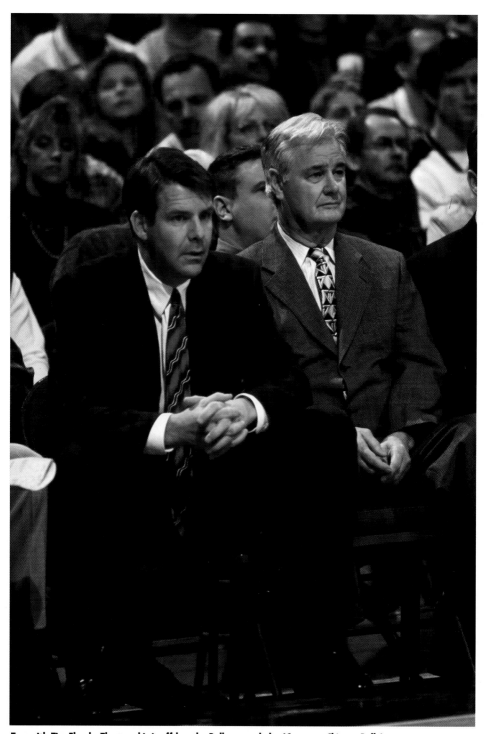

Tex with Tim Floyd. The two hit it off but the Bulls struggled. *(Courtesy Chicago Bulls)*

**Tex with Shaquille O'Neal and Phil Jackson.** *(Photo by Dan Gluskoter)*

The Laker bench shares a light moment. Kobe Bryant is at left, during his broken hand period early in the 1999-2000 season. Assistant coach Frank Hamblen, left, and trainer Gary Vitti, right, book-end Phil and Tex. *(Photo by Dan Gluskoter)*

Tex in his element. *(Photo by Dan Gluskoter)*

A Laker gets a wake-up call. *(Photo by Dan Gluskoter)*

A frequent sight. Tex and Phil "conferencing" early in the Laker season. *(Photo by Dan Gluskoter)*

Figuring it out during a Laker timeout. *(Photo by Dan Gluskoter)*

◆ ◆ ◆

Jerome Richard Krause, the son of a Russian Jewish immigrant, grew up in Chicago and was in many ways the archetypal Chicagoan. Outwardly tough, brusque in personal relationships and perhaps, at 5'5", driven by a Napoleonic complex to succeed, Jerry Krause was a sports nut without the physical tools to excel as an athlete. He learned instead to excel on the margins of sport — as a back-up catcher in high school and then at Bradley University, where he also assisted the basketball program charting plays. What he lacked in the physical realm, he made up for with brains and chutzpah. Jerry knew what was going on and he knew who had it going on. He soon became a favorite of scouts, who learned to trust his opinions. Always hungry to learn, Jerry pumped them for information. He became a scout himself.

Nobody outworked Jerry Krause. He had what he called the "two-cocktail rule" — when other scouts were enjoying their second cocktail, he was down the road looking for more talent. In the competition with other scouts, Jerry learned when to talk and when to keep his mouth shut. Wearing a trench coat and hat, he looked every bit the spy and picked up the nickname "Sleuth." He had an eye for talent, frequently finding it in places other scouts overlooked. Among his many finds were two Division II players, Jerry Sloan from Evansville, one of the greatest Bulls players in history and Earl Monroe from Winston-Salem State, another NBA Hall of Famer.

Krause respected people who seemed unusually dedicated to their profession and was drawn like a magnet to Tex Winter. They met while Tex was at Kansas State; Jerry was fascinated with the triangle, pumping Tex relentlessly for information on how it worked. Tex found Jerry to be a quick study and he was only too happy to talk triangle basketball with someone as consumed with the topic as Krause. They spent hours together reviewing game films and became friends. Jerry considered Tex a basketball genius, frequently referring to him as such. Years later when asked to list his favorite books, Krause included Tex Winter's *The Triple-Post Offense*; when asked to list the top coaches of all time he responded, "Red Auerbach, Red Holzman, John Wooden, Alex Hannum and Tex Winter."

Krause became general manager of the Chicago Bulls in 1976, but his tenure quickly soured in a media frenzy over whether or not he had offered DePaul coach and hometown favorite Ray Meyer the Bulls' head coaching job. Unpopular with the Bulls' administration and ownership, he was promptly fired.

After a short stint scouting for the Los Angeles Lakers, Bill Veeck, owner of the Chicago White Sox, brought Krause back to his hometown in a baseball capacity. The team was purchased by Jerry Reinsdorf in 1981 and four years later, when Reinsdorf bought the Bulls, he made Jerry Krause his general manager.

Jerry Krause was back. Krause's work ethic, loyalty and eye for talent convinced Reinsdorf he could handle the job. The first call Jerry Krause made was to Tex Winter. "I saw Jerry quite a bit at Northwestern," said Tex. "He told me several times he'd be calling me if he got a G.M. job in basketball. When I saw the report on TV, I told Nancy, 'The next call will be Jerry Krause asking me to take a job.' Sure enough, it was Jerry."

---

**"Jerry was an only child. He spent a lot of time alone. He always had big dreams."**

---

Jerry Krause wanted Tex Winter to be his first acquisition as the Bulls' G.M. Jerry showed the tenacity of a bulldog — at times begging for help, at times invoking a mythical promise that Tex would join him when he got a team. Tex hesitated initially, not especially impressed with the package he was offered. On the other hand, NCAA rules were increasing the likelihood he'd have to become involved in recruiting at LSU if he kept his full-time position there. The Bulls offer was an intriguing opportunity. "Make it worth my while," he told Krause as he warmed to the idea. When the offer was raised substantially, he told Krause, "That sounds more like it." Simple as that, it was back to the cold Chicago winters and freezing keisters.

◆ ◆ ◆

The Chicago Bulls were a lackluster basketball operation. They were 27-55 for the 1983-84 season, failing again to make the playoffs, failing also to attract fans. Their abysmal record placed them third in the NBA draft lottery, directly behind Portland, who owned Indiana's pick and Houston, who had an even worse record than the Bulls. Houston chose Hakeem Olajuwon; Portland, on the theory that big men were the future of the NBA, chose Sam Bowie. That left the Bulls with the leftovers, which happily enough for them, included a North Carolina product named Michael Jordan, who had foregone his senior year at the university to turn pro.

Midway through the 1984-85 season, Reinsdorf bought the team, fired the G.M. in the first two weeks and hired Jerry Krause. Jordan had already made the All-Star team and was well on his way to Rookie of the Year honors and a 28.2 points per game scoring average. Krause fired head coach Kevin Loughery when the season ended — he wasn't one of Jerry's guys. In the course of one season, the Bulls had acquired Michael Jordan, changed owners, G.M.s and coaches — and hired Tex Winter.

Tex was in for a wild ride. Stan Albeck, hired to replace Loughery, was a nice enough guy, but Tex was unsure where he stood with Stan. Jerry Krause had supposedly cleared Tex's position and status with Stan, but Tex knew from his time at Long Beach State the frustration of having your assistant picked by a higher-up. Tex continued to think of himself as a consultant, there to help Stan in any way he could and be a fundamentals instructor for the players. If Stan wanted to use the triangle, that was fine; it was his call.

Tex found Stan Albeck to be a good coach. He knew the NBA, its systems and the Bulls' opponents. While he ran the same plays as most other NBA coaches, he also understood the importance of defense and conditioning. Tex knew of Jordan from his time at LSU — the Tigers had played Jordan's Tar Heels and gave them a pretty good run. Beyond Jordan's obvious physical talent, Tex saw a competitiveness and basketball savvy not found in many players. Tex liked the fact that Jordan had not hesitated in taking the game-winning shot against Georgetown in the national championship final in 1982. It was indicative of the fearlessness he saw in Jordan— a player unafraid to take the ball with the game on the line. Jordan was a smart, hard worker — other qualities Tex admired.

The 1985-86 season started poorly. The Bulls went 0-8 in the preseason, in the middle of which Quintin Dailey, one of their stalwarts, requested admittance to a drug treatment facility. The situation was symptomatic of a larger drug problem on the team. Jerry Krause traded David Greenwood for the aging George Gervin to improve the backcourt and fill in for Dailey. The move did not sit well with Michael Jordan, who became more upset when the Bulls waived his friend and confidant, Rod Higgins.

Jordan took it out on the Cleveland Cavaliers in the first Bulls home game, scoring 29 and leading the Bulls to a one-point victory. Watching Michael play was thrilling for Tex, who marveled at Jordan's acceleration, jumping ability and variety of moves to the basket that left defenders grasping at air. Despite Jordan's relative youth, Tex saw natural leadership qualities as well as perfectionistic traits. Jordan was a hard worker — and he wanted to win. His drive and work ethic contrasted sharply with that of older players who had learned to accept losing and were merely putting in time.

As good as Jordan was, Tex realized he could be even better. Michael needed to work on his jump shot. If he could add a consistent shot to his repertoire, his driving moves would be even more effective. He also needed to learn how and when to pass. With all the special skills Jordan possessed, he couldn't make a simple chest pass.

Chest-passing was not on the Jordan agenda the following evening as he scored 33 in leading the Bulls past the Detroit Pistons, 121-118. Late in the fourth quarter, Jordan escaped on a breakaway, only to be caught from behind and slammed to the floor by the Pistons poster-child bad boy, Bill Laimbeer. Laimbeer had made no attempt on the ball; his target had obviously been Jordan. Further, in typical Bill Laimbeer style, he seemed totally indifferent to the fate of his prey.

An enraged Jordan came after Laimbeer and the benches emptied. Tex did what he could to keep players on the bench, as visions of LBSU-UNLV flashed through his mind. Moments later, he was separating coaches, as Albeck and Pistons' coach Chuck Daly squared off. In his second game back in the NBA, Tex Winter survived his first riot. Little did he know he had witnessed the opening salvo in a physical, bitter rivalry with the Detroit Pistons that would drag on for years.

As traumatic as the game with the Pistons had been, it paled in comparison to an episode that occurred in the Bulls' following game against the Golden State Warriors in the Oakland Coliseum. This situation would set in motion a chain of events within the Bulls' organization that would play out over a period of years, not only leading to Stan Albeck's firing, but to a running gun battle between Jerry Krause and Michael Jordan that would last more than a decade. Tex Winter would see it all, survive it all. But it would tax his acquired wisdom and acumen to the fullest and it would not always be fun.

Michael Jordan crumpled to the Oakland Coliseum floor. At first it was similar to any number of mishaps that occur on a basketball floor — a player falls, slips, or is pushed. But this time Jordan needed help walking to the bench, then to the locker room. It didn't seem significant, but it was. Jordan had a broken navicular tarsal bone in his left foot, a break so tiny it didn't show up on X-rays. The precision of a CAT scan was required to reveal the damage. It would be a minimum of six weeks before Jordan could return and there were no guarantees because the navicular tarsal receives a minuscule blood supply and therefore, can be very slow to heal.

The Bulls lost four straight after the injury. Quintin Dailey was rushed out of rehab and made inconsistent contributions before the team suspended him for continued drug use. With the Bulls' record at 5-9, Jordan went home to North Carolina rather than accompany the team on a two-week road trip. The Chicago papers made a story of his "desertion." Jerry Krause asked him to return. Jordan refused, saying he couldn't stand to watch his teammates playing so poorly game after game.

With the Bulls struggling at 8-17, speculation arose that Jordan would return by early January. But a physical revealed the bone had not mended. The Bulls announced he would be back by February 1, then slipped the date to February 14. The Bulls continued their slide, taking a 17-33 record into the All-Star break. Tex felt growing tension on the team and within the organization. Jordan had made comments about what he saw as the team's lack of effort. Meanwhile, many players were openly hostile about Jordan's refusal to stay with the team during his convalescence.

Tex wondered if the team could jell when and if, Jordan returned. The Bulls' shot at the playoffs was slowly drifting away and there were those, probably including Jerry Krause, who thought the Bulls should write off the season in the hopes of picking up a high draft choice in the off-season. While trying to win games at this juncture made little sense to some, to Albeck and Winter it was a code of honor to try to win. Anything less was unthinkable.

Jordan returned to Chicago March 10 and passed tests which showed the strength had returned to his left foot. He had worked hard in therapy and had secretly been playing basketball in North Carolina. Later that day, he practiced with the Bulls. But bad news followed. A CAT scan revealed a small crack was still present in the bone. Doctors estimated a 10 to 20 percent risk of serious injury if Jordan returned to basketball to finish the season. If he rested until next season, the odds would be closer to one in 100.

But Jordan had caught the basketball bug. With three specialists, Krause and Reinsdorf advising against, Jordan insisted he knew his own body and was ready to play. He was willing to risk his career to prove it. Bad feelings abounded. Jordan felt he was being treated like a piece of property instead of as a human being. Reinsdorf and Krause resented the accusation that they were tanking the season for a draft choice. Eventually a compromise was reached — Jordan would play seven minutes per half — and no more.

Jordan played 13 minutes in his first game back. When the game went into overtime, he asked Stan Albeck if he could play. Albeck, on strict instructions from Krause, refused. The next day, Jordan was asking for 10 minutes a half.

As management gradually yielded to Jordan's requests for expanded playing time, Tex noticed a collateral problem in the team concept. The Bulls were executing the half-court triangle effectively — until Jordan entered the lineup, then it was Katie bar-the-door. The Bulls had won their last three ballgames before Michael's return, now they were struggling again. Michael hadn't gotten his game completely back yet; he was missing a lot of shots. The change in pace from the offense without Michael to with Michael was just too much for the team to effectively absorb. There were rumblings in the media that a number of Bulls players were unhappy with the schizophrenia they were feeling on the court.

The coaches were caught in the middle. Tex agreed with the specialists that Jordan was taking too big a chance in coming back early. He felt for Stan Albeck who had Jordan bugging him for more minutes and management telling him to hold the line. As Jordan's game improved, it became more difficult to take him out when his time was up — especially in key situations with the game on the line.

With Jordan lobbying for more minutes in the media and accusing management of purposely blowing off the playoffs for a draft choice, his playing time was gradually increased. However, precisely tracking Jordan's playing time was a persistent problem for the staff. Since the NBA rounded leftover seconds to the next minute, there were times Albeck found himself in trouble over a few seconds.

The matter came to a head in a hard-fought game with the Indiana Pacers late in the season. Jordan had been on a fourth quarter tear, leading the Bulls back into a game they thought they had lost. With 31 seconds remaining and the Bulls down a point, Jordan's time was up. Albeck pulled him. Jerry Krause was sitting directly behind the bench, but Albeck never looked his way. Krause said later he would have given the OK. Others said Albeck was trying to make a point. The incident undoubtedly contributed to Albeck's later firing. Loyalty was paramount to Jerry Krause and the stress of the situation seemed to bring out the worst in everyone.

With a spot in the playoffs on the line and the largest crowd of the season on hand at Chicago Stadium, Jerry Reinsdorf finally relented and let Albeck use Jordan as he saw fit. The Bulls came back on the Washington Bullets, edging them, 105-103, for their spot in the playoffs. Jordan shot poorly, just 12 of 36, but his late-game heroics carried the day. He paid respect to Jerry Reinsdorf for allowing him more playing time, but Jordan would carry a grudge against Jerry Krause for years to come.

> **"The thing with Michael my first year with the Bulls was an eye opener, although to a lesser degree I had experienced a similar situation with Elvin Hayes. The coach has to find a way to get along with the star — it's part of the job."**

Tex marveled at the dynamics of the situation, realizing full well how much the game was changing. It almost didn't make sense. How was it a young player in his second year could stand up to management, indeed, the owner of the franchise? Where did he get the gumption to stand up to his veteran teammates? How was a coach expected to coach when a player's minutes were dictated from above? How do you weave a superstar's talents into a team concept he doesn't seem to fit?

The issue of Jordan's role was complicated by his incredible performance during the playoffs. With the Bulls overmatched by Larry Bird and the Boston Celtics, Jordan took over. He scored 30 points in the first half of Game One, finishing with 49. The Bulls lost, 123-104. He scored 63 in Game Two, erasing Elgin Baylor's single-game playoff scoring record of 61. It may have been the greatest postseason performance in the history of the game, but again the Bulls lost — this time in double overtime. "I think he's God disguised as Michael Jordan," said Larry Bird afterward. "He is the most awesome player in the NBA."

Jordan came down to earth in Game Three scoring only 19, as the Bulls lost, 122-104, to end the series. Despite Jordan's heroics, the Bulls had been swept. When he performed magnificently, they came close; when he didn't, there clearly wasn't enough team game to make a go of it against a team like the Celtics. Tex saw this as the critical issue in the Bulls' future — how to integrate Jordan's unique talents into a team concept. While the rest of the world marveled at Jordan's performances, Tex worried about the larger issue of how to turn such performances into wins. It didn't matter how great Jordan was if his play didn't translate into victories. Tex saw Jordan's drive to personally excel with an equally strong drive to win. Jordan loved winning, hated losing — not just in the typical sense that could be said of anyone, but in a deeper, more visceral sense. Jordan was a player driven to win. Maybe he could be convinced to compromise his personal exploits for the sake of winning. Maybe Jerry Krause could pick up a player or two to help Michael share the load.

Jerry Krause agreed with Tex's assessment. They thought a lot alike. That was why Jerry wanted Tex to fly to Arizona to check out a new head coaching prospect named Doug Collins.

*Basketball raises blood pressure. Tension runs high because the play is so fast and because the fortune of a team can change in a matter of moments. The elevation of one moment changes to despair in the next. The basketball coach lives in a constant world of such moments.*

— Tex Winter, *The Triple-Post Offense*, 1962

---

*I had to incorporate my ability into a system that made the team better. Doug never really had a system because he relied on individual talent. In that sense, I needed the right players around me to make the team better.*

— Michael Jordan, *For the Love of the Game*

# CHAPTER EIGHT
# CALVES TO BULLS

Few players epitomized the emotional side of basketball as did Doug Collins. He was a slasher, a scorer and play maker. A relentless competitor, he played hurt and he played hard. He had the moves and he was quick. In a game increasingly dominated by black athletes, Collins seemed to fit in — a black man trapped in a white man's body.

He exuded energy and will. Yet despite these qualities, Doug Collins' career was a series of "almosts." Almost Olympic hero, almost NBA champion, almost coach of the World Champion Chicago Bulls.

A member of the U.S. Olympic Basketball Team, Collins fought the Russians in the 1972 Munich Olympics. The United States had never lost a war or an Olympic basketball game. Both records were about to fall. Just as the Americans were struggling to disengage from Vietnam with some semblance of "honor," amateur American basketball was facing relentless pressure from Soviet and communist bloc countries that were increasingly physical and professional. In both cases, it was only a matter of time.

But Doug Collins had done his part. He was Davy Crockett at the Alamo, Westmoreland fighting the ants, hamstrung by LBJ. Doug stole the ball with six seconds left, the U.S. down 49-48 in a game it had never led. Fouled with three seconds left, he sank the game tying free throw. The timeout horn went off as he released the second — it didn't matter,

Doug sank it anyway. The Soviets in-bounded the ball, but two seconds later the referee stopped play, awarding the Soviets a timeout. They were given a reset to three seconds and they scored. The U.S. record of 62-0 in Olympic competition had fallen.

For Americans, whether players, fans, or casual observers, there was only one way to cope with the loss — denial. We won the game, the Russians *stole* it. Heck, U.S. Coach Hank Iba had his pocket picked while filing the official protest. The game became a paradigm for what we had always feared — that we could build a country better than the Communists in every way, but that they could still cheat us, steal from us and walk away with the globe. Now they were beating us at our own game, in fact *stealing* it. The team voted unanimously to refuse their silver medals. And Doug Collins' sinking of the two most important free throws in U.S. basketball history became but a footnote.

Tex Winter saw a lot to like in Doug Collins. Collins was a local boy. He had played college ball at Illinois State and was an All-American there. The #1 draft choice of the lowly Philadelphia 76ers, Collins had started, much like Jordan, with a losing franchise. He was a key ingredient of the 76ers' rise to respectability and eventually to the NBA Finals. Collins had shown he could meld with his teammates, heavyweights of the day — George McGinnis, World B. Free, Daryl "Chocolate Thunder" Dawkins and, finally, Julius Erving. But most of all, Collins, like Jordan, was a competitor.

Jerry Krause sent Tex to Arizona to check him out. "Jerry thought Doug would relate well to the players, having been one," Tex related. "He asked me to spend a day with Doug to confirm that he would fill the bill. We knew Doug would be a popular choice with the fans — he had a good image and was well-known in the Chicago area. I found him to be extremely intelligent and enthusiastic. What he lacked was coaching experience. All he had was some assistant time at Arizona. He was a gamble."

Krause gambled and Collins took over the head job. His energy and enthusiasm were contagious — especially with Michael Jordan. Collins saw Jordan's potential, perhaps as he had seen Julius Erving's unique ability to take over a game with his intimidating moves to the basket. During the 1986-87 season, he cut Michael loose. Jordan would respond with a staggering 37 point-per-game average — more than a third of his team's points. He would lead the league in 11 categories — score over 60 points on two occasions; 50 or more in three consecutive games.

"In Michael Jordan, we have the sleek roadster, the Corvette," said Collins. "The rest of the guys are the bruisers, the Mack trucks."

Early on it became apparent Collins would support his star's exploits. When the Bulls handed Atlanta its first loss in November on a last-minute Jordan miracle, Collins said, "When Michael takes it, there's no such thing as an impossible shot."

The effort took a tremendous toll on Jordan, with teams working him over at both ends of the floor. By March, he was tired and nursing a number of nagging injuries. "I'm in pieces right now. I've never felt worse as a pro."

As the numbers piled up along with the accolades, voices of criticism arose. Larry Bird, who the previous year had called Jordan the best player in the league, amended his comment in *Hoop* magazine. "When he came into the league, I thought Jordan would be a great all-around player, but his game has completely changed. Right now, the only thing he does is shoot 30 times a game. I'd never want to play like that … It's too much of a load."

Wilt Chamberlain would question Jordan's shooting ability. An April 16 game against Atlanta epitomized the Jordan problem. Not only would he answer Chamberlain's criticism by becoming the first player since Wilt to reach 3,000 points in a season, but he would score a league-record 23 consecutive points. He would finish with 61, his third consecutive game with 50 or more. Most telling, though, was that the Bulls lost the game.

It was a bad omen for the playoffs, where the Bulls were swept by the Boston Celtics. Jordan commented, "They stood around as if to say, 'Let's see what Michael can do.' It shouldn't be that way. If they expect me to average 37 points next year, well, I don't want to do it."

Despite his protestations, Michael Jordan had radically changed the game, challenging conventional wisdom. He had rendered his teammates irrelevant, beating double and triple teams by himself. "He borders on being too good. He's causing a lot of things that have always been taught in basketball, particularly relating to the team concept, to be reevaluated," admitted Tex. "I'm questioning these things myself and I've been coaching 40 years."

It is difficult to exaggerate Jordan's impact on the game at that point. He was filling arenas wherever he went; the Bulls set a new home attendance record. For many fans, division titles and playoff pairings meant little compared to the one-man exploits of Jordan. The cult of Michael Jordan had begun and it would prove addictive.

Tex saw the relationship between Collins and Jordan as tenuous at times. Though similar in their drive to win and their seemingly insatiable competitive zeal, Collins seemed to live out his fantasies through Jordan and the two butted heads on occasion. During an intrasquad scrimmage in training camp, Jordan accused Collins of cheating his team by a point, ostensibly so Jordan and his team would have to do the extra running that came with losing. Jordan stormed out of practice in a fury. Two days later, after the incident had become a media event, the two made up in a press conference.

The Bulls added two key components to the team during the 1987 off-season — Scottie Pippen and Horace Grant. Pippen was a gifted athlete who could handle the ball and score; Grant was a physical presence who could rebound. Jerry Krause performed various machinations to obtain both players, trading for a draft choice to get Pippen, passing on North Carolina University's Joe Wolf to get Grant.

Scottie Pippen's virtues were touted by Billy McKinney, Tex's feature player at Northwestern. Billy was the Bulls' director of player personnel at the time. Krause asked him to personally check out Pippen, a relative unknown from Central Arkansas University. "Billy sent back glowing reports on Scottie," said Tex, "and Jerry traded up to obtain the draft choice necessary to get him. It was a brilliant piece of teamwork."

"We never scouted Horace Grant," Tex said, "he was not a prospect. Horace was the work of Johnny Bach. Johnny was looking at Joe Wolf films and kept noticing Horace cropping up in the games against

Clemson where Horace played. I liked Joe Wolf, but I had too much respect for Johnny to discount his opinion. When we looked at the films, it was obvious Johnny was onto something. Joe was a good player, but Horace was exceptional."

The difficulty was getting Krause to agree. It would have been easy to take the expected path and draft a highly-touted white player from Michael Jordan's alma mater, North Carolina. "Jerry held out until the final minutes," Tex recalled. "He and Jerry Reinsdorf were out in the hall trying to decide what to do. I reminded Jerry the coaching staff was unanimous in our support for Horace Grant. Mr. Reinsdorf told Jerry to go with his gut feelings."

Krause deferred to the coaching staff and added Grant to the earlier selection of Pippen. The maneuvers would pay off and be recognized — Jerry Krause would be named NBA Executive of the Year and the Bulls would finish with a 50-win season.

Despite the success of the 1987-88 season, the Bulls developed a problem — a group of bullies known as the Detroit Pistons. Beginning on a cold January night in Chicago Stadium, the feud would last three years and end only after the Bulls were twice denied entrance to the NBA Finals and the Piston franchise was relegated to years of obscurity. Jordan and Joe Dumars of the Pistons crashed into each other while going after a rebound. Dumars went down; Jordan, with the ball, attacked the basket. Rick Mahorn, the Pistons 6'10", 255-pound forward attacked Jordan, throwing him to the floor. The Bulls Charles Oakley grabbed Mahorn and the two shoved each other toward the Chicago bench. Coach Collins, employing the sound military tactics that come with experience, lassoed Mahorn from behind. He was rewarded with a punch in the face.

The Bulls would win that night, but the Pistons would knock them out of the playoffs that year and the play would continue to be rough. Early in the series, Bill Laimbeer, the Detroit center, set an illegal pick that caught Jordan in the privates. Jordan lashed out at Laimbeer, missing with a cat-like right cross, but picking up a technical foul. In Game Five, a Jordan elbow knocked Piston point guard Isiah Thomas unconscious. The two never cared much for each other to begin with. Thomas, a native Chicagoan, was reportedly jealous of Jordan's popularity in his hometown. However, Thomas had the last laugh; the Pistons took the final games of the series with relative ease.

Michael Jordan was not happy with the Jerry Krause's 1988 off-season maneuverings. He lost a friend when the Bulls dealt Charles Oakley to the New York Knicks for Bill Cartwright. Jordan saw Oakley as one of his few teammates who would stand up to the Pistons; he saw in Cartwright an aging and injury-prone center. What's more, the Bulls had drafted another center, Will Perdue, whom Jordan saw as lacking the physical toughness to make it in the NBA. Jordan would not hesitate to come down on Perdue in practice when the rookie got out of line.

The moves posed a larger problem for Doug Collins during the 1988-89 season. He would have to develop a low-post, half-court offense, in which he had little experience. He didn't understand it. Moreover, he didn't like it; the structure reminded him of Henry Iba's tactics in the Olympics. It didn't work then and it would surely be a waste of Michael Jordan's talent now. Collins began stressing. He wasn't eating or sleeping. He broke out in a telltale rash when nervous, developing a gaunt, unhealthy look.

> *"I have a lot of respect for Doug. He was an aggressive player and dynamic coach. We didn't always see eye to eye, but then we came from different basketball experiences. He's one of my favorite sports commentators. He knows the pro game and can verbalize it."*

He moved Jordan to point guard, exhausting him and privately blaming him for the Bulls' lack of a fast-break offense. His players accused him of taking credit for success and blaming them for failure. He began losing his temper with players, officials and his own coaching staff. He became increasingly controlling, directing more plays while ignoring the advice of assistants Winter and Jackson and frequently exploding into anger and tears. In essence, he ignored Tex in practice, giving him noncoaching tasks to perform. His relationship with General Manager Jerry Krause deteriorated. Rumors had him belittling Krause behind his back. He wanted Krause out of the locker room and off the team bus. He took his grievances to team owner Jerry Reinsdorf. Krause began keeping a book.

It was a difficult time for Tex Winter. A practice purist, he made the mistake of critiquing Doug's practices and while the critique contained balanced comments, they were not appreciated by Coach Collins. As a result, Tex no longer sat with the team on the bench; his view was from the stands, his observations available only at halftime.

Tex empathized with Collins' situation. He liked Doug and supported his right to run the team in his own way. That's what head coaches have to do. Doug was sharp and highly motivated. Part of the problem was he seemed to expect his players to be just as smart and just as fanatical. That wasn't possible. Doug was working under tremendous strain, without a great deal of coaching experience — that great teacher of perspective — to fall back on. Now Collins seemed to be rejecting the friendship and mentorship that Tex's experience brought to the team. Tex had written about such situations some 35 years before. "Tension creates undue fatigue and a mental attitude that blocks the coach's ability to make decisions and analyze situations. This brings on general disorganization which makes for less efficiency in carrying out the duties of coach. He becomes irritable, thus spoiling his relationship with his team and his associates."

The Bulls slipped to 47-35 in the regular season and the Cleveland Cavaliers took them to the fifth and deciding game of their playoff series. Jordan had promised victory; Collins feared for his job. The fourth quarter of the final game was a back-and-forth affair in Cleveland until Craig Ehlo scored off a screen to put the Cavs up by one with three seconds left. In the ensuing timeout, Collins drew up a play for Dave Corzine, hoping to surprise the Cavs. Jordan interrupted, demanding the ball. Collins relented and drew up a play for Jordan. Michael made it work, eluding two defenders to catch the ball, launching a leaning jumper with Craig

Ehlo in his face. Miraculously, it went in.

But Jordan would run out of miracles against the Pistons. With "Remember the Jordan Rules" posted on their team bulletin board, the Pistons employed a sagging defense designed to thwart Jordan's forays into the middle. Often double-teamed, when Michael did break free he would encounter weak-side help from Dennis Rodman, an intimidating shot blocker. When Collins criticized Jordan for taking too many shots in the first four games, Jordan sulked, taking only eight shots in Game Five — which the Bulls lost. To add to the Bulls' woes, Rodman was proving himself an able defender, able to stay with and often neutralize Scottie Pippen. But the Pistons were always physical. A Bill Laimbeer elbow in the first two minutes of the final contest took Pippen out of the game, sealing the Bulls fate.

Though he didn't realize it, Collins' fate was also sealed. Shortly after the NBA draft was completed, he was fired in a five-minute session with Krause and Reinsdorf. Both sides agreed not to talk about the reasons, citing "philosophical differences." But the differences were not about Aristotle's view of reality.

Collins' many pluses had become outweighed by his increasing minuses. He had neglected the development of younger players and had not made the most of the Bulls' major off-season acquisition, Bill Cartwright. This, despite the fact he had one of the league's most renowned big men coaches in the country in Tex Winter.

Collins had not made much of his staff, either, becoming paranoid about assistant Phil Jackson, whom he saw as his rival and ignoring Tex in practice for daring to point out his coaching mistakes. Jackson suffered through the silent treatment while Tex was sent on scouting trips to cool tensions. Collins wanted his assistants to be low-profile with the media. "I wasn't planning on coming back the next year," said Winter. "I didn't feel I was contributing and I certainly didn't want to be a burden to Doug."

Collins, initially viewed as a player's coach, had clearly strained relations with his players and lacked patience with developing players. There were innuendoes that he had become a player's coach in lifestyle only, that players had plotted to catch him in a compromising position and get him fired. Also, there was truth in the allegation of "philosophical differences." Despite the resources of Jackson and Winter, there was little evidence that Collins ever developed a philosophy. "There were personal and professional reasons for his firing," said Tex. "Doug committed to things he didn't follow through on. The triangle was an issue — he geared too many plays around Michael. Michael couldn't have lasted playing that way."

The firing was a shock to Chicago. The photogenic, animated young coach was popular with fans —more popular than Jerry Reinsdorf, who had threatened to move his Chicago White Sox out of town. "I was surprised they let Doug go after three years," said Winter. But Reinsdorf had been put off by Collins' going behind his general manager's back and by Collins' increased grandstanding, his apparent desire to be "the next Mike Ditka" as Reinsdorf called him, with all that implied. "Collins failed an elementary test of professional survival," wrote Ray Sons of *The Chicago Sun-Times*. "Sometimes you just have to do it the boss's way."

Though he would be loathe to admit it, Phil Jackson knew the piece about doing it the boss's way. Krause had called him in 1985 to interview for an assistant position under Stan Albeck. Jackson was coaching in Puerto Rico at the time and failed to change wardrobe for the interview. He arrived in flipflops, chino pants and an Ecuadorian straw hat with a parrot feather. And, of course, he was bearded. Krause wanted the two men to talk X's and O's but the conversation never got that far. Albeck told Krause, "No way."

Two years later, when Krause hired Jackson as an assistant under Collins, he told him what to wear — and to shave. Jackson was the Bulls' second choice for the head job at the time and his hiring under Collins was a kind of insurance policy in case Doug faltered.

Jackson had been coaching the Albany Patroons in the CBA and was Coach of the Year there in 1985. He had been named coach of the CBA All-Star team that played the Soviet National Team in 1986. But he had grown tired of "the power, money and self-glorification of the game I love," and resigned his coaching position in 1987. Retreating to his home in Montana, he had just filed for unemployment when he got the call from Krause.

The 43-year-old Jackson was a two-time Division II All-American at North Dakota where he played under Bill Fitch. He was a New York Knicks second-round pick in 1967 and spent 13 years in the NBA — 11 with the Knicks. He played mostly off the bench, averaging 6.7 points. He played on the 1973 title team, but missed playing on the Knicks 1970 championship team due to a back injury. It may have been for the best. Kept off the roster to protect him from the expansion draft, Coach Red Holzman adopted Jackson as an assistant. Though he played in practice, Jackson also scouted opponents, discussed strategy and learned how to view the game from a team perspective. Holzman was a proponent of team defense, believing team defense built teamwork. The lesson was not lost on Jackson. Phil thought he would like to be a coach.

Phil was in Montana when he got the call for the head job with the Bulls. Other teams had expressed an interest in Jackson, particularly the New York Knicks and Phil had made it no secret that he was interested in a head job. However, the Bulls had forbidden teams to talk to him until after the draft. Now the draft was over, Collins was gone and the Bulls were offering the job to Jackson.

Calling it "the best decision I ever made," Jackson signed a four-year pact that he viewed as a graduate school in basketball. The Bulls immediately signed assistant coach Johnny Bach to a one-year contract. Bach was a defensive specialist. The Bulls also offered a contract to a man Jackson described as "the innovator of the famed triangle offense, a system that emphasizes cooperation and freedom — the very values I'd spent my life pursuing off the court and dreamed of applying to the game." The man was Tex Winter. But he had yet to accept the offer.

"I took some time to consider the situation before I signed on," said Tex. "Being an assistant can be difficult. I sometimes thought Doug Collins resented the fact that I had been sent to Arizona to check him out and then became his assistant. But I had a great relationship with Phil while we were assistants. We talked a lot of basketball and had worked together in the summer leagues, often toying with the triangle, which he embraced. Phil respects people. He treated me like an elder statesman, which I appreciated."

Jackson, like Winter, hoped to build a team concept that would depend less on Michael Jordan's individual talent. "I'd like to see him use less energy," Jackson said at the time of his hiring. Jackson wisely called his superstar upon taking the job. "Congratulations," was the response. "Let's go win the championship."

Almost immediately, the issue of the 1989-90 season became how to go about winning a championship. Scottie Pippen adorned the cover of the team's pocket schedule and Jordan fretted that "team basketball" was an attempt at what he called the "de-Michaelization" of the Bulls. The situation was exacerbated when Jerry Krause opined that the Bulls might have won two championships by now had they drafted Hakeem Olajuwon instead of Jordan. Jordan was peeved as well by Krause's preoccupation with the drafting of Toni Kukoc out of the European league, as if his addition was some sort of missing ingredient.

Though Jackson was an able psychologist, liked and respected by the players, his task was daunting. He knew the actual success of teams with a scoring champion was not good. Teams with Wilt Chamberlain, Bob McAdoo and Dominique Wilkins were competitive but were routinely stymied in the playoff series. Jordan had never heard of Phil Jackson when he joined the team as an assistant and he was not particularly interested in the team exploits of the New York Knicks in the Stone Age of the early '70s.

"The players today can do things they couldn't do 20 years ago," Jordan said at the time. "The game isn't played like Tex Winter or Phil Jackson taught it. Those concepts don't work against bigger, faster players who jump higher. You don't need that with players who create."

With that kind of attitude from his superstar, Jackson could not commit to Tex's triangle. The immediate problem was convincing Jordan that he could be a great player away from the ball, that he didn't need to wear himself out bringing the ball up the court when he could simply run ahead, dragging the defense with him, opening up the court for a ball handler. There was also the problem of Bill Cartwright and the low-post offense. "I had to learn how to deliver the ball to Bill," Jordan admitted in his 1998 book, *For the Love of the Game*. "It took awhile before I started to appreciate what Bill gave us."

Getting the ball inside to Cartwright was a start. He could score. On defense, he was holding opposing centers below their scoring averages. He was also showing himself to be physically intimidating to the opposition, the trait Jordan had valued in his friend, Charles Oakley. Naturally playing with his elbows away from his body in an erratic, unpredictable manner, Cartwright was racking up an impressive number of elbow victims. Opposing teams were begging him to wear elbow pads, a request the Bulls denied.

"My advice was that these guys should get out of the way," said Tex. "I thought it was an attempt at a psyche job. Bill was aggressive, yes and at times even awkward, but he was not a dirty player, nor was he hurting anyone intentionally."

Tex's larger job was to adjust the aging center's offensive game. "We asked him to become a feeder first, a ball distributor from the post. This was not easy for Bill because he was also a scorer. He had to quickly distinguish between shooting and passing opportunities. It is based on footwork; it takes a lot of drilling."

The work paid off. "I was wrong about the Charles Oakley-Bill Cartwright trade," Jordan wrote later. "I loved having Charles on the team, but Bill made the difference."

Jordan, though, was making a major difference. In a late March regular season game, he scored a career high 69 points against the Cavaliers. Incensed that the Cleveland crowd cheered his injury early in the game, Jordan vowed to make them pay.

In the playoffs, Jordan averaged 43 points against the Philadelphia 76ers, easily eliminating his rival, Charles Barkley, from the competition.

Despite Jordan's continued scoring exploits, the Bulls felt like a different team. It was most noticeable in the tight situations that are a constant in NBA competition. Where Collins had exacerbated those situations, filling them with drama and tension, the even-tempered Jackson created a more peaceful environment, especially in the team huddles of close games.

He had a mentor in Tex. As far back as 1962, Winter had written about the importance of relaxation and "letting go." Tex wrote that relaxation could be learned — a coach's knowledge and experience were critical in recognizing and combating tension. The two coaches shared the belief that the ability to relax was part of a team's maturation process.

The Bulls had reason for confidence as they faced their old nemesis — the Detroit Pistons — in the conference finals.

*"Phil and I work well together, even when we were both assistants. Of course it helped that we had Michael and Scottie to make us look good."*

◆   ◆   ◆

Detroit had a media plan. They released tapes showing questionable fouls being called to protect Jordan. They maintained that they alone had the system to stop him. The stats backed them up. Jordan routinely scored five points less against the Pistons than against the rest of league and he had an extra miss for every 10 shots taken.

Jordan, refusing to admit "the Jordan Rules" could stop him, charged gamely into the teeth of the Pistons defense in losing Games One and Two of the series. With fewer fouls being called, Jordan would take 43 shots — and miss 26 of them. The Pistons clogged the middle with big bodies. Dennis Rodman was quick to move in whenever Jordan drove the lane, eager to draw the offensive foul. "The Flopper," as Jordan called him, was also doing yeoman defensive work on Scottie Pippen. They seldom left Michael without a double-team, Joe Dumars fronting his every move, Isiah Thomas ready to jump in and help. The Pistons taunted Jordan for his baldness and raised his selfishness in the media. Even Michael's teammates, "The Jordanaires" as they were sometimes called, reacted to the situation and Michael's negative comments about them, saying, "when we win it's him, when we lose it's us."

Of the Pistons, Jordan later wrote, "Their game was to intimidate, to divide and to conquer an otherwise united team by forcing players to react emotionally. The Pistons tried to get you to play angry, which meant you were playing out of control. All that pushing and shoving was their way of getting the minds of opposing players off the game plan. That's what Dennis Rodman was all about. He would try to get inside a player's head and take that player out of the game mentally. Once he had distorted the guy's thought process, the physical part was easy.

"Chuck Daly, who coached Detroit at the time, had his own plan for me. The Jordan Rules were a set of defensive principles the Pistons applied to stop me. As far as I could tell, the plan involved running as many players as possible at me whenever I touched the ball and then hitting me as hard as possible every time I touched the ball. Some rules."

Jackson relieved the tension of the opening game losses by splicing the game film with scenes from *The Wizard of Oz*. The heartless Tin Man, brainless Scarecrow and cowardly Lion were intertwined with the Bulls' numerous shortcomings of the two games. He told his team to think of the Pistons defense as a zone and stop charging into the teeth of it. The Bulls responded with wins in the next two games. "I called him Cecil B. de Mille after that," said Tex. "For me, the message was about courage."

But the Bulls would lose the series in seven games, Game Seven a nightmare come true for Michael Jordan who felt abandoned by his teammates in the clutch. Scottie Pippen, reduced to a shadow of himself with a migraine, shot one for 10. John Paxson was little help — he had sprained his ankle in the previous game. Jordan himself was playing with a number of nagging injuries and his remaining teammates were unable to pick up the slack.

The situation did not bode well for the future of the triangle. Where had his teammates gone when Michael Jordan needed them? Moreover, what would prompt Michael Jordan to later say, "In the years between 1989 and 1993, I became a man."

*Competition is keen and merciless. The coach's position is precarious at best.*

*Having proven himself, he is called upon to prove himself again and again.*

*— Tex Winter, The Triple-Post Offense, 1962*

## CHAPTER NINE
# EASY AS 1 — 2 — 3

There is nothing easy about NBA basketball.

It is an extremely physical game and seems to become more so with each passing season. Thanks to weight and conditioning training, the players are demonstrably bigger and stronger — and probably faster and quicker. There are no zone defenses in the NBA, at least in theory. If you beat your man, you will be met by someone else helping him out. Beat him often enough and you will be double-teamed. Good players welcome the legalized mugging of the double-team, because a weaker player might lose vision and panic, but good players see through the phalanx of hands and arms to take advantage of the open man.

Defenses are improving in the NBA. The days you could glide through the lane and finish a dunk without being assaulted are long gone. Coaches like Pat Riley have decided that's not going to happen. Glide through the lane these days and you'll more likely get knocked on your ass.

Playing with injury is common, not to mention the aches and pains that accompany running up and down a hardwood floor and periodically having to "hit it" in quest of a loose ball. Loose balls take a heavy toll. For some unfathomable reason, all rules are suspended when a loose ball occurs and players are free to jump on each other and foul each other in ways that are never allowed when the players are upright. It looks a lot like football, minus the equipment and turf. Good players dive for the loose ball; good players play hurt.

Playground basketball, where most NBA players get their start, is a game of confidence and intimidation. Only the strong survive on the playground. Winners get to play, losers sit it out and watch. It is essential to win and there are no referees. You get the calls by being louder and more vociferous than the other guys. The playground teaches you how to get into the other guy's mind. The NBA is full of playground survivors. Every year there's a fresh crop of youngblood wannabes, guys the veterans see as spoiled and ungrateful. They could also be faster, better and making more money.

Ah yes, the money. By reasonable standards, there is lots of it. More than enough to last a lifetime … almost unimaginable amounts of money … and plenty of family and friends to spend it with. There is Mama's house, the cars and the crib. There is gold, leather, frankincense and myrrh — and opportunity. Yes, there is opportunity. Franchises, restaurants, car dealerships, life insurance and stockbrokers — hordes of professionals with every conceivable scheme to turn lots of money into even more. And of course one needs an agent— someone to negotiate on one's behalf for a modest percentage of the take. Patrick Ewing had it right when he said during the 1998 lockout that players make a lot, but they have a lot of expenses. In the end it is all relative. No matter how much you make there is almost always someone with less game making more.

It is the owners' fault. They're the ones making the real money, guys who couldn't touch the rim on a stepladder. Guys with names like Prescott and Theodore. Big money men who are good with a balance sheet. They are tough, greedy bastards who know how to negotiate. They have teams, too, damned good ones, with G.M.s and a band of accountants and lawyers. To them, it is a business and you are the property. You're trade bait. Rub them the wrong way, fail to meet expectations and you're off to the Timberwolves in January.

And whose side are the coaches on? Follow the money. They work for the G.M., or worse, they *are* the G.M. They all have their pet systems and philosophies. Good luck if your game is all playground freelance; just hope you don't draw one of those controlling, set-play kind of guys. You either fit, they adjust, you're miserable — or you go. They can help you meet your incentive clause — or not. One minute they're your friends, the next minute they're in your face. They're feeling pressure, too. In the end, it's the coaches who pay for failure. Players are rarely fired. With coaches, it's only a losing streak away. Communication is difficult. It's a guy thing. Sometimes you just want to do what Latrell Sprewell did — strangle somebody.

If you're a star with a good public relations representative, you might get away with it. If you're a journeyman, don't even think about it. You're way down the food chain. If life is good, you're seeing some minutes, at best as some kind of sixth man where you can satisfy your ego as a contributor. But it's a 13-man roster and for every five guys on the floor, there are eight on the bench. Eight guys who in any other venue, from the NCAA to the European League would be superstars, who could drop to the CBA and be a wunderkind. By any reasonable standard, you're at the top of your profession.

But the NBA is not a reasonable profession. This is not youth league where Johnny gets to play a quarter. Here, after years of being "the man," you are just an also-ran, with your family and friends wondering if you'll ever get out of that warm-up suit. OK, the money's good and you have a front row seat for the action. It's small compensation for the humiliation of the pine.

But compensation comes in many packages. NBA players are much in demand by groupies, partiers and wife wannabes. It's not as hard to connect with a player as you might think and for some reason, sex doesn't seem to have quite the deleterious effect on a basketball player as it would have on a boxer. The opportunity is always there and a skilled practitioner can live the life of a sultan. Marriage is a tough row to hoe for an NBA player, but divorce is also costly — not to mention what happened to Magic Johnson, who was diagnosed HIV-positive in 1991. Still, the temptations are innumerable; there is always somebody offering a toot or a toke.

In the end, your livelihood depends upon performance — measurable performance. Statistics are kept on everything in the NBA and there's nowhere to hide. If you're one of the guys who "does those 'other' things well," you'd better be able to prove it. In a game that at its core is team-oriented, there's heavy emphasis on individual stats. You may be able to cook the numbers at the office, but in the NBA, a free throw either goes in or stays out and you don't get partial credit for bouncing it around the rim.

Your game is a public spectacle, an average of 15,000 sets of eyes per game, more if there's TV. Highlights at 11. Media events. Interview requests. Reporters. A write-up the next day. Box scores and lots of analysis, always someone there to explain what happened. The only consolation is, with an 82-game schedule, there's no time to think. You are shuttled from city to city with such speed that the past quickly melds with the future. You change time zones like average people change clothes. Time zones and hotel rooms, buses and planes. Try Minneapolis to Miami or Orlando to Toronto. Passports? And you experience it all with an average 6' 7" frame. You are a freak. You are gawked at. Nothing — not a bed or a chair, a bus seat or toilet — is made to accommodate your outrageous size. If you are successful, there are another 20 or so playoff games ... still a chance to see Salt Lake City in June.

Given the alternatives, NBA basketball is a great career. Many of the players never graduated from college. So there's always Army ball or the CBA. Larry Bird rode shotgun on a garbage truck for awhile. Of course, playing in the NBA and winning in the NBA are two very different things. Consider this: there are 29 NBA franchises and 28 of them either fail to make the playoffs or lose their last game. Moreover, in the last eight years, only three franchises have won NBA championships. Consider that it took Michael Jordan seven years in the NBA to win a championship. And it was easy?

Beneath the surface of NBA teams, battles are waged. Opinions vary, ranging from matters of basketball philosophy and strategy to arguing the relative value of players and how the players should be used. These matters go to the soul of a franchise. The 1990-91 season brought these issues to a head for the Chicago Bulls. General Manager Jerry Krause once told Tex, "If we have two people that think alike on all issues, one of them is unnecessary."

One of the mysteries of the period was the relationship between Tex and fellow assistant, Johnny Bach. Bach had been a successful college coach both at Fordham and later at Penn State, where he had coached the triangle. Both men were of the same generation and had similar views on the game. Though a New Yorker, Bach fancied western-style attire. Tex was not so inclined; in fact, he had never owned a pair of boots. People often mistook the two, calling Johnny "Tex," and Tex "Johnny."

Bach jumped to the pro game earlier than Tex and favored pro-style concepts. Bach carried the title "defensive coordinator" and Tex "offensive coordinator." Tex thought the titles misnomers, having long preached the philosophy that a good defensive team required a sound offense and vice versa. The reality was that the Bulls staff made little distinction between the assignments of the two positions. The staff worked together in a give-and-take atmosphere where all coaches had input.

Johnny Bach was fascinated with Michael Jordan. He saw in Jordan the consummate warrior, the ultimate basketball expression, a player who changed the game. Jordan played on a higher level, with more dedication and more fire. Johnny admired how Jordan could humiliate an opponent, finding ways to beat him *mano a mano*, even taking on the double-team. He would inspire his teammates to follow his lead. His talents should be exploited, the stage should be set for him. He would come through. Bach called it "the archangel offense."

Tex didn't buy the cult of Jordan. Exploiting Jordan had worked to a point, but the point had always ended short of an NBA championship. More Michael wasn't going to get it done. Basketball is a team sport. Everybody brings something and to win consistently, including the big games, you have to be hitting on all cylinders. That was the beauty of the triangle; it kept everyone involved — including the opposing defense. It took advantage of Jordan's unique talents without wearing him out. Doug Collins had put all his eggs in one basket and in spite of Jordan's talent, it wasn't enough.

Tex and Phil Jackson were on the same page. Jackson's playing experience under Red Holzman convinced him team offense was the way to go. The Bulls already had an established fast-break attack, but they often struggled when confined to half-court. Teams like the Pistons would key on stopping Jordan, leaving the remaining Bulls to create on their own. Jackson agreed the triangle was the answer for the Bulls. He recognized that in Tex Winter, he had an offensive master, capable of elevating Holzman's rudimentary motion game to an art form. The problem would be convincing Michael Jordan — especially with Johnny Bach pumping him full of machismo.

---

**"There are always differences of opinion between members of a coaching staff and a variety of ideas about what's best. The head coach has to sort it out and decide what's best. Then he has to sell it to the team. That's why he gets paid the big bucks."**

---

Jordan came to the 1990-91 season with a renewed sense of purpose to beat the Pistons and win the championship, but also with some skepticism about whether the triangle was the way to do it. Last season started with the same attempt at "de-Michaelization." Hadn't his teammates let him down in the final showdown with the Pistons?

"Phil did a great job selling Jordan on the triangle," Tex said. "He pitched it as an attempt simply to take some of the pressure off. Michael was trusting; he could have sabotaged the concept had he wanted to."

The Bulls were slow to adjust. The triangle concept goes against the grain of individual stats and the individual accomplishment that the NBA rewards with fatter paychecks. Learning the system is a methodical, tedious process requiring drilling and attention to detail. It takes time for the pieces to fit and for the players to see the opportunities that arise. In the case of the Chicago Bulls, it would lead to their losing the first three games of the season.

There were other problems. Michael Jordan wanted a better supporting cast. He campaigned for the Bulls to acquire Walter Davis, a former North Carolina Tar Heel, who Jordan thought could take on some of the scoring burden. The Bulls coaching staff voted unanimously against the move. Tex thought Davis's team skills were suspect, especially his defense. "Walter Davis was a tremendous player in his day, an All-Star. Any team would have been happy to have him," said Tex. "But by the '90s, he was on the downside of his career, as time would tell. Michael idolized him at North Carolina, but he was overestimating his talent at that point. I think Michael was a little nostalgic."

Although the decision had been made on the recommendation of the coaching staff, Jordan blamed Jerry Krause for the decision. He also was still peeved about his general manager's preoccupation with acquiring Toni Kukoc from Croatia. Jordan took his concerns to the Bulls owner, Jerry Reinsdorf. Reinsdorf backed his G.M. and chastised his superstar for disparaging his teammates. They, too, had beefs. Pippen was underpaid and felt the Bulls were slow in renegotiating his contract. Cartwright and Paxson were in the final year of their contracts. Others were concerned about playing time.

Despite the internal warfare, the triangle made possible the Bulls' best regular season record in franchise history, 61-21. Jordan's scoring average for the season was down a couple points, but Scottie Pippen's rose an equal amount. The Bulls had obliterated substandard opponents, but struggled against the best teams, finishing a mediocre 21-18 against teams playing .500 ball. Results against the formidable Pistons were mixed. They were clobbered by the Pistons in December, 105-84; but squeaked by them later in the season, 95-93. They would defeat them again on the last day of the season in a game marred by fighting and physical play — a harbinger of the playoffs to come. They finished the regular season as the best-shooting Bulls team in history, hitting 51 percent of their shots. They also set team records for assists and three-point shooting.

Still, implementing the triangle had been a struggle. Some nights Jordan would get hot and take over the offense. Jackson would put him on the corner of the triangle where it would be harder for him to get the ball. Some nights he would just take Jordan out. Jackson had been somewhat successful in convincing Jordan to run ahead of the ball, dragging defenders away from the ball handler. Tex supported Phil were he could, but at times, even Phil wanted to experiment. With Tex away for the NCAA Final Four, Jackson ditched the triangle, allowing Jordan to handle the ball at the top of the offense. The result was 28 first-half points for His Airness and disgruntled teammates who thought he was showing off.

Tex saw another means of keeping Jordan in the triangle. He saw in Michael all the tools of an effective post-up player — someone who could establish himself inside and score or pass off among the big men. Michael was tough, strong and could jump. Tex had always believed the triangle to be most effective with a variety of players on the post. That was the beauty of the triple-post at Kansas State with Parr, Boozer and Frank — all big men who could rotate at post.

"We recognized Michael could beat people from the post position and that it would probably lengthen his career," said Tex. "He worked extremely hard on his post-up skills and in typical Jordan fashion, he mastered those skills. It probably did as much as anything to bring him into the triangle. Posting up gave him a new bag of tricks, something to further challenge his game and dominate his adversaries."

Having glided by the Knicks and 76ers in the early rounds, the Bulls faced their old nemesis, the Detroit Pistons, in the Eastern Conference Finals. In the previous three years of playoffs against the Pistons, the Bulls had successively improved — winning one, two and three games. Thanks to the triangle and their developing maturity, they were about to go 4-0. Game One was telling. Leading by three points going into the fourth quarter, Jackson started his second team — and left them in for six and a half minutes. The result was a nine-point lead and proof that a well-disciplined group of less talented players could run the triangle — and make it work.

"That move was typical of Phil," Tex recalled affectionately, "and even I cringed when he tried that one. But we believed there were times when the second team could run the offense better than the starters. They tended to stay with the triangle in a more disciplined fashion. They had to — they didn't have the same talent as the first group. The trick was to know when to give them the chance. I credit Phil with that particular decision. It took guts and he was right; they did a great job."

Still, Detroit defended the triangle better than anyone in the league.

They were deep in guards, so they were especially adept at pressuring the ball handler. The Bulls' coaching staff thought they saw a solution. Why not let Pippen bring the ball up court? If the Pistons wanted to match him with a guard, they would face a serious mismatch if Pippen established himself near the basket. Paxson, on the other hand, was an excellent jump shooter and could be positioned off on the wing.

The Pistons responded with their signature knock 'em down, beat 'em up approach. They were hit with three flagrant fouls in Game Two and would totally lose their composure by Game Four. Laimbeer pushed Paxson out of bounds in the first quarter; John responded with 10 straight points. In the second quarter, Rodman shoved Pippen from behind, knocking his head to the floor, resulting in six stitches. But the Bulls were not to be denied. They rolled over the Pistons, 115-94. The Piston starters were removed from the game early, leaving the floor to avoid the humiliation of congratulating the victors. "It was very strange," said Tex, "when the Piston starters, who had been removed from the game walked right past us on their way to the locker room. There were still minutes on the clock and they were conceding. In all my years of coaching, I had never seen that happen."

After three years of being eliminated by the Detroit Pistons, the Bulls finally returned the favor. The changing of the guard was complete; the Pistons began what would become a decade of decline. The Chicago Bulls, using a team concept called the triangle, were a franchise on the way up.

The Bulls had home-court advantage against Magic Johnson and the Los Angeles Lakers in the 1991 NBA Finals. It did not last long. During the opening game in Chicago Stadium, the Bulls came out tight and seemed to lack confidence. With his teammates struggling, Jordan tried to take over, throwing the triangle even further out of sync. By the end of the third quarter, he was tired and asked for a breather. This was uncharacteristic of Jordan and a cause of concern to Tex Winter. "It didn't happen often," said Tex, "but Michael was smart enough and honest enough to sometimes ask out of a game. It could be caused by fatigue or just the feeling that his effort was counterproductive."

Magic Johnson was tiring, too and the Bulls pulled within a point with nine seconds to go. Jordan launched a jumper from 18 feet, which took several tantalizing caroms off the rim before bouncing out. The loss was a warning shot to the team. Despite their recent success with the Pistons, they had entered play at a new level — the NBA Finals. Former Laker coach Pat Riley predicted Laker Finals experience would be decisive. It was virgin terrain for the Bulls' franchise and time for the coaching staff to get to work.

Johnny Bach had been watching tapes of the Lakers' previous series with the Portland Trail Blazers. He confirmed what Tex Winter had already noticed —the Trail Blazers were successful double-teaming the Lakers low along the baseline, rather than up top. After watching the tape of Game One with the Bulls, he was convinced some defensive changes were in order. Tex Winter agreed. Phil Jackson was not so sure. Did it really make sense to scrap their defensive scheme after a two-point loss? The Bulls practiced the new defense for two hours before Game Two. It opened up a new possibility. Why not put Pippen on Magic Johnson?

Despite the hype of a Jordan-Johnson match-up, it made sense to try Pippen on Johnson. Tex called them "big facilitators," large, unselfish players who could handle the ball and get it to open teammates. Pippen lacked Johnson's flashiness, but he made up for it with his defensive capability. "On the defensive end, Scottie is clearly exceptional," Winter believed. "Pippen can not only help, he can recover. He can guard his own man and help with team defense. We noticed that in certain situations, Magic Johnson would give up his dribble. He'd bounce the ball twice and look to pass. That was a good time for Scottie to smother him — and there's nobody better at trapping than Scottie Pippen."

With Jordan in early foul trouble in Game Two, Pippen got his chance guarding Magic Johnson. The results were astonishing. The younger, less experienced Pippen held Johnson to four of 13 shooting while scoring 20 points himself and adding 10 assists. The Bulls routed the Lakers, 107-86.

The Bulls were onto something. A simple adjustment had reaped tremendous dividends. "Adjustability," Tex Winter had termed it some 30 years previous in his basketball bible, *The Triple-Post Offense*. He called it "the most important quality of my philosophy of life as well as basketball." For Tex, basketball was a proving ground where players and coaches learn the importance of adjusting to the many and varied situations that present themselves. Reactions and modus operandi that served a team well at one time might not do so again. Winter understood full well the benefits of careful analysis, revised plans and practiced implementation. It worked in basketball; for him, it worked in life.

The Bulls were expected to wilt under the pressure of facing three consecutive games at the Los Angeles Forum. Just the opposite occurred. In a series played amidst Hollywood celebrities and unparalleled hype, the Bulls proved the oddsmakers wrong — taking three consecutive games from the home team Los Angeles Lakers. The Bulls were world champions. They had defeated the Detroit Pistons and traveled uncharted waters in crushing the Lakers, compiling an unprecedented 15-2 playoff record.

Tex saw the victory as the culmination of six years of hard work and confirmation that the triangle could triumph at the professional level. He took particular pleasure in the fact that the Bulls had proven the critics wrong — you could win in the NBA without a dominant center, you could win with a leading-scorer guard. But you had to have team.

"I think the championship is going to get rid of the one-man stigma," Jordan said after the final game. "We have been trying to get rid of that stigma for awhile."


The publishing of Sam Smith's *The Jordan Rules* after the 1991 season offered an inside glimpse of "a turbulent season with Michael Jordan and the Chicago Bulls." A fascinating read, Smith's book made it abundantly clear how tough life was in the Bulls' camp. The egos, the money issues and the various power struggles were laid out in detail for the world to see. "Mountains out of molehills," was Tex Winter's response to the book. He saw many of the locker room and behind-the-scenes quotes as bantering typical of any team. But he was annoyed that one of their own, perhaps more than one, was passing along family secrets. While Tex was seen as a good interview by members of the media, he was not a gossip — he always downplayed team squabbles like the good parent he was. Tex recognized intuitively that you can't survive in an environment such as surrounded the Bulls with loose lips or an inflated ego. This philosophy was one of the keys to his longevity.

The Krause/Reinsdorf management team was not pleased with their portrayal in the book. Neither was Michael Jordan, who shunned Smith for some time after the book was released. It made an interesting backdrop for the 1991-92 season.

The Bulls got off to a strong start, winning 15 of their first 17, establishing a team record 14 consecutive wins. They were nearly unbeatable at the All-Star break at 37-5, on a pace to challenge the 1972 Los Angeles Lakers for most victories in a season — 69. Though they would fail to reach that mark, finishing at 67-15, the Bulls set a team record for road victories at 31 and tied their previous record of 36 home wins.

Easily disposing of the Miami Heat in the first round of the playoffs, the Bulls faced the New York Knicks, who had eliminated the Pistons. The Knicks borrowed a page from the Piston playbook, establishing a physical style of play that assaulted Jordan whenever he drove to the basket. The Knicks took the Bulls to seven games. They were followed by the Cleveland Cavaliers, who were eliminated in six.

The Portland Trail Blazers were the Bulls' victims in the NBA Final, the team that had passed on drafting Michael Jordan almost a decade before. With their non-physical style of play, the Trail Blazers never had a chance. The team's star, Clyde Drexler, was being compared to Jordan. It was a poor comparison. Jordan scored 35 points in the first half of the first game. While the Trail Blazers would rally to win Game Two in overtime, they were never really in the series.

In the final game, played in Chicago, the Bulls found themselves down 17 points in the second half. "It was obvious the starters were flat — not getting the job done," said Tex. "I leaned over to Phil and said, 'We've gotta do something; shake things up.' "

Jackson responded with a makeshift lineup of Pippen, Armstrong, Bobby Hansen, Stacey King and Scott Williams. They got it done. "It was a drastic move," admitted Tex, "but it had to be done. Fortunately, the guys were ready when duty called. Bobby Hansen hit a big three for us and Stacey King was tremendous."

When the fans refused to leave Chicago Stadium after the victory, the players returned to party on the scorers' table. "It was a big thing," recalled Tex, "but there were incidents around the city that got out of hand."

Only two teams had won three NBA Championships in a row — the Minneapolis Lakers of George Mikan fame and the legendary Boston Celtics of the late '50s and early '60s. Jordan and Pippen started the 1992-93 season tired, having played in the Barcelona Olympics. They were given some accommodation by Phil Jackson and were excused from one of the team's two-a-day workouts in training camp. Horace Grant took exception.

By some reports, the team was fighting boredom throughout the 1992-93 season. They would finish the season at 57-25, well off the previous year's pace and only third best in the league behind New York and Phoenix. "It wasn't boredom so much as fatigue," Tex felt. "We were a tired ball club. To the fan and weekend player, the NBA looks pretty glamorous and sometimes it is. What the fan doesn't see and the weekend player doesn't experience is the drudgery — traveling, practicing, playing injured, even playing the number of games on the schedule. The mind and body take a beating. You pay a price."

After sweeping Atlanta and Cleveland in the early playoff rounds, the Bulls dropped their first two games to the New York Knicks. Jordan, who had been spotted in an Atlantic City casino in the wee hours before Game Two, shot only 12 for 32. But he recovered. The Bulls won the next two games, each by 20 points. Jordan scored 54 in Game Four and the Bulls went on to sweep the remainder of the series.

As the Bulls prepared to meet Charles Barkley and the Phoenix Suns in the 1993 NBA Finals, allegations surfaced that Jordan had amassed some $1 million in gambling debts. It didn't seem to affect the Bulls' play — they beat the Suns twice in their opening road games, an NBA first. The Suns rallied to steal a triple overtime contest at Chicago Stadium.

The Bulls dominated the sixth and final game of the series before going cold. Phoenix led by two with 14 seconds and the Bulls in possession.

The play, drawn up for Jordan during the timeout, was covered. Pippen drove the lane, dishing to Grant who passed outside to John Paxson.

"The last play was so typical of how we wanted our offense to work that year," said Tex. "We had the best player in the history of the game in Michael Jordan. Because he's never afraid the take the last shot, he makes the first building block — one that the other team absolutely must focus on. Then you have Scottie Pippen, the perfect complement to Jordan. He's a skilled ball handler and unselfish to a fault. So we wanted him to handle the ball in that situation. If he can get the ball to Michael, fine. Michael's going to create the play, even if he doesn't finish it.

"If they overguard Michael that's fine, too — we have Horace Grant making a signature move cutting along the baseline. With the defense collapsing, Scottie got the ball to Horace, who now has two choices — take the ball to the basket or pass out to the spot-up shooter, John Paxson. In this case, Horace wasn't clear to the basket so he passed to John. John is all set to catch and shoot the ball. When the defense is occupied like that, somebody is going to be open — and there's nobody we want more in that situation than John Paxson. Chances are John Paxson will hit that shot."

Paxson drilled the shot. The Bulls had their three-peat, the third in NBA history.

*The first objective of the coach and players should be a complete mastery of the individual fundamentals. The second objective is the integration of the players into a team. Once this is done, the house has been built on a solid, sound foundation. The team will play with the confidence and poise so essential to success.*

— Tex Winter, *The Triple-Post Offense*, 1962

## Chapter Ten
# Flying Without Michael

From the halfway point of the 1992-93 season, Tex Winter began hearing rumors Michael Jordan would leave basketball. Tex, like many others, was skeptical. Maybe, as some said, Jordan was just angling for more money. He knew Jordan had a lot of good years left if he chose to play them. Sure, Michael was tired and disillusioned. But as long as the Bulls maintained the capability of winning, he knew the pull on Jordan would be immense. Michael loved winning.

Tex sensed problems during training camp. The team had lost its connectedness. He felt it most from Horace Grant. Grant had complained about Jordan and Pippen receiving preferential treatment in training camp after the Barcelona Olympics. Grant wanted equal status. However, the coaching staff didn't think he deserved it. Grant was a follower — part of the supporting cast and no more. Grant was listening to people who told him he was just as key a component as Jordan or Pippen, but not paid as much, or appreciated.

Still, an important issue was raised — were all members of the team to be treated equally, or was it justifiable, in light of the circumstances, that Jordan and Pippen be rested a bit during camp? Tex was against favoritism, but this seemed to be a special case. Still, it was having an adverse effect on Grant and affecting team unity.

> **"Transitions are fraught with difficulty — especially when a team has done well and lost a key player or lost its edge. It takes just the right adjustments to keep functioning at peak performance. It's a very tricky thing."**

The team had moved into Berto Center, a multi-million dollar training facility Tex had helped design. The new venue was proving to be both a blessing and a curse. Tex had insisted that all three courts be NBA regulation distances. Normally the cross courts would have been shorter in length, but Tex had insisted — he wanted the players to deal in full scale every time they practiced. He made sure the wood floor had a solid cushion to save the players' legs. A running track circled the floor. Toss-back machines, which Tex co-invented with Ken Mahoney, a former K-State player, lined the walls. Now there was no reason the players couldn't perfect the two-hand chest pass.

The weight room was state-of-the-art. Tex believed players should spend four days a week there during the off-season — two days working endurance and two on strength. He had believed this for 40 years, long before it was fashionable. He had done his own research with a kinesiologist — it was all in *The Triple-Post Offense*.

Though Tex might not admit it, Berto Center also caused problems for the team. Now they were located with management and the nine-to-five crowd from whom they'd previously had some distance. Phil had a screen installed to shelter the team from the press during practice, but management was an omnipresent factor. It was in the weight room, in fact, that Jerry Reinsdorf would first approach Horace Grant in the legendary discussion that would lead to Horace leaving the team.

Throughout the season, personal conversations among the Bulls were getting out — conversations on the team bus, in the locker room, or during practice that Tex thought should have stayed confidential. Tex wondered if players who couldn't maintain confidentiality off the court could be trusted on the court. Usually the players could work out their differences as long as they were winning. Players don't have to be close personally as long as they trust each other in that special world of the basketball court. Out there, you know each other in a different way. You know each other's strengths and weaknesses — you communicate in a different way. Out there, a well-set pick means "I love you," a blown pass off the fast-break means "You're dirt. I don't respect you."

Tex saw that Jackson and B.J. Armstrong were feuding. Armstrong touted his superior speed and penetration ability and was upset about sharing time with John Paxson. What Armstrong failed to acknowledge was Paxson's tenacity and superior role playing. Tex agreed Armstrong was the more talented player. He was younger and more aggressive. But with Jordan and Pippen in the lineup, there wasn't enough ball to go around. Paxson could play without the ball, getting himself into position to hit open shots whenever Jordan got stuck and needed an outlet.

Tex thought B.J. was overly sensitive to criticism. He took things too personally, reacted emotionally and then sulked. Tex felt that accepting criticism was part of being a professional, part of being an athlete. It was given to help the player help the team — period. Jackson was about as good at sugar-coating criticism as anybody Tex had ever seen, but Armstrong wasn't handling it. "B.J. was young at the time and like all good players, he wanted desperately to fit in and to play," said Tex. "I've talked with B.J. several times since then and I think he understands now that John was a perfect fit for the system. Having played on different teams, B.J.'s become a big believer in the triangle."

Despite the dissension, the 1992-93 season had been a success. The Bulls had accomplished the three-peat. The players had survived the season without serious injury. It made sense to keep the streak alive.

But tragedy struck. In July, 1993, Michael Jordan's father, James, was brutally murdered. James was a well-known figure to Tex and the players — he often traveled with the team. "James had a strong influence on Michael's life," Tex recalled. "He was both a father and a buddy to Michael. He was a friendly and light-hearted man. He and Nancy hit it off."

Nancy Winter remembered James as a warm-hearted, affectionate man

— always looking for an opportunity to hug and say hello.

Rumors circulated that James Jordan's death may have been precipitated by his son's gambling debts. The rumors were unfounded and unfair — and they further devastated Michael, who was angry with the press for reporting them. It further sapped his appetite for another season in the spotlight.

He waited until two days before training camp to announce his retirement. Jackson had tried to talk him into calling it a sabbatical, suggesting options for sparing Michael some of his normal burden. But Jordan was fixated on the 82-game schedule and the 20 or so playoff games that would probably follow. "Few people realize the commitment it takes to play an 82-game schedule in the NBA," Tex said. "Michael Jordan was never one to give it anything less than his best."

The late-breaking decision left the Bulls in the lurch. Jordan seemed to take some satisfaction in surprising Jerry Krause, which he most certainly did. Newcomer Toni Kukoc was reduced to tears. He had left his home in Croatia to play with the Bulls and Michael Jordan. Now he had apparently lost that chance. Free agents Bill Wennington and Steve Kerr also signed with the Bulls in the hope of playing with Jordan. Those hopes were dashed.

The city of Chicago did not take the news well. *The Chicago Tribune* ran advice from grief counselors on how to cope with the loss. An economist estimated lost business and service opportunities at $100 million. Oddsmakers cut the Bulls championship chances from 5-2 with Jordan to 25-1 without him. NBA history provided ample proof that a retiring superstar left his team with significantly fewer victories the following year.

Tex was philosophical about the development. "Michael needed to get away from the game for awhile. With the '92 Olympics, he had been playing competitive basketball for two years without a break. Despite the fact that he called it retirement, I personally thought he would come back at some point. We still had a very good team without him, certainly not as strong a team as we had with him, but this was a situation beyond our control. In basketball, you learn to live with these things and do the best you can."

It was obvious the team was in trouble. While Tex saw in Toni Kukoc the kind of player who, like Jordan, had the fearlessness to take the last shot, it was going to take some time for him to adjust to NBA basketball and American life. He would also have to overcome the image that he was Jerry's kid; Jordan and Pippen had already ganged up on him in the Olympics to prove their point. Now Pippen was riding him in practice, just as Jordan had done to so many others before him. Tex questioned whether it was the right approach. Toni had been a bona fide star in Europe, but Tex saw him as weak in the fundamentals of basketball. It was as if he had grown up too fast and missed a few classes along the way. He'd also formed some bad habits that would be hard to break.

"Toni was a very fine talent," remarked Tex, "but he was naive about the NBA. He was the Michael Jordan of Europe and had been playing at that level since he was 15 or 16. He could shoot the three, he had great vision and he could deliver the ball. The strange thing was, he was 6'11" and he only played the top of the floor — he never played inside."

Jerry Krause thought Toni needed weight training to bulk up a bit for the mega-bodies he would meet in the NBA. Jackson wasn't so sure — he wasn't a weight-training advocate. Although Tex had been a weight-training proponent for 40 years, he sided with Jackson on Kukoc's training plan. There was really no need to bulk Toni up if he wasn't going to play an inside game. Toni needed work on fundamentals. The big question remained, "Was he worth the money?"

Money is a major issue in the NBA and there are just enough salary anomalies to drive everyone to distraction. Forget your company pay scale. There are great players playing for relative peanuts and a number of bums that are grossly overpaid.

Consider Scottie Pippen's situation. By 1994, he had played in three NBA championships and a gold medal Olympic team. He was the 1994 All-Star Game MVP. He had a five-year deal worth $18 million — a little over $3 million a year. Good money, yes, but not nearly as good as it would have been if he'd allowed his original contract to run out after the 1992-93 championship season. For Scottie, it was a choice of having the security of renegotiating his original contract or playing it out, risking the possibility of a career-ending injury and going for the really big bucks. Scottie opted for security. In retrospect, it was a poor choice.

Enter Toni Kukoc. While Scottie Pippen had been busting his ass taking care of business, the general manager of the Bulls, Jerry Krause, was courting Toni Kukoc. Showering him with gifts and telling everybody how great he was. Toni signed a six-year contract at $4.3 million a year.

He comes to practice, but he's "a project." You can bully him and yet he's making more money. You're doing the work, he's making the money. Does the word "slave" come to mind? It did to Scottie Pippen. "But I'm no slave to anyone," he told Sam Smith in Second Coming. "This is my job; I'm not their slave. You do the work and say nothing and they'll be thinking they're your master."

Imagine owning a franchise. Go ahead, be Reinsdorf. Take Jerry Krause as your G.M. The good news is you're rich and you're winning. It's also the bad news. Because you're rich, you're expected to foot the bill for excellence; because you're winning, you won't be seeing any draft choices. You have to negotiate a maze of salary cap rules that could break the Clinton legal defense team into factions.

You must judge talent, player potential, character and motivation. What's the right mix of players and at what point in their careers? There are plenty of tempting possibilities out there looking for a big pay day and a soft place to loaf. You get lots of advice from players, fans and the press. And of course, there are other owners with similar problems, some of them desperate to buy a winner. You can pretty much count on having to match whatever your dumbest, or wealthiest, competitor offers.

Now put yourself in a coaching position. You're supposed to be the boss, but the guys on the floor are making more than you are — way more. How good does your hundy feel when a player is making 10 million? When a player makes more during a home stand than you'll make all year? The jewelry in his locker is worth more than your car. If you have any difficulty in this sort of upside-down situation, this would not be the job for you.

The Miami Heat crushed the Bulls in the first game of the 1993-94 season in Chicago Stadium. Michael Jordan was present in the stands for the game as the Bulls conducted their traditional ceremony, unfurling the championship banner from the year before and presenting the players their rings. The loss made for an awkward evening and triggered talk of acquiring another player to get them through the season. Jeff Hornacek, Byron Scott and Derek Harper were among the contestants — with Scottie Pippen assuming Jordan's role of badgering management for a better supporting cast.

In a surprise move that was unpopular at the time but would pay dividends later, the Bulls dealt Stacey King to Minnesota for the amiable Australian center Luc Longley. With Kukoc and Longley on board, the Bulls were taking on an international flavor.

The Bulls were a respectable 21-10 at the trading deadline — better than expected. The outcry for another player had cooled. While they lacked the confidence necessary to win consistently on the road, they were winning at home. Scottie Pippen had stepped into the leadership role and was playing well, without trying to be Michael Jordan. He was the standout MVP at the NBA All-Star game and would average 22 points on the season, a career high. Reserves Steve Kerr, Bill Wennington and Pete Myers were playing well —for near the minimum salary — a real bargain, especially for Myers, who was logging serious minutes at Jordan's former position.

John Paxson and Bill Cartwright suffered the most in Jordan's absence. They were forced to pick up the slack with injured and aging bodies. Both played considerably more than they were accustomed to and without the rest periods they had enjoyed in the past.

The Bulls were not without their usual array of sideshows. Horace Grant, in the last year of his contract, suffered a variety of injuries and illnesses that limited his playing time and created a media war with Phil Jackson. B.J. Armstrong continued whining about losing playing time to John Paxson. Will Perdue wrote an article for his local paper complaining about Jerry Krause's presence on the team bus. Krause took it personally. Perdue would be off the roster for the playoffs.

Tensions ran high as the team struggled to maintain its previous status — and incidents were frequent. Scottie Pippen was arrested on a gun charge and would later insinuate that Chicago Bulls fans were racists, because he was booed more than Kukoc. He opined that the Bulls made a mistake in paying Kukoc so much money while failing to satisfy Grant.

Even the normally steady Tex Winter got into it with back-up center Scott Williams during practice. Words were exchanged and it appeared Tex was willing to fight the 6'10" Williams before Jackson moved to break things up. Jackson kept a close eye on Williams — he had nick-named the center "Psycho."

Tex had his moments with Pippen as well, feeling at times Pippen was ignoring him — one of the not-so-subtle snubs coaches endure when players take advantage of their exalted status. Comes with the territory. Maybe Scottie was miffed because Tex disputed a "Player of the Game" award.

"It's tough to stay on a even keel when a team has the kind of success the Bulls had up to that point," said Tex. "Too many egos."

Meanwhile, Jordan announced his intention to play baseball. Possessing three NBA championships, he felt he had little to prove. His father had always wanted him to play baseball and Jerry Reinsdorf, who also owned the White Sox, was willing to give Jordan a chance. "My feeling was that he should give it a whirl," said Tex. "He probably needed to try something else and get it out of his system."

Even without Jordan, the Bulls won 55 games in the 1993-94 season, no mean accomplishment. "We played better as a team," said Tex, "but that's not to be critical of Michael. We didn't have any choice. His absence necessitated more reliance on the system and we still had some super athletes."

Not that they always pulled together. In Game Three of the Eastern Conference Semifinals against the New York Knicks, Scottie Pippen refused to finish the game. Jackson had designated Kukoc to take the final desperation shot with only 1.8 seconds remaining and the Bulls trailing by a point. Kukoc had confirmed throughout the season that despite his shortcomings, he shared with Jordan that same fearlessness in face of the last shot — regardless of consequences. But Pippen wasn't buying it. He felt it was his turn, but he was being snubbed. He refused to get off the bench, thinking the Bulls had little chance anyway and that he could make a point by staying put. Ironically, Kukoc made the shot and the Bulls won — that is, they won on the scoreboard. In the locker room, there was much to be worked out.

"I was disappointed," said Tex. "We were all disappointed."

Publicly apologetic, Pippen saw the incident as further evidence of his maltreatment by the Bulls. A tearful Bill Cartwright, thinking himself in his last season as a player, questioned how Pippen could come so far with his teammates, only to abandon them in the clutch. Matters were made worse by the fact that the Bulls had been down two games to none at the time — to the New York Knicks.

Both Phil Jackson and Bill Cartwright had played for the Knicks and the rivalry had become intense. Jackson and Knicks coach Pat Riley took very different approaches to basketball and life. Riley favored a very physical approach to defense; he was flamboyant, intense and highly paid. Jackson thought Riley's defensive tactics were destroying the game, that Riley was a media creation without much substance. There was no love lost between the two and the teams clashed frequently on the floor.

It was not the only clash the Bulls were involved in. They were not favorites at NBA headquarters, either. The Bulls had sued the league successfully to keep their games on WGN, a local Chicago station. They also had defied league directives to make players available to the media during the playoff series. With Michael Jordan in your corner and several championships in tow, perhaps the Bulls were seen as Bull-ies to the league hierarchy.

There were ways to get even. The assignment of officiating crews was a prime example.

Referees have a difficult time. They have countless opportunities to influence the outcome of a game and there are countless types of contact to decipher. It is a sensitive area with the league — players and coaches are fined when their criticisms cross the line. It would be nice to think officiating is objective and consistent, that all refs call a game pretty much the same and that they harbor no grudges. The reality is quite different. Teams know the crews; the crews know the teams. Like any human endeavor, there are problems.

The Bulls had a long-standing beef with Hue Hollins, a veteran official who seemed to be assigned more than his share of Bulls games. Games are assigned by the league through a confidential process and the officials' schedules are kept secret to avoid undue influence. The Bulls had complained about Hollins, having lost a previous playoff game where their opponent shot twice as many free throws. Free-throw numbers are usually a pretty good indicator of a problem.

In the fifth game of the Knicks series, the Bulls had a one-point lead and had only to stop New York from scoring — and not foul. After the final shot — a miss — Pippen bumped the arm of the shooter, Hubert Davis. It seemed harmless enough. Hollins called a foul. Davis canned his free throws. A dubious call had cost them the game and the edge in the series. "You'd be laughed off the playground if you made that call," was Tex Winter's opinion on the matter. The Bulls went on to lose the series in seven games.

In a season during which they had won just two fewer games than they had the season before with Michael Jordan on board, losing to the Knicks was an especially painful experience. The situation called for change. No one could possibly forecast the changes that lay ahead.

The Bulls prepared for the 1994-95 season by trading Scottie Pippen; well, almost trading Scottie Pippen. The time seemed right for Pippen to go. His image was tarnished by the 1.8-second incident and the phantom foul that lost Game Five. It was obvious Pippen was ready to go. As good as he was, he'd become a thorn in the flesh. The Bulls thought they could get a top-flight player for Pippen. They thought they could get Shawn Kemp from Seattle. In fact, they thought the deal was done. But word of the trade leaked in Seattle and fans mounted a campaign to save the popular Kemp from leaving. The SuperSonics owner changed his mind about the deal just minutes before it was to be signed. Pippen and Kemp would stay where they were and Scottie Pippen would add one more perceived slight to his growing list of grievances. And he was about to lose his supporting cast.

Horace Grant followed through on his threat to leverage free agency, signing with the Orlando Magic for about $5 million a year. The loss of

Grant left a bitter taste with Owner Jerry Reinsdorf, who insisted he had made a verbal agreement with Grant during a private meeting at Berto Center. Reinsdorf called a press conference to explain that the Bulls had done everything they reasonably could to keep Grant, who had exaggerated injuries during the season and cost the Bulls home-court advantage during the playoffs. Grant saw himself feuding with a slave-owner mentality, one that expected him to play through serious injury and illness, regardless of the consequences to his career. It was an ugly parting, one that Horace Grant would later avenge on the court.

Bill Cartwright retired before the 1994-95 season only to unretire and sign with Seattle. He would play one more year there. John Paxson retired and stayed retired, coaching during the Bulls' summer league before finding his way to the broadcast booth. Scottie "Psycho" Williams was released.

The Bulls declined to renew assistant coach John Bach's contract. Phil Jackson brought the news to Bach himself. Jackson was tired of listening to Bach complain about Krause; tired as well of Bach's "defensive guru" status when he felt at least equally knowledgeable and responsible for the Bulls defense. Johnny had never fully supported the triangle offense — he had been known to contradict Jackson's timeout advice, telling Jordan to "forget the triangle." Perhaps equally damning, Johnny had never cultivated a relationship with Jerry Krause. Tex Winter saw his fellow coach's release as another instance of the transitory nature of sport. You were there one minute, part of the team and five minutes later, with little explanation, you were released.

The Bulls picked up free agent Ron Harper during the off-season to shore up the team. Harper had been a scoring guard for Cleveland and had overcome a serious knee injury. His acquisition at almost $4 million a year made Pippen fourth on the Bulls payroll behind Kukoc, Armstrong and now Harper. Harper hardly seemed to be worth it. His lateral movement seemed poor in training camp and it appeared he could pose what the Bulls needed least — a defensive liability. Ultimately, however, Ron Harper would work out. Either way, he was going to be a highly-paid Bull for a while — his contract ran through the end of the millennium.

Scottie Pippen held a benefit basketball game in September in soon-to-be-abandoned Chicago Stadium. It would be the last event in the old stadium before the opening of the United Center, the Bulls' new home. Ticket sales were slow until the day before the game, when Michael Jordan announced he would participate. A frenzy of ticket sales ensued. Since the game would not be televised, it was be there or be square.

Michael's welcome home was resounding. A thunderous ovation met him at warm-ups. His first warm-up basket was cause for celebration. He played on the visiting team, at times guarding his host, Scottie Pippen. As in practice, they went at each other hard. But defense was not the order of the evening — Jordan's team won, 187-155, with Jordan scoring 52 points. As the game ended, Jordan knelt and kissed the Bull at center court. It was time to go back to baseball.

The Bulls opened the season November 4, 1994, with an 89-83 win over the Charlotte Hornets. The first game at the United Center ushered in a new era in Bulls basketball. Gone were the intimate confines of Chicago Stadium with its balconies, obstructed views and art deco decor. Gone too was the infamous sixth-man effect that came with packing some 18,600 Bulls fans into its confining space. There was nowhere for the noise to go except back and forth between the floor and the ceiling. It was loud — and there was an intimacy between players and fans.

The new season found the Bulls ensconced in the new $175 million United Center — complete with cash machines, a $5 million scoreboard and 216 luxury suites. The luxury suites were key — their price tag allowed the Bulls to finance the facility without tax dollars. The United Center offered a different feel and sound. While seating only 3,000 more fans than Chicago Stadium, the new facility's interior was over one-third larger. There was room to move around and plenty of entertainment to induce one to do so, not to mention three times more restrooms as the stadium. It just wasn't as loud.

The Bulls were 23-25 at the All-Star break. They were losing a lot of close games, but were able to beat the better teams. Tex thought Phil Jackson seemed almost serene, especially compared to the previous season, when he seemed frazzled — on edge. Phil had lost a close friend during the off-season and had done some soul-searching, clarifying his values.

The season was progressing better than expected. The Bulls were not as strong as they had been in past seasons, but they weren't exactly bottom dwellers either. Tex enjoyed working with the group, trying to maximize practice, realizing they would have to get out everything to win the close ones.

It was the off-court stuff that made it difficult. Pippen and Krause were now openly feuding and it was affecting Scottie's play. Pippen was struggling with his composure, exploding into episodes both in the press and on the court. Pippen wanted to be traded. Before a game in which he had to be restrained from going after a referee, Pippen told a *Daily Herald* reporter, "I might have to do something to make them get rid of me." The Bulls were ready to accommodate. A deal was worked out with the Los Angeles Clippers. Pippen nixed it.

On March 3, 1995, Michael Jordan walked out of spring training in a huff. He was quitting baseball. In a season of change, things were about to get radical.

*Much can be learned by studying the moves of the great individual players in the game of basketball today. What makes them different from the average player?*

— Tex Winter, *The Triple-Post Offense*, 1962

*Tex tells me to come back for practices. He tells me that even if I don't want to play in the NBA anymore, that if I want to I should just be a member of the practice team ... He's just trying to entice me. But he knows me — he knows what to say.*

— Michael Jordan, *Rebound: The Odyssey of Michael Jordan*

## CHAPTER ELEVEN
# RETURN OF THE JEDI

Professional baseball lost Michael Jordan over a parking spot. It was no great loss perhaps, for Jordan was an aging .200 hitter with a mediocre arm — a minor leaguer. Had it been anyone else with his performance credentials, his loss would not have been noticed. But this was Michael Jordan and everything was noticed. "The Jordan Watch," as it was aptly named, provided the nation a daily update on the latest statistics of America's favorite athlete. Hadn't he improved? Hit .259 for the Birmingham Barons the last month of the '94 season? Stolen 30 bases? And wasn't there a new pop in his bat in the spring of '95?

Whatever Michael Jordan might or might not have accomplished in the new sport of his choice, baseball was clearly not ready for him. The '94 World Series was canceled due to the players strike and in the spring of '95, the owners were planning on filling the major league ranks with minor leaguers. In a league devoid of big-league players, Michael Jordan would be the perfect draw.

But Jordan would not be cast in the role of a strikebreaker. First, he was banished from the clubhouse for refusing to wear the White Sox uniform. Then he lost his parking spot. He could park down the street outside the protected lot — and would have to wade through the mobs of fans who would invariably be waiting. It was the last straw.

A vigil began at the Michael Jordan monument outside the United Center. Jordan began attending Bulls practices, something he had done from time to time while in baseball. But this time he was running wind sprints afterward. Eventually, practices were canceled because of the media crunch. The possibility of Jordan's return quickly became the biggest news story in the country. President Clinton bragged the economy had produced 6.1 million new jobs during his presidency, adding, "If Michael Jordan goes back to the Bulls, it will be 6,100,001 new jobs."

"It was an opportune moment for Michael to return," Tex Winter reflected. "In many ways, the time off had been good for him— a mental and physical respite. If we could get him back with 20 or so games left in the regular season, it would give him a chance to get his game back and be ready for the playoffs."

A week into the maelstrom, Phil Jackson announced the matter was in Jerry Reinsdorf's hands — a remark that earned him a gag order from the Bulls owner. Jackson wanted Jordan back in a bad way; the Bulls had been losing too many close games. He longed for a closer like Jordan. Winter was more ambivalent. Certainly he wanted Michael Jordan on their side. But he wondered what effect Jordan's return would have on the team. Pippen and Armstrong had developed as ballplayers and leaders in Jordan's absence. He wondered if there would be enough basketball to go around. He wondered if Jordan would try to fit in — or take over.

Jordan, meanwhile, was using his leverage to obtain the best contract he could from Reinsdorf. Jordan was tired of earning less in salary than other players in the league and he saw his negotiation with Reinsdorf as a sort of competition, one he could win. If nothing else, the stock value of the companies Jordan endorsed would soar upon his return.

With the Bulls three-quarters of the way through their season at 32-31, Reinsdorf and Jordan came to an agreement. He would play his first game March 19, 1995, in Indiana, against the Pacers. Jordan's agent issued a two-word statement on behalf of his client: "I'm back."

But it wasn't the same Jordan who came back. Wearing the number 45, his baseball number, Jordan seemed to be acknowledging he was a different player than when he had worn number 23. It showed. He seemed slower; his shots weren't falling. He shot seven for 28 his first game back in an overtime loss to the Pacers. His teammates seemed to defer to him, encouraging him to shoot again and again. "The Bulls were a good team until I came back," he said afterward.

Jackson canceled the shoot-around before Jordan's second game, opting instead for a team meeting in the hotel ballroom with a local stress reduction expert, Dr. George Mumford. Tex supported Jackson in his attempts to bring the team together. He knew Jackson sometimes took flak for being unorthodox in his approach. He knew the reality was quite different. The media described the session as "group meditation." However, the Bulls had worked with Mumford before. Mumford knew what he was doing — the team needed reflection time together. Jordan's return was certainly causing stress. Individual roles were changing and players were losing minutes. As far as Tex was concerned, the situation called for just the kind of timeout Jackson scheduled.

Later that evening against the Boston Celtics, Jordan seemed to regain his former self. It was the last time the Bulls would play in the venerable Boston Garden. Like Chicago Stadium before it, the Garden was being replaced by a new facility. Jordan usually preferred playing in the old arenas. Though his playing time was limited due to foul trouble, he seemed to have his game back, scoring 27 points. Late in the game, he took an alley-oop pass from Pippen and slammed it home. The Bulls won, 124-107 and the team performed well.

Jordan's first game in the United Center, in front of a hometown Chicago crowd that was hyped to a frenzy, was an anticlimax and harbinger of problems to come. The Bulls were hosting the Orlando Magic, complete with Shaquille O'Neal and former Bull Horace Grant. It was the first time Horace would play his former teammates; he had missed two previous opportunities due to injury. Phil Jackson made a point of mentioning that fact when asked how the Bulls would defense Grant. Horace did not appreciate the obvious allusion to his alleged malingering while a Bull. He and his teammates would out-rebound the Bulls 53-35 en route to a 106-99 victory. Jordan was a miserable seven for 23 on the game. He also missed free throws, saw his shots blocked and had difficulty performing down the stretch. He complained afterward that he felt uncomfortable in his first game at the United Center. He looked it. "I know I can play the game of basketball," Jordan said after the game, as if to reassure himself.

What happened in the next two games was a microcosm of the intoxicating high the Bulls would experience on the roller coaster ride of the 1995 season as they came to rely on their prodigal superstar. In a close game at the Omni against the Atlanta Hawks, Jordan had the ball stripped away by Steve Smith. Mookie Blaylock scooped it up and went the length of the floor, laying it in. The Hawks led 98-97 with 5.9 seconds remaining in the game.

The Bulls called timeout and drew up a play for Jordan. Steve Smith, still guarding Jordan, asked him who was getting the ball. "Pippen," Jordan responded. Jordan took the ball instead, driving the length of the floor on Smith, faking him out of position before nailing an off-balance 14-footer for the win. It was vintage Michael Jordan. Jordan lovers everywhere let out a collective sigh of relief. Michael could still do it. Superman was back — and the situation was about to get even better.

With the Knicks naively single-teaming Jordan at Madison Square Garden, Jordan scored 55. The evening was all Michael, all the time. "Michael saw the Garden as a basketball mecca — he played his best ball there," said Tex. "That night he made up his mind to put on a show."

It was the most Jordan would score against the Knicks in his career. With the Bulls winning the contest, 100-82, the math was easy — Jordan had scored a whopping 55 percent of the Bulls points, shooting 37 times. Scottie Pippen shot 12 times during the game; Michael Jordan shot 11 times in *the first quarter* — more than the rest of the Bulls, less Pippen, *would shoot in the entire game*. In the third quarter, Jordan, in a scoring frenzy, waved off a substitution from Phil Jackson. Television cameras caught him berating teammate Pete Myers for taking a shot. The cult of Michael Jordan had returned. Like relapsing alcoholics, the Bulls and their fans drank deeply of a heady intoxicant that night. It would lead to more binges, strange episodes and unpleasant mornings after.

Tex saw the chemistry of the team being inexorably altered. Longley, Kerr, Kukoc and others had not played with Jordan before. They were deferring to him and their contributions diminished as a result. Pippen and Armstrong had flourished in Jordan's absence. Now the superstar was back and the pecking order was being shuffled.

Pippen left his spot in the limelight to assume his previous supporting role. Even while the primary scorer, Pippen had remained popular with his teammates because he was much more willing than Jordan to share the ball. Armstrong, who had matured into a confident ball handler and scorer, was now expected to position himself in a corner and wait for Jordan to pass. He was to share those duties with Steve Kerr. Neither player was seeing as many open shots with Jordan back.

Jordan didn't trust Longley and wanted Will at center, despite having panned Perdue in years previous. Longley was increasingly subjected to Jordan's ire as the season progressed. It was Longley who would have to prove himself. Pete Myers, who had replaced Jordan, was returned to the bench from whence he came. His selfless play had fit in well with the tri-angle offense, but his talent was no match for the returning superstar.

The triangle itself was in trouble. Jordan wanted to scrimmage during practice and noted that teammates Toni Kukoc and Corie Blount hadn't learned the triangle in the 18 months he'd been away. Corie Blount seemed a hopeless case. Though a talented player, Blount's style of play was ill-fitted to the triangle and he exhibited little progress in learning it. He would be essentially given away to the Los Angeles Lakers in the off-season. Toni Kukoc was another story. He needed to handle the ball to get his game going, but with Jordan back he was seeing much less ball. Jordan saw potential in Kukoc, but realized he would be a liability at power forward because of his less physical style of play. Jordan favored Dickey Simpkins at that position and Kukoc was in jeopardy of losing the starting position he had enjoyed.

"It's always been a fine line with Michael," said Tex. "The seventh prin-ciple of the triangle philosophy is that the offense is only sound when it gives individual players the freedom to contribute with their unique skills. With Michael, there were awesome skills. Normally, I supported his contributions and the individual exploits didn't bother me, as long as the other guys weren't standing around watching one man."

---

**"Phil and I thought Michael would see the light and realize he couldn't carry the team. Phil gave him a lot of rope. Unexpectedly, he just kept pulling. We maybe misjudged the depth of his tenacity."**

---

There was another problem. Jordan, who was shooting 44 percent on the road, was shooting a paltry 33 percent at home in the United Center. The "at home" seemed to be part of the problem. Home was Chicago Stadium across the way, in the process of being torn down. The United Center didn't feel like home — it was cavernous and impersonal. Even it's name "United" seemed alien; it wasn't named for the town or the Bulls, but for the airline that helped finance its construction. Jordan had trouble accepting the new venue, as if he resented the Bulls having played there without him … resented Jerry Reinsdorf designing and building the place without his input.

The analysis of the United Center problem led to numerous explanations, many of them supported and seemingly encouraged by Phil Jackson. The lights were "too bright," the temperature "too warm," the rims "too tight," the atmosphere "too impersonal." It was an "arena" rather than a "stadium." Jordan was known to spend off-time hanging from and bouncing balls off the rims in an effort to loosen them up — as well as experimenting with shooting with the lights out. He was convinced the glare of the lights was clouding his vision.

Tex had heard it all before. Teams often doctored their home court, much as Muhammad Ali's people loosened the ropes before his "Rope-A-Dope" fight against George Foreman in Zaire. With the ropes loosened, Ali could lean back for support while Foreman punched himself out. Similarly, a fast-break team might want an over-inflated ball and tight rims because the ball bouncing out of the basket more often and coming hard off the rim might favor a fast-break team. Home teams were always looking for an edge, from the noise and distraction created by their crowds to the color of the visiting locker room. That was stuff you had to deal with. Tex thought the whole United Center problem was overblown and dangerous. After all, it was the Bulls' *home* court.

"I thought Phil encouraged the whole discussion too much," said Tex. "It seemed to me to be purely psychological and the less excusing the better. My response was, 'How come the other guys are shooting so well here?'"

Having lost the final game of the season to the Milwaukee Bucks, the Bulls headed to the first round of the NBA Playoffs in Charlotte, North Carolina. Jordan shot a miserable 11 for 29 against the Bucks and it was hard to blame his poor performance on the United Center — the game was played in Milwaukee.

Jordan's up-and-down performances led to a wealth of analysis, among which was stated that the United Center bugaboo was only symptomatic of Jordan's fading skills. The coaching staff shared concern about Jordan's effect on the team; they were clearly not a close-knit team since his return, with flashes of anger and frustration often apparent. Now they were traveling to Jordan Country — North Carolina, to play the upstart Hornets, including trash-talking Alonzo Mourning and the highly-paid Larry Johnson. Johnson and Mourning were emblematic of the new NBA — young, unpredictable beneficiaries of a reward system that paid on potential, before their NBA performance was established.

The Hornets had a weapon of fear in John Bach, who had been hired as an assistant by the Hornets after leaving the Bulls. Bach knew the Bulls inside and out — the offense, the defense and the psychological strengths and weaknesses of Bulls players. Bach was a champion of hard play, machismo and intimidation. He would set the defensive scheme, most probably double-teaming Jordan, then focusing on Pippen and Armstrong, making the remaining Bulls responsible to score. Bach would challenge Mourning, "the Tasmanian Devil," to be on his game. He would have the Hornets ready; it would be point of honor for him.

Having Bach in the other huddle made many players queasy, but Tex had a deeper understanding of the situation. He knew Bach understood the triangle better than most thought. He and Johnny worked both offense and defense, sharing ideas and feeding off each other. It wasn't as if John coached only defense and Tex coached only offense. They knew each other well; they knew each others' systems well, too. But none of that mattered to Tex. That was the beauty of the triangle. The defense names the play. Whatever they throw at us, we can counter — if we play properly. It doesn't matter what they know.

Game One went into overtime and was a problematic win for the Bulls. Pippen played miserably, getting into foul trouble early and scoring only eight points. Will Perdue logged only 16 minutes as the starting center. Luc Longley, his replacement, scored 14 points and played well, although he seemed to draw Jordan's ire throughout the game. Kukoc was visibly backing off the Johnny Bach-type challenges the Hornets were throwing at him. The Hornets, one of the poorest rebounding teams in the league, almost doubled the Bulls' rebound production. Jackson requested that the rims be checked, thinking the Hornets must have softened them to help their cause. The league said they were fine. The Bulls were relying increasingly on Jordan, who scored 48 points, showcasing his skills before the North Carolina crowd. It was worse at crunch time — Jordan scored 10 of the Bulls' 16 overtime points.

The situation came to a head in Game Two, which the Hornets won easily, 102-89. With Jordan continuing to star, the remaining Bulls struggled. Mourning single-handedly out-rebounded the entire Bulls' front line. With Perdue not looking to score, Mourning was free to roam, helping others on defense. At the prompting of Johnny Bach, Larry Johnson man-handled Toni Kukoc, who shot three for 12 while the attacking Johnson scored 25. The Bulls shot a sorry 12 for 42 in the second half. Something needed adjusting, Tex thought and it wasn't the rims.

Jackson was fed up with Perdue and Kukoc, announcing they would be replaced as starters for Game Three. Luc Longley and Jud Buechler, Jordan's two least favorite players, would start the game. Buechler, a little-used player making the minimum NBA wage, would replace the highly-paid Kukoc. It was not the kind of change that would please Jerry Krause. But Buechler had stood up well to Larry Johnson in the minutes he played in Game One and Jackson thought he was worth the risk. Jordan and Kukoc showed their dismay by sulking through practice.

"It was a tough situation," said Tex. "It always is when you make player changes. Perdue especially had a high opinion of himself. Players must have big egos; you don't see much humility. I supported the move to Longley — I may even have suggested it. I wasn't so sure about Buechler for Kukoc. I think Phil used the changes as a wake-up call for the two players and the team. Playing time is the single greatest commodity a coach has to allocate. It's a key component in motivating players. It has to be invested, not squandered. In exchange for playing time, players are expected to contribute. When they stop contributing, for whatever reason, it's the coach's job to put someone in who can."

Jackson reversed his decision to start Buechler, figuring that two player changes were too much for the Bulls to assimilate. Whether by serendipity or design, Jackson hit on just the right formula — the Bulls destroyed the Hornets in Game Three at the United Center, 103-80. Kukoc scored 22 on nine for 10 shooting. The Bulls put Jordan on 5'3" Muggsy Bogues, primarily a playmaker and poor shooter. The move allowed Jordan to help Longley by double-teaming Mourning, who suffered through two of nine shooting and was held in check on the boards. With Jordan's point production reduced to 25, Scottie Pippen joined the flow, playing well for the first time in the series with 14 points, five rebounds — and nine assists.

The fourth and deciding game of the series was a lesson in just how tenuous the Bulls' grasp of excellence could be at the United Center. In the third quarter, with the Bulls trailing, Jordan asked to be taken out of the game. It was a particularly ugly quarter — the Bulls scoring just 11 points — the lowest point production for a quarter in franchise history. "They kept throwing the ball to me," Jordan said. "They had to realize they have to walk on their own two feet if we're to succeed."

Jordan returned in the fourth quarter to score seven of the last nine points as the Bulls hung on to win, 85-84. In the end, the game seemed more about which team would play worse, the Hornets missing two makeable shots in the final seconds.

Rumor had it Jordan was rooting for the Orlando Magic as the next Bulls' opponent because it would mean fewer games in the United Center. He was about to get his wish.

◆   ◆   ◆

The Orlando Magic was a talented team, albeit a stumbling one. Even with Shaquille O'Neal, Anfernee Hardaway and Nick Anderson, they seemed to have lost their edge down the stretch, losing eight of their last 13 games.

The Magic's spiritual leader in the series against the Bulls was Horace Grant. Grant had stood up to the pressure in the previous series against the Boston Celtics, canning two critical free throws in the waning moments of the deciding game. And it was Grant who had the most to prove against the Bulls. He had something to show Jackson, Jordan, Krause and Reinsdorf.

Jackson had picked on him, made light of his injuries. Jordan had treated him like a second-class citizen, challenging his importance to the team while exalting his own. Krause and Reinsdorf had questioned his integrity and let him go. Grant suggested Jordan had lost his edge. Jackson, he said, had ridden him unnecessarily while sparing Jordan and Pippen. Krause and Reinsdorf had stepped on him. The feelings of animosity were mutual. There were egos on the line.

The confluence of egos made the crazy events of the final seconds of Game One almost comic. With the Bulls ahead, 91-90 and Michael Jordan possessing the ball with 18 seconds remaining in the game, the Magic should have been looking to foul, but they were looking for the ball. All Jordan needed to do was hang on to it. Instead, he put on a dribbling exhibition. Nick Anderson sneaked up on Jordan, knocking the ball to Anfernee Hardaway, who passed ahead to — guess who — Horace Grant. To the delight of the hometown fans, Grant slammed the ball home for the lead.

Now one point down with 6.2 seconds remaining, the Bulls had another chance to win the game. Jordan, as expected, took the ball and drove to the basket. However, what happened next was unexpected. As the defense collapsed, Jordan dumped the ball off to a surprised Scottie Pippen. The ball bounced harmlessly out of bounds — Pippen had been moving toward the basket in hopes of a rebound. It seemed an odd time for Jordan to share the basketball.

Postgame analysis of the situation was swift and would evolve into a full-blown media circus. Phil Jackson "checked the lunar charts and celestial stations of the stars," concluding the whole thing might have been a mirage. The ball was supposed to go to B.J. Armstrong at the 16-second mark, as Armstrong was the team's best free-throw shooter. Inexplicably, Jordan kept it instead. Jackson had never known Jordan to lose track of a teammate in that situation.

Tex wondered if Jordan had been distracted by the loud, disorienting music or whether Jordan had succumbed to fatigue. "It was embarrassing," Tex admitted later. "Michael took such pride in how he finished a ball game. He was the best there ever was at it ... and this was his worst finish ever. But Michael was strong enough to see the situation as a challenge and to re-commit. Part of the strength of Michael Jordan is his tremendous confidence."

Jordan himself was stoic. "I won't make excuses. With the game in my hands, I couldn't deliver. The next couple of days I'll think about it. Then I'll let it go."

Horace Grant used the interlude between games to pick at Scottie Pippen's frustration. Besides the issue of whether Pippen could have anticipated Jordan's strange pass in the final seconds was the larger issue of Pippen's role with the Bulls. Pippen was rebounding and recording assists, but unlike his other teammates, was not getting shots. Grant opined that the Bulls took advantage of Pippen's selfless work, that they would ruin his career.

But it was the Hornet's Nick Anderson who set off the main charge. Grant had encouraged Anderson to challenge Jordan before the series and Anderson had done just that. He had posted up on Jordan in Game One and embarrassed Jordan by asking for the ball. It was Anderson who sped up from behind and knocked the ball away from Jordan at the critical moment. And it was Anderson who made the following comment after outscoring and outplaying Michael Jordan in the first contest:

"Age catches up with you. When Michael was a 28, 29-year-old player, he was like a space shuttle taking off. Now he's still trying to rev up, trying to get ready. Before he retired, he had quickness and explosiveness. Not that it's not there now, but it's not as sharp as when he was number

23. He still does some things, but not like number 23 did. Number 23, he could just blow right by you. Number 45, he revs up, but he doesn't really take off. He looks tired. Shots he normally makes, he somehow doesn't make now. And I didn't see him go to the basket with his right hand. I don't know if he's injured or what, but I'm not seeing number 23."

Game Two belonged to Michael Jordan. In response to Anderson's comments, he came out wearing his old jersey, number 23. He heated up quickly, hitting a three-point shot and a jumper and guiding the Bulls to an early lead. He went on to score 38 points, shooting a torrid 11 for 13 in the second half, leading the Bulls to a 104-94 win. Late in the game, Jordan, having blocked a shot, punctuated the event with a vintage dunk. This time, he seemed all the way back.

The Jordan return to number 23 didn't surprise Tex. In fact, he hadn't even noticed the change until someone brought it to his attention after the game. He knew Michael Jordan without having to look at his number.

While Tex agreed with some of Anderson's analysis, he also knew Anderson's comments would challenge Michael. Anderson should have let sleeping dogs lie. It was basic sports psychology. You had a good game against Michael Jordan? Keep your mouth shut. If the press probes about Michael's game, repeat the litany that Jordan's the best ever. Sure, Michael had lost a little and tired a bit more easily, but he had entered the season past the halfway point and was trying to dominate younger, better conditioned players. The point was, Michael was trying to do too much and it was hurting the team. On some days Jordan was his old self, but over the distance Tex thought they were better off playing team ball.

The media was in a frenzy. Jordan's incredible performance highlighted his defiance of league rules on two counts: one, he was wearing white patent leather shoes while his teammates wore black; two, he had changed his jersey number without authorization. The league wanted him back in his number 45 jersey and in the same color shoes as his teammates. Jordan compromised. He changed shoes but continued wearing number 23. Jordan had stopped talking to the press after the debacle of Game One, but he milked the media coverage of the controversy, showing up for warm-ups in his chosen attire just minutes before the five o'clock news in Chicago.

Chicago loved it. Owner Jerry Reinsdorf agreed to pay Jordan's fines. Tex saw the situation as a byproduct of the cult of the super hero. Yes, Jordan was unique in his competitive ability to respond to challenge. There truly was no one quite like him. But basketball is a team sport. What draws attention to one player, lifting him above the rest to the point of distraction detracts from the team, causing an almost chemical change that can sour the effort. The number change Tex understood. It was just Michael's way of accepting a challenge and shutting Anderson's mouth. He admired Michael's courage.

But Tex was ambivalent about the shoe thing. In a way it was grandstanding, putting self above team. He wondered if the fragile infrastructure of the team could withstand much more. On the other hand, this *was* Michael Jordan. Tex thought the league was being picky about the shoes. As ugly as they were, they did have *some* black on them. He sided with Michael. The league had some pretty ridiculous rules. Michael was involved in a power struggle; the NBA leadership had tried to downplay the importance of Jordan's return. The shoes and the jersey were Jordan's way of challenging the NBA structure. Tex thought the league could use an occasional challenge.

The start of Game Three, played at the United Center, seemed to confirm what Bulls fans had hoped for — that the Bulls had vanquished the Magic in Game Two and that the series was now reduced to mopping-up operations. In the first five minutes, the Bulls went up by 10; the crowd was in a frenzy. They would shoot 63 percent the first quarter. Jordan was on fire.

But they couldn't sustain. In the excitement of the game, the Bulls began running with the much younger Magic. Tex noticed it first. He knew the dangers. When teams run, scoring can be volatile. The Bulls needed to slow down. Michael was going to wear himself out.

In the words of Sam Smith, "The Bulls had become the Pistons and the Magic had become the Bulls." In former days, the Pistons had fought the Bulls to keep the score down, forcing them into a half-court game, fouling them hard, slowing the pace of the game. Now it was the older Bulls who needed to slow down the Magic. The "three-headed monster" of Perdue, Wennington and Longley fouled Shaquille O'Neal at every opportunity, sending him to the free-throw line. One of them might foul out, but surely not all three. O'Neal would have to make his free throws.

As Tex feared, Michael ran out of gas. He was pulled in the third quarter, the Bulls down 10. Without him, the Bulls pulled to within a single point by the end of the quarter. Sometimes it was better without Michael. Tex knew, sometimes he just tried to do too much. He seemed to be on a personal quest at the expense of the team. Short-term gain for long-term problems. It was a shame, too, because Orlando was a perfect subject for the triangle. Tex could see the Magic was vulnerable to good ball movement.

Back in the game in the fourth quarter, Jordan would not score in the last six minutes. With 90 seconds remaining and a chance to tie the game, Horace Grant swiped the ball from him. Grant finished the game with 18 points and 14 rebounds. The Bulls lost, 110-101.

The loss seemed to break Jordan's spirit. He reportedly sulked in practice — and took a third fewer shots in Game Four. The "other guys" — Pippen, Armstrong, Perdue and Kukoc — took over. A less overbearing Jordan and better ball movement led to a 106-95 win. It was vintage Tex-ball, everybody scoring, everybody participating. It wouldn't last.

For whatever reason, Jordan chose to reassert himself in Game Five. He would shoot eight times in the infamous third quarter, in which the Magic erased a 12-point halftime deficit with a 35-20 spurt. Pippen was pushed out of the offense; he would shoot only five times in the second half. There appeared to be tension between the two players. The supporting cast had troubles, too. Bill Wennington, the normally steady-shooting center, shot two for 11 on the game, missing key shots down the stretch.

Things couldn't be going better for Horace Grant. With the Magic so loaded with scoring talent, Jackson decided to focus the defense elsewhere. Grant had a field day, hitting 10 of 13 for 24 points. The Magic won, 103-95. "I'm happy no one is guarding me," Grant said at the time. "I'm having a ball out there. That's Phil's philosophy, 'Let Horace beat you.'"

In fact, that was exactly what Phil Jackson had been thinking. He knew

Horace well from his time as a Bull and figured he'd shy away from pressure shots in the playoffs as he sometimes had with the Bulls. You couldn't focus on everybody because the Magic had too many weapons.

Under media and fan pressure, Jackson changed tactics for Game Six, played at the United Center. The Bulls needed a win to avoid elimination and to send the series back to Orlando. This time Pippen would guard Grant more closely. Though the move effectively stymied Grant, it opened up the floor for a rain of three-pointers from Hardaway and Anderson. Still, the Bulls seemed to have the game in hand. They led by eight with only three minutes remaining in the game. But the Bulls would not score again.

The last 90 seconds featured a Jordan air ball, a desperate Jordan dish to Longley after attacking into the teeth of the Magic defense and a Jordan turnover — his 41st of the 10 postseason games. Horace Grant brazenly waved a towel from the bench as the Magic rolled to a 108-102 victory. The Magic completed an incredible 14-0 run in those final three minutes. Grant was hoisted atop his teammates' shoulders before a stunned Chicago crowd. Many thought he deserved the series MVP. When asked who taught him to play basketball, he responded, "Johnny Bach."

The end of the Bulls' season burst a balloon of expectations. Jordan's triumphant return to the team, his flashes of brilliance, his courage in reclaiming number 23 were overshadowed by the team's crushing defeat. It was obvious Horace Grant's defection had been the difference. Obvious as well that Grant had crafted the perfect revenge. Jerry Krause spoke briefly to the team after the game. He was angry. He didn't want to do this again next year, he said. Owner Jerry Reinsdorf admitted publicly that Horace had "stuck it to us." He began planning for next year's season the following day.

Changes would be necessary. There was speculation whether Jordan would return. The Chicago media questioned the utility of the triangle. Tex wanted Phil to ask Michael what he thought. Did Michael want the triangle back? Would he come back if the triangle continued as the offense of the Bulls' future? Tex wanted Phil to ask. He wanted the truth, but he thought Michael might hedge if Tex asked him.

> "I never wanted the triangle to get in the way of the team, and I knew Michael might not tell me what he really thought. I thought it best that Phil ask him. It worked out better than I thought — we got a real commitment from Michael."

Phil came back from the discussion with a positive response. Jordan was committed to the triangle. By deferring to Jordan, Tex had gained a conscious commitment from Michael. Michael would have the off-season to think about that commitment and what it would mean for the team.

Other changes were in store. The Bulls thought they needed bigger guards. They would let B.J. Armstrong go in the expansion draft. They saw the future in Ron Harper and wanted him to work especially hard during the off-season. Harper had just begun to get comfortable with the triangle when Jordan had returned, cutting Harper's playing time. They wanted Harper to be ready to maximize the extra minutes he would be offered next season. Tex thought Luc Longley was the center of the Bulls' future, but he needed help at power forward, someone like Horace Grant to rebound and do the dirty work. Such a player would take a load off Scottie Pippen as well. Such a player does not grow on trees, Tex knew, even in the NBA.

The Bulls were willing to deal Will Perdue. Under normal circumstances, they could not expect to get much for the back-up center. However, they were about to enter into an agreement that would be anything but normal.

*The players can make the coach's job pleasant or they can make it impossible. If the outstanding players on the team are also people of high moral character, clean-cut, ambitious and hard working, the rest of the players will follow suit.*

*No cut and dried rules can be given for discipline. This is determined by circumstances. The effectiveness of any method depends largely upon the coach and his relationship to his team, the individual concerned and the total situation.*

*Don't take yourself too seriously. A sense of humor can lighten the burden and smooth the rough spots.*

**—Tex Winter, The Triple-Post Offense, 1962**

# Chapter Twelve
# Send in the Clowns

Tex Winter voted no on the trade for Dennis Rodman. The Bulls agonized over the decision for weeks, even asking Jordan and Pippen what they thought of the deal. It was a classic double-bind: Rodman had the potential to be the part of the equation the Bulls needed so desperately to fill — that of a physical, rebounding, power forward who didn't need to fight over shooting the ball with Jordan and Pippen. Rodman also had the potential to become the Bulls' worst nightmare — a sideshow so disruptive that the delicate Jordan/Pippen high-wire act would come crashing down, taking the circus tent with it.

Dennis Rodman grew up in the Dallas projects. His father, Philander Rodman, left home when Dennis was three. By his own admission, he was "goofy and shy." Like many of the kids in his neighborhood, he expected to wind up "dead or in jail." He worked the graveyard shift as a janitor at the Dallas-Fort Worth Airport until he was jailed for stealing watches. In tracking down the watches, police found not a single one had been sold — Dennis simply gave them away. Rodman was spared a six-month sentence when the watches — 50 in all — were recovered from family and friends.

The ordeal had a sobering effect on Dennis. He questioned whether the way up was really through "stealing and dealing." Although he had difficulty making the junior varsity team in high school, Dennis took up basketball again. He was helped by a miracle of sorts — now 6'8", he had grown a whopping nine inches since high school. He tried out for a local junior college team and was offered a scholarship after 15 minutes. He played well for the school, but flunked out after a semester. Not wanting anything to do with college, Dennis went back to wandering the streets, refusing to answer recruiters' calls. Only Lonn Reisman and Jack Heddon showed up at the door. They convinced Dennis he needed to get out of Dallas.

Southeastern Oklahoma State University in Durant, Oklahoma, was a long way from Dallas for Dennis Rodman. He lived with a white family in a town of 6,000. That sometimes caused problems, but the family provided much-needed support and this time, he managed to keep his grades up. Dennis found acceptance through basketball; indeed, he found notoriety. No one in Durant, Oklahoma, had ever seen anybody play basketball like Dennis Rodman. He was an NAIA All-American three years in row, averaging 25 points and 15 rebounds per game. He was taken in the NBA draft as the #27 pick by the Detroit Pistons.

Rodman was seen as a project by the Pistons. He grew up among wolves — Bill Laimbeer, Rick Mahorn and John Salley. Rodman especially admired Laimbeer's style of play. Laimbeer feared and respected no one; he played hard and physically and he whined a lot. He was a jerk and didn't care who knew it.

Dennis fought to fit in. He was helped by the Pistons' head coach, Chuck Daly, who saw the possibilities in his awkward, yet determined young player. Different as they were, Daly and Rodman seemed to click. Daly put a premium on performance and as long as Dennis produced, he didn't seem too concerned with lifestyle issues. Under Daly's tutelage, Dennis quickly became a rebounding role player. In only one season of his seven with the Pistons, Rodman averaged more points per game than rebounds. He also learned to play defense, taking on bigger players and shutting them down.

The Pistons became an awesome playoff team, successfully contesting Larry Bird's Celtics and Michael Jordan's Bulls. They would win NBA Championships from Magic Johnson's Lakers and Clyde Drexler's Trail Blazers. Dennis would win Defensive Player of the Year honors and make the NBA All-Star team. The Pistons of those years were tough and intimidating. They got inside your mind. They were wolves who had learned what it took to win.

When Daly lost his coaching job, Rodman felt betrayed — cheated by the NBA and the Pistons' new management. The team was losing players and seemed to be coming apart at the seams. Rodman's rebounds were down. The previous year, his average of 18.7 rebounds per game was the highest in the NBA in 20 years. Toward the end of the season, he contemplated suicide. He came away from the near-death experience determined to live life his way — regardless of the consequences and what others might think. No more Mr. Nice Guy.

Rodman had contract issues. He felt he was underpaid. He saw marquee players around the league making two and three times his salary without producing. They knew how to score; he knew how to win. He was keeping track. The Pistons lost 16 of 20 of the games Rodman missed his final year; at one point they were 17-12 when he played, 0-12 when he didn't. He was willing to sit out a year to get what he thought he deserved from the Pistons. They traded him to San Antonio instead.

The San Antonio organization was not the right place for Dennis, but perhaps few places are. Management never figured out how to handle Rodman. Coach John Lucas bent team rules in an attempt to appease him. Playing alongside David Robinson, a Naval Academy graduate, the contrast in behavior was all the more marked.

Still unhappy with his contract, Rodman reported to training camp with his hair bleached blonde. Though he continued rebounding, his points per game dropped to a career low 4.7. During the '94 playoffs, he was suspended for hip-checking John Stockton of the Utah Jazz. It was bad publicity — the big, bad, black guy beating up on the clean-cut little white guy. Dennis compounded the situation by leaving the team during the suspension and staying with his girlfriend, Madonna. The Spurs lost miserably without him, 105-72. Despite his 20 rebounds, they lost again upon his return. The series over, Rodman left the team without saying good-bye and exited in a limousine with Madonna, still in his uniform. Was Dennis on drugs? There were doubts as to whether his coach, John Lucas, could ever control him. Lucas, by the way, was replaced by Bob Hill.

Rodman played 49 games under Coach Hill; 43 were wins. The statistic was deceiving. Hill and Rodman were bad ju-ju. Management wanted Hill to keep Dennis on a tighter leash, to instill discipline. It didn't work. Dennis became a coach's worst nightmare — skipping team huddles, taking off his shoes during games and going off on Hill. During an interlude between playoff series', Rodman took off for a gambling spree in Las Vegas. Though the Spurs at first didn't know where he was, Rodman's picture was soon on the cover of *Sports Illustrated*. Had Rodman bailed out on the team? An accompanying article described his Vegas exploits. During the Western Conference Finals, Rodman received a one-game suspension by his own team for insubordination. When the series was lost, Dennis left the team immediately, as he had the previous year. The Spurs were ready to peddle him — if they could find a taker.

Jerry Krause was intrigued when he heard Rodman was available. He went to Jerry Reinsdorf, who, while expressing misgivings, gave the go-ahead to explore the opportunity. But he wanted Rodman checked out. He was willing to take a risk, perhaps, but he wanted to know the odds.

The Bulls called Rodman's friends, former coaches and teammates, eventually getting permission talk to Dennis' psychiatrist. Despite the episodic chronology, much of what they heard was positive. Krause invited Rodman to Chicago for lengthy discussions conducted at his house. Dennis let Krause do most of the talking. He found much of what was said redundant and at times, insulting. Krause took him down the litany of problems Rodman had with the Spurs. Listening to Dennis, there was a strange logic to many of the incidents. Rodman had been at war with the Spurs' coaching staff and management; therefore, his antics were the acts of a desperate and disoriented malcontent. Krause wanted to be sure such a war did not erupt with the Bulls. With their different philosophy and tenor, the Bulls' staff just might be able to handle Dennis, he reasoned. Phil Jackson had been a renegade, so maybe he could relate. Despite his reservations, Krause liked Dennis.

Dennis liked Jackson. Krause had been right — the two did relate. Jackson gave Rodman a copy of the team rules, asking him to look them over and let him know if there were any problems. Dennis found the rules similar to those of other teams; however, the way they were presented was different. Jackson had no ax to grind; he wanted Dennis on the team because he knew what he could bring to the floor. Lifestyle issues were downplayed.

While events were proceeding smoothly behind the scenes, Chicago was in an uproar over the Rodman possibility. Could it be the Bulls were taking on public enemy #1, Dennis Rodman, formerly of the Bulls-bashing Detroit Pistons? Could Chicago, the city of Mike Ditka, Richard Daly and Jerry Sloan embrace the alternative lifestyle of Dennis the Menace? What effect would Rodman have on the team?

"I had the same concerns as the fans," said Tex. "There are character issues in every walk of life. The incident that stuck in my mind was when Dennis pushed Scottie from behind in the playoffs, causing him to need stitches and endangering his career. That had nothing to do with lifestyle or hair color. For me, it's a character issue. There are just some lines you don't cross in basketball or you jeopardize the integrity of the game. I harbored serious doubts about bringing Dennis in. Certainly I could see the upside, but my opinion at the time was — it wasn't worth the risk."

Scottie Pippen still wore the scar under his chin from Rodman's shove, yet he and Jordan saw the advantages of having Rodman aboard. His style of play would complement their games. He didn't need the ball, but more importantly — he knew how to rebound. Pippen and Jordan assented to the trade. It didn't mean they were enamored with Dennis, who showed up at the announcement press conference sporting bright red hair with a Bulls logo embedded in the back. Skepticism was confirmed when it was widely reported Rodman and his teammates weren't talking during training camp. Maybe it had been the wrong move.

---

**"I take a lot of ribbing from my old K-State players. I was a stickler for character and perception issues. They see it as poetic justice that I've gotten to know Dennis Rodman."**

---

◆  ◆  ◆

Tex Winter's Berto Center office is part library, part Hall of Fame. Pictures of his successful teams line the walls. Some of them are as obscure as they are ancient — the 1947-48 Kansas State freshmen, a 1952 shot of a team called *Ponce de Leon*. The Kansas State freshmen Tex coached would form the nucleus of the team that took on Kentucky for the national championship a few years later. With *Ponce de Leon*, he was the first Division I coach of a long line to coach a summer in Puerto Rico.

There's a 1982 photograph of the officers and board of the National Association of Basketball Coaches, which Tex chaired that year. Pictured with him are a host of college coaches, including Bobby Knight, Eddie Sutton, Dean Smith and Jud Heathcote.

Occasionally, Steve Kerr would borrow a book. Otherwise, Tex is the sole patron of his personal library. His books on coaching include Red Auerbach's *Basketball for the Player, the Fan, the Coach* and John Wooden's *They Call Me Coach*. Phog Allen's 1937 title, *Better Basketball* and Everett Dean's 1942 entry, *Progressive Basketball*, provide historical context. For motivation there is *I Can* by Ben Sweetland and David Abrahamsen's 1957 version of *The Road to Emotional Maturity*.

On his desk, along with accompanying video cassettes, is Dr. Tom Amberry's, *Free Throw — 7 Steps to Success at the Free-Throw Line*. In November, 1993, Amberry, a retired podiatrist, made 2,750 consecutive free throws, finally stopping without a miss. The effort took 12 hours and was accomplished in view of 10 witnesses who signed sworn affidavits attesting to the count. Amberry *was 71 years old at the time*. His record was published in the 1996 *Guinness Book of Records*.

Amberry's products are designed to help readers become 90 percent free-throw shooters, to set up practice routines and hit clutch free throws under pressure. Improvement at the free-throw line is said to increase 3-point accuracy, build total game confidence and develop the "shooter's touch."

Amberry broke the previous record of 2,036 set by Ted St. Martin in 1977. St. Martin also has a technique book on the market — *The Art of Shooting Baskets*. St. Martin began shooting free throws in earnest in

1971, when the official record stood at 144. It wasn't long before he broke the record, running off ever increasing strings of 200, 245, 927, 1,238, 1,704 and finally 2,036 — a record that would stand 16 years.

Amberry and St. Martin offer significantly different approaches to free-throw shooting, at times contradicting each other on even the basics. Amberry is the more cerebral of the two, perhaps because of his medical background. He emphasizes ritual, recommending exactly three bounces of the ball, along with looking at the inflation hole and pretending it is "the black hole of the universe." St. Martin is content to extol a healthy body and a mind free of drugs. Amberry says the feet should be centered on and square to the basket; St. Martin says right foot forward, centered on the basket. St. Martin says eyes focused on the back of the rim; Amberry says they should focus on the "cylinder of air through which the ball must pass." St. Martin advocates "very little knee bend;" Amberry recommends bending "more than you think."

Amberry emphasizes the importance of "elbow in," despite the unnatural feel. St. Martin says "elbow in" is overemphasized. St. Martin recommends a $3\frac{1}{2}$ to 4-foot arc; Amberry says the amount of arc varies with a player's height, between 35-45 degrees. St. Martin says the ball should rotate $1\frac{1}{2}$ times; Amberry just wants "plenty" of rotation. It's no wonder so many players have trouble with free throws, if even the experts can't agree.

Tex Winter worked with Dennis Rodman on free throws. Realizing you couldn't "make" Dennis Rodman do anything, Tex employed classic reverse psychology, walking off the court after practice, making Dennis ask him to come back and work with him. One thing not many people gave Rodman credit for — he was a hard worker.

Tex would review the fundamentals as Dennis shot. He wanted the right foot slightly forward and turned in to free the right shoulder, locking the shot on line. Tex never talked about "elbow in" — that was taken care of by squaring the ball up and using the index finger to bisect the seams at a 90-degree angle. The proper grip took care of the elbow, one less thing for the shooter to think about. Knee bend should be natural and consistent from shot to shot, no need to go too deep. Tex spoke in terms of ball "trajectory," never arc or height. It was the ball's trajectory that was important and he wanted it high over the basket. Dennis should focus on the basket — not the rim. The ball should rotate naturally, no need to attempt counting. While Tex could tolerate some unorthodoxy in a player's shooting style, there was no need to with Dennis — he had perfect form.

After Dennis hit 10 in a row, Tex moved him on to the real point of the session — pressure shooting. Since Dennis had mastered the fundamentals, it was the mental side Tex concentrated on. Tex saw Dennis as a contradiction. He wanted attention, but was also extremely self-conscious. Tex often wondered what the team psychologist was learning about Dennis, but that was confidential. Tex knew self-consciousness made for poor free-throw shooting, regardless of fundamentals.

Tex practiced with Dennis in pressure situations, having him "shoot two" with the team down a point. If Dennis hit, he shot for the win; if not, he shot to tie.

Rodman would work himself into the situation, reacting to hits and misses as though a game really were on the line. He would never become as consistent as Tex hoped, but in his three years with the Bulls, Dennis came to be known for his pressure shooting at the foul line.

Tex, like many of the Bulls, was slow to warm to Dennis in training camp for the 1995-96 season. "Dennis was a loner, anyway," recalled Tex. "We extended a welcome to him, but no one was going to go out of their way to kowtow to him. We were successful before he came and he was going to have to prove himself like anybody else. It took a while for us to overcome the animosity we felt toward him, having been the subject of his shenanigans for so many years. I personally felt the irony of having to coach him, after having expressed reservations about bringing him to the team. But it was my job to coach him, so I focused on what he could do for the team on the court. Otherwise, I left him to his own devices."

In the Bulls' first preseason game, Rodman drew a delay of game foul for throwing the ball into the stands. He yelled something at the referee, drawing a technical foul. It was exactly the kind of antics that concerned

Tex Winter about the new guy. Jackson laughed off the incident.

"Basketball is entertainment and Dennis is a clown," quipped Tex. "He makes people laugh, he surprises. Sometimes the coaches are the straight men; sometimes we laugh too, sometimes we don't. Stuff would bother Phil like it bothered me, but Phil Jackson was absolutely the best coach I've ever seen at handling distractions. He always chose his battles well and he knew when Rodman was testing him. He had a sixth sense about where to draw the line with a player and with the team. He kept communication lines open; sometimes he'd talk with Dennis, Michael or Scottie individually."

Jackson had a relaxed approach to player infractions as well. Where Rodman was fined $500 for being late for practice in San Antonio, the fine with the Bulls was $5. There were ways of working off the fine during practice, such as in free-throw shooting drills. Jackson would let Rodman pick two teammates to shoot against three players of his choosing. As mediocre a shooter as Rodman was, with Kerr and Jordan on his side, he found he still had a chance to win. What's more, when he found coming to practice a few minutes late was no big deal, he started coming on time.

The Bulls' second preseason game gave them a flash of the Dennis Rodman the Bulls had hoped for. When Indiana's Reggie Miller made a move to fight Scottie Pippen, he found he would have to fight through Dennis Rodman to get to him. It was the kind of presence the Bulls were counting on.

"That's one of the beauties of basketball," Tex said. "A lot of what happens off the court can be overcome by what happens on the court. The main thing is how the players relate as teammates on the floor."

> **"Dennis worked hard on the court and hard in practice. But I'm glad Phil had the major responsibility for managing the antics. That stuff was difficult for me to put up with. I had to separate Dennis the player from Dennis the problem child. In the end I found that I liked him — not the antics — but the person."**

Jordan and Pippen had clearly returned ready to make a statement to the league. Jordan had worked out ferociously during the off-season, in preparation for the rigors of an 82-game regular season. Pippen had worked out personal problems and appeared more focused and at ease playing in Michael's shadow. The Bulls won their first three games with Rodman in the lineup. Then the unexpected happened. Rodman mysteriously collapsed in practice, the victim of a calf injury. He would miss the next month of the season. As if to make a point to their ailing power forward, the Bulls continued on a tear, boosting their record to 13-2. Throughout Rodman's convalescence, Phil Jackson was philosophical and supportive. "Dennis will be back when he's ready," Phil said.

As Rodman prepared to return to the lineup, news of a *Playboy Magazine* spread with Dennis and his girlfriend hit the media. In the accompanying article, Dennis claimed Michael Jordan had been seduced by the pedestal, but that it was Rodman who brought real excitement to the game. Though the media feasted on the hubris, the comments seemed to leave the team largely unfazed. It was just Dennis being Dennis.

Rodman returned early in December for a game at the United Center against the New York Knicks. Perhaps in celebration of the occasion, he had dyed his hair bright green. For a while, it appeared dubious whether Rodman's presence would add anything to the Bulls' repertoire besides color. They trailed by seven points at halftime. But Rodman's energy and 20 rebounds got the crowd into the game and the Bulls rallied to win, 101-94.

Especially satisfying for Rodman was the Bulls' 106-87 destruction of the San Antonio Spurs two nights later. He pulled down 21 rebounds, exalting in the turn of events. He would make much of the different fates of the two teams in the coming months. San Antonio slid into mediocrity without Dennis Rodman, while the Bulls were headed for the record books.

The Bulls went on a roll, winning nine in a row upon Rodman's return. Most significant was a 112-103 victory over the Orlando Magic — a team that had beaten them four straight, including the embarrassing playoff losses of the year before. The new and improved Bulls dominated the game. Jordan and Pippen led the scoring with 36 and 26 respectively and Rodman picked up 19 rebounds — part of the 80 in the first four games of his return.

The only chink in the Bulls' armor was their repeatedly slow game starts. They appeared to toy with opponents, dangerously at times, before turning up the heat. This tendency caught up with them in Indiana where the Pacers vaulted to a 24-point first half lead. The Bulls second half rally fell short and their 13-game winning streak came to an end in a 101-94 loss. Phil Jackson suggested they start their next winning streak the following game, when they entertained the Pacers at home. The Bulls obliged, routing the Pacers, 120-93, suggesting the previous loss had been a fluke.

Tex Winter was pleased with the direction of the team, especially since the bench had begun contributing. He knew the starters could not carry the team the entire season, that injuries of one sort or another were bound to crop up and it would be the bench that would have to pick up the slack. The players were getting to know each other, extending defenses ever further with the triangle. It was an intelligent team. Even Rodman had impressed Tex with his basketball knowledge. Dennis had picked up the triangle more quickly than most. The problem was Dennis had no interest in being part of the offense, except to rebound. He'd leave his spot in the triangle in order to position for the boards. He was a genius at finding the basketball in a rebound mode. However, Tex wished he would complete his game by joining the offense. As good as he was, he could be even better.

Tex marveled at Rodman's physical abilities. When going for rebounds, at times he looked as if he were on a pogo stick, sometimes jumping three or four times, tipping the ball closer with each jump, until he finally could grasp it. Like Jordan, Rodman was an exceptional physical specimen — strong, wiry and blessed with incredible reflexes. He could have been a world-class quarter-miler, or maybe a hurdler.

Tex was alternately entertained and embarrassed by Rodman's "extracurricular activities" — the antics designed to draw attention to himself and get into his opponent's mind. Some of it was entertainment. Still, Rodman's antics kept him on edge. He had already been ejected from one ballgame, getting into a tussle with Seattle's Shawn Kemp. At least he had picked on someone his own size.

It was difficult at times to be part of a sideshow that was taking away from the game of basketball. In a way Rodman was a wash — as a player he was exceptional, producing tremendous results. As a person, he had a lot to work out. Dennis was conflicted. On one hand, he was shy and self-conscious; on the other, he craved attention. It was an explosive mix.

Tex marveled at the degree of acceptance Dennis received from the fans, especially in Chicago. He had gone from arch-enemy to hero in a matter of weeks. A billboard with his likeness had to be taken down because it was stopping traffic. The level of adulation was sobering — this from the tough town of Chicago.

Rodman was also doing well in the All-Star balloting and he especially hoped to make the Eastern squad as the game was scheduled to be played in San Antonio. Dennis wanted desperately to return triumphantly to the city and franchise that had rejected him, trading him for the lowly Will Perdue. But here Dennis had a problem. Since he hadn't been voted to the first team, he would have to rely on the coaches ballot to make the squad. The coaches rejected him for the fourth consecutive year. Rodman saw it as an NBA conspiracy and headed for Las Vegas on a gambling spree.

Tex Winter saw it differently. It wasn't "the NBA" speaking, it was the coaches. They were simply repaying Rodman for the abuses he had heaped on their profession and the game of basketball. What Rodman put the San Antonio coaches through would not soon be forgotten. Rodman cost John Lucas his job and he subjected Bob Hill to public embarrassment. The coaching profession was stressed enough in the

NBA. Dennis Rodman was a coach's worst nightmare — good enough on the floor to be alluring, crazy enough in every other venue to be dangerous. Why would the coaches give Dennis Rodman anymore limelight?

The Bulls were an unprecedented 42-5 at the 1996 All-Star break, triggering comparisons with great teams of the NBA past. The 1972 Los Angeles Lakers held the league record for regular season wins at 69. Bill Sharman, Tex's teammate at USC, had coached the Lakers that year. Now Tex had a chance to be part of the team to break it. The question was — should they even try? Phil Jackson had been known to rest his starters for the playoffs during previous years. Would going for the record consume emotional and physical energy better saved for the playoffs? Would it distract? What good was the record if you went into the playoffs and got beat? Ultimately, events would dictate how the cards were played.

On March 10, the Bulls were manhandled by the New York Knicks at Madison Square Garden, losing by 32 points. If that weren't bad enough, Scottie Pippen reinjured his ankle, adding to his list of nagging injuries which included his back and knees. Pippen had been playing sensationally and seemed on an MVP track. Even Jordan had begun referring to Pippen as the team leader, referring to himself as one of the "supporting cast." Despite Pippen's desire to continue playing, the Bulls persuaded Pippen to take a 10 day rest. Toni Kukoc would move into his starting position.

Kukoc stepped up big, averaging 20 points in his first two starts. Dennis Rodman stepped out. Called for a foul in the first period of a game against the Nets in New Jersey, Rodman put his hands down his trunks in a show of disrespect. It netted him a technical. The angered Rodman charged the referee and butted him with his head. Rodman continued his tirade after ejection, overturning drinks and shoving around courtside chairs. The league responded with a heavy fine and a six-game suspension.

Tex, like the rest of the team, was angry with Rodman's irresponsibility. His actions jeopardized the team's effort and would cut short Scottie Pippen's rehabilitation. An upside was that Toni Kukoc was getting plenty of playing time, proving himself to be equal to the task. He shot over 50 percent during Rodman's absence, averaging nearly 20 points a game. Tex liked the Bulls' bench. It was important to have players who could step in and produce; important to the team's success and to let Dennis Rodman know he wasn't the only show in town.

Luc Longley, the 7'2" Australian, was also working out well, averaging almost 10 points a game and taking up space on defense. Tex found him an excellent passer who played well at the apex of the triangle, though he missed a lot of easy shots. Longley had spent time on injured reserve and missed 20 games over the regular season. The Bulls had banked heavily on Longley in trading Will Perdue and they were never quite sure which Longley would show up. Still, he was developing. The Bulls also had Canadian-born Bill Wennington to spot Longley as the situation dictated. That made three foreigners on the squad — Kukoc, Longley and Wennington — not counting Dennis Rodman, who was clearly from another planet.

The Bulls finished the 1995-96 regular season a remarkable 72-10, an NBA record. They had banished the United Center bugaboos of the previous season, running their home record to 40-2, ironically losing the final home game on a Hue Hollins call in the final seconds — the same Hue Hollins who made the phantom call on Scottie Pippen to end the '94 season. The loss cost them a share of the best home season record in league history; the Boston Celtics still held it at 41-1. Phil Jackson had been resting his players at the time. Perhaps it would pay dividends in the playoffs.

Tex was concerned about Alonzo Mourning of the Miami Heat, the Bulls' first foe in postseason play. Mourning joined the Heat from Charlotte and had boosted his scoring average to over 23 points per game on the season. He had a strong interior-post game, boosted by moves Tex thought were traveling. But his biggest concern was putting Mourning on the free-throw line where he was good for almost three out of four on his career. "Keep it out of his hands," was Tex's advice. The Bulls double-teamed Mourning.

Pat Riley was another story. Riley had guided the Heat to the postseason in his first year as the team's coach. *The NBA Guide* called him "simply the best in the business … the most driven man in the NBA … almost possessed." His style contrasted with that of Phil Jackson and they did not like each other. Riley brought his trademark physical style of play with him from his coaching years at New York where, of course, he had run up against the Bulls. The Heat and the Bulls already had an ugly meeting during the regular season; it was obvious the players didn't like each other either.

They would like each other even less after the best-of-five series, which the Bulls won in three games. Mourning and Riley were ejected at the end of Game One. Under pressure from the United Center crowd and Dennis Rodman's continuing antics, Mourning missed four consecutive free throws early in Game Two. Jordan was later knocked to the floor going to the basket, injuring his back. Despite the pain, he scored 26 in Game Three and Pippen stepped up with 22 points — including a triple-double. The Heat displayed plenty of attitude; they just didn't have the horses to pull it.

The New York Knicks had more horses, among them Patrick Ewing, Anthony Mason and Michael Jordan's old teammate — Charles Oakley. Having grown up under Pat Riley, they knew something of the physical style of play required to challenge the Bulls. Jackson planned to counter the Knicks' muscle by starting Dennis Rodman over the less physical Toni Kukoc, who was mired in a shooting slump. Rodman countered that strategy by dressing in drag for a local promotion for his newly-released book, *Bad As I Wanna Be.*

Tex was flabbergasted. Here they were preparing for the bullies of the NBA and their power forward is prancing around in some kind of tutu wearing more makeup than Tammy Faye Bakker. It didn't make sense. Had the world gone mad? It certainly seemed upside-down.

Tex frequently discussed Dennis with Phil Jackson. Tex felt he got along with Dennis, especially when the subject was basketball. He continued to find Dennis a willing pupil and a hard worker. The off-the-wall behavior just didn't fit. Phil's theory was Rodman suffered from Attention Deficit Disorder, or ADD, a genetic condition that affects concentration and shows itself in a variety of social disorders. Boredom, problems with authority, hyperactivity and the urge to place one's career in jeopardy were all ADD symptoms that Dennis exhibited in spades. ADD sufferers were typically relentless in their chosen career pursuit, a characteristic that also fit Dennis on the basketball court. Even the trips to Las Vegas made sense, fulfilling a need for action and distraction. Would shock treatment help, Tex wondered?

The Bulls tried to downplay the affair. It was just Dennis being Dennis. A publicity stunt. Besides he looked kinduv ... cute. Maybe. But something was affecting the Bulls.

"The Knicks spread their defense," said Tex. "Normally we wouldn't mind, because it allows us to spread our offense, opening up the post area for cuts and rebounds. The problem was, we weren't shooting the ball well."

Tex watched as the Bulls rode Michael Jordan's 44 points in Game One. He cringed when Patrick Ewing flattened Jordan as he went to the basket and wondered how long Michael's back would hold out. Game Two brought more balanced scoring as the Bulls Ron Harper hit for 15 and contributed to the Bulls' tenacious defense. Tex admired Harper's ability to pick his shots and find the right role for himself at any given moment in the team's offense. Dennis Rodman had stepped up big in Game Two as well, countering the Knicks' muscle with 19 rebounds. Tex appreciated the fact that Dennis accomplished the feat *sans* tutu.

The Bulls lost Game Three in overtime at Madison Square Garden. Jordan scored 46, playing virtually the entire game. He finished with back pain and was otherwise exhausted, as evidenced 24 hours later in Game Four when he would slip to seven of 23 shooting. The rest of the Bulls were shooting poorly as well. Tex thought the Knicks were "snakebiting" — tapping the Bulls as they released their shots, not hard enough to draw a foul, but a bothersome physical presence nonetheless. Rodman again pulled down 19 rebounds and showed some versatility as well, finding Bill Wennington open off the triangle late in the game for open shots, leading to a Bulls win.

The Bulls ended the series in Game Five at the United Center, winning 94-81. Perhaps in testimony to the endless possibilities of the triangle, it was Dennis Rodman's seven points in the third quarter that helped put the game out of reach. Dennis then put himself out of reach, drawing a second technical in the fourth quarter en route to ejection. He exited with what had become his signature flourish, tossing his jersey into an approving crowd. The incident raised the question of which Dennis Rodman would show up for the Orlando Magic series — and Horace Grant.

The tension leading up to the series was palpable. It would be the big rematch. Towel-waving, carried-off-on-the-shoulders-of-his-teammates Horace Grant was back. Only this time, the Bulls had an exotic weapon of their own — Dennis "The Worm" Rodman. Who was the better power forward? Debate raged. *The Chicago Sun-Times* ran a front-page comparison of the two. They had an article choosing Grant over Rodman because of his superior scoring ability. Maybe Dennis took it personally. Whatever the reality, in Game One, Rodman took it to Horace Grant unmercifully, grabbing 21 rebounds and answering the scoring charge with 13 points. Grant tallied but a single rebound and never scored. Late in the game, he collided with his own player, Shaquille O'Neal, hyperextending his elbow. He was lost for the series. The only towel-waving was one of surrender from the Magic. Despite the occasional counterattack, they were never in the series, dropping four straight. Though they downplayed the revenge factor, the Chicago Bulls redeemed themselves from the humiliation of the previous year — and prepared to meet the Seattle SuperSonics in the 1996 NBA Finals.

Tex liked the way the Bulls matched up with Seattle. The SuperSonics were a good team, yes, with excellent shooters that included Hersey Hawkins, Gary Payton and Detlef Schrempf. Sam Perkins and Shawn Kemp provided muscle as well as scoring power. But for the first time in the playoffs, Luc Longley would be the biggest physical presence on the floor. The SuperSonics didn't have a center in the mold of Mourning, Ewing or O'Neal.

The wild card was Rodman, who had been ejected in a regular-season meeting with the Sonics for losing it with Shawn Kemp. Kemp was a handful; he and Dennis were like two heavyweight fighters that really didn't like each other. Ali and Liston come to mind; Rodman, the loud mouth instigator as Ali; Kemp, the brooding powerhouse as Sonny Liston. Putting them on the same floor would be volatile and there was no telling what might happen. Tex had been counseling Dennis about "extra-curricular activities," the unnecessary things he did to draw attention to himself or nettle opponents and referees. He wondered if it did any good. Tex thought they should match Longley with Kemp and save Dennis for later.

The other factor was complacency, for the Bulls were 10-1 favorites in the series. Tex hated complacency. He'd seen it cost teams a lot of games over the years, and the Bulls were ripe. Way too much talk about the "best team ever." Lose a couple games and they'd be "the biggest bust ever."

Phil went with Luc Longley on Kemp. A Sonics back-up, Frank Brickowski, attempted to bait Rodman into a scuffle. It backfired and Brickowski was ejected. The Bulls carried the day, 107-90. Sonics coach George Karl denigrated Rodman's contributions in his postgame comments, suggesting Rodman's antics were bad for the game.

Maybe so, thought Tex, but this time our guy kept his composure.

As if in response to Karl's comments, Rodman poured it on in Game Two, his 20 rebounds covering the especially poor shooting of the Bulls. His record-tying 11 offensive rebounds led the way to a 92-88 victory.

Game Three, a Chicago victory played out in Seattle's Key Arena, seemed to signal the end of the series. The Bulls built a huge lead, then seemed to toy with the Sonics' counterattacks. Rodman began his extra-curricular activities in the second half, rubbing it in the face of the Sonics and their fans. But it was Brickowski who was again ejected, this time for a flagrant foul. Everything was coming up roses.

The NBA rehearsed the awards ceremony before Game Four at Key Arena on the assumption the Bulls would sweep the series. At the time it seemed a safe bet. In addition to the Bulls' regular season of record 72-10, they had compiled an amazing 14-1 playoff record. The "greatest ever" chorus began anew.

Tex Winter felt himself being swept along with the tide. He could sense danger on the horizon, but the pull of optimism was overwhelming to the team. He cautioned against over-confidence but his words were taken as those of the team worrier. He didn't feel he was really getting through. Maybe he, too, had been affected by the team's success. Rationally, he knew better. Ron Harper was hurting and the Sonics Nate McMillan, who had been sidelined with injury, was reportedly ready to play. Tex knew a subtle shift like that could change a series, but no one was inclined to listen. He hadn't cared for Rodman's showing off at the end of Game Three, either. How would Shawn Kemp react to that? Ali had beaten Liston twice; he hadn't had to go best of seven.

Kemp was furious. He harangued his teammates about giving up in Game Three and challenged them to commit to the rest of the series. Shawn Kemp can be a scary guy. His anger served to awaken the Sonics. They took the lead midway through the first period and never looked back. As Tex had feared, Harper's knees were slowing him down and the Sonics got a huge lift when Nate McMillan entered the contest late in the first period. The Sonics celebrated by running up a 21-point lead in the second quarter. Harper had to leave the game; the Bulls were never really in it.

Game Five was played without Ron Harper and the Bulls missed his defensive presence. It was a close game until the Sonics ran off 11 straight points in the fourth, winning 89-78. The Bulls again shot poorly from the floor, hitting only three of 26 from beyond the three-point arc. Worse, Tex thought the team seemed fragmented and frustrated, taken aback by the sudden turn of events. Rodman especially seemed angry, perhaps responding to the baiting of the crowd. The scoreboard had been flashing pictures of him in drag while the rock tune, "Dude Looks Like a Lady" played over the loudspeakers.

Practice in Chicago seemed to steady the Bulls. Tex took the squad through the fundamental drills and rehearsed the triangle, pointing out opportunities the players had missed the last two games. Ron Harper indicated he would play, which seemed to further focus the team. If Harper could do it with the pain he was suffering, how could the other guys give it less than their very best?

Harper was introduced as a starter before Game Six, an event that set off a frenzy in the crowd that never let up. He would play 38 minutes. Michael Jordan found an additional motivator — it was Father's Day and he dedicated his effort to the memory of his dad, James Jordan.

Who knew what motivated Dennis Rodman? He would grab 19 rebounds and tie his own record of 11 offensive boards. In a game of spurts, Dennis would crest on the biggest wave, accepting a Pippen feed off a break, scoring and drawing a foul. He hit the free throw for a 15-point third period Bulls lead.

Other spurts followed, including a 9-0 Sonics run that put the outcome in jeopardy. It was quickly dashed with a rain of three-pointers from Pippen, Kukoc and Kerr. Jordan led the team with a modest 22 points and seven assists. Tex thought it was the perfect combination — modest scoring from Michael with maximum ball sharing. Everybody got a piece of the basketball and everybody came through. The Bulls simply had too many weapons and when they were synchronized — the effects were staggering. Carrying the "best team ever" moniker had almost cost the Bulls the championship, but in the end, even Tex Winter had to admit, "We were awful good."

*We don't talk to our team much in terms of winning and losing games. We do, however, talk to them a great deal about effort. The last thing we say to the team before it takes the floor is "Go out there and play to the very best of your abilities — individually and as a team. If you do this the score will take care of itself and regardless of the results we'll be mighty proud of the effort."*

— Tex Winter, *The Triple-Post Offense*, 1962

## CHAPTER THIRTEEN
# FORGOTTEN CHAMPIONSHIP

In any other era, the 1996-97 Chicago Bulls would have been a legacy unto themselves, a team having a season for the ages. Yet because history is relative, the team and its accomplishments have become more of a centerpiece, wedged between the incredible 72-10 Bulls of Jordan's first full season back and the equally incredible 1997-98 Bulls which culminated with the last shot of Jordan's career. The 1996-97 Bulls were incredible; but even if you were paying attention, their exploits have probably become a bit of a blur. The problem is there's simply too much to take in — and too much to keep track of.

Picture the six Chicago Bull NBA Championship trophies on a mantle and put a space between 1-2-3 and 4-5-6. The space represents the year Michael Jordan was playing baseball and the year he came back after mid-season. No trophies for those years. So trophy #1 represents the win over Los Angeles, #2 over Portland, #3 over Phoenix, #4 over Seattle, #5 and #6 over Utah. That's the other problem: for the first five championships, the Bulls defeated a different opponent in the Finals. But they repeated over Utah, which has further contributed to the blur. It's a nice problem to have.

Fortunately the term "double three-peat" was invented to describe the Bulls dynasty. They won three championships in a row, twice.

◆　◆　◆

The Bulls finished the 1996-97 season at 69-13. They started the season at 17-1 and were 42-6 at the All-Star break. They swept Washington in the playoffs and beat both Atlanta and Miami in five games.

The biggest question of the season seemed to be, "What will Dennis Rodman do next?" He started off well, presenting Phil Jackson with an expensive, customized motorcycle as a token of his appreciation. Dennis could be generous. But he refused to shake the extended hand of NBA Commissioner David Stern at a pregame ceremony where the Bulls were presented their championship rings from the year before. Dennis could be rude.

Dennis was also getting big. He had his own *World Tour* with MTV during the off-season — an iconoclastic, rebellious party show directed at teens. He opened a kinky bar in downtown Chicago. His second book, *Walk on the Wild Side*, came out at playoff time. He scheduled a parade for a bookstore signing, complete with floats and a group of costumed gays. The parade fizzled when local store owners objected; the book didn't do so well, either.

*Bad as I Wanna Be* had been informative, entertaining and edgy, but *Wild Side* was over the edge and creepy. It revealed an angry Dennis Rodman, unhappy with the Bulls' management, NBA Commissioner David Stern and even select sports commentators. It made clear Dennis wanted the best of all worlds — the freedom to create controversy as he saw fit and to be loved for it by everyone. Not everyone loved Dennis Rodman. His first wife published her own book, *Worse Than He Said He Was*, which painted the downside of life with The Menace. There was also an unauthorized autobiography. Dennis was getting a lot of ink.

On the floor, the Bulls were clearly a better team with Rodman in the lineup. They had opportunities to experiment both with and without his presence. In December, the team suspended him for two games for excessive profanity during a live postgame interview — a game in which he had been ejected. In January, he took an 11-game suspension for kicking a camera man in the groin during an out-of-bounds sequence. He received mandatory counseling and settled out of court with the cameraman for $200,000. The cost of the suspensions was in the neighborhood of $1 million.

---

**"It's easy to forget what it takes to be a champion. The championships do sort of run together — but that doesn't take away from what it took to get there."**

---

Jordan opined that perhaps Rodman's off-court enterprises were distracting him. Dennis called Michael an expert on the subject, citing his movie *Space Jam*, his new cologne and myriads of endorsements. He offered that he had never had a legitimate conversation with either Jordan or Pippen but that "we respect each other's auras and give each other space."

The Bulls got even more space from Rodman when he went down with a knee injury with 13 games left in the season, setting the stage for a brilliant Krausian maneuver that added to the Bulls' weaponry down the stretch.

Brian Williams had been around. He'd played for two high schools, two colleges and in the space of his five-year NBA career — three different teams. He had walked away from the Los Angeles Clippers and failed a physical with the Dallas Mavericks — he'd apparently injured a knee in a skydiving accident. He had averaged nearly 16 points a game with the Clippers and at 6'11", had the kind of presence and inside game the Bulls needed with Rodman out. After the season, he would sign a multi-million dollar contract with the Detroit Pistons.

Krause got him to play out the last nine games of the regular season for $30,000 and the chance to go for a ring. Williams seemed to meld perfectly with the Bulls and demonstrated an array of skills and acumen that left the basketball world wondering, "Where did they come up with this guy?" The move looked especially good when Rodman struggled a bit during the playoffs after knee surgery and suffered a foot injury against the Miami Heat.

"Hiring Brian Williams was a great move," recalled Tex. "He was tough, aggressive and had good rebounding skills. Jerry came up with a key guy for us when we really needed somebody to step in for Dennis."

Stress levels were high during Game One of the 1997 NBA Championships. Karl "The Mailman" Malone, the big power forward for the Jazz, had recently been named the league MVP. "The Mailman delivers," was an oft-heard phrase around the league. However, MVP was an honor usually reserved for Michael Jordan. The Jazz presented an ominous threat to the Bulls.

The Bulls were out of their offense for much of Game One and Tex was not happy about it. Worse, the Jazz were getting away with illegal back picks, wily John Stockton running up behind the Bulls defenders and bumping them off their man. The usually composed Winter was screaming at the refs, "Watch the back picks!"

An official came over to the bench during one timeout. Tex was still gesturing.

"That's enough out of you!" the referee warned.

"Well, read page 44, section 33. It's in the rule book!" Tex replied.

The ref whistled a technical.

"It was a real bad feeling," Tex said later, "to be in the NBA Finals and have a technical called on you is not what you want to have happen. On the other hand, the rules need to be enforced and that's all I was asking for. I wasn't cussing or being disrespectful, but sometimes the truth is harder on an official than swearing."

Jackson found the tech amusing, laughing off the incident with his usual aplomb. Coping with Rodman's antics for three years made the occasional outburst from Tex a relative breeze. At least now the officials knew that someone cared about the rule book and would be watching for illegal picks. The Jazz would have to be more careful, knowing the Bulls staff would be keeping tabs. The league would later rescind the technical and the accompanying fine.

The Bulls still had their hands full. The Jazz were playing well, especially Malone, who was having little difficulty scoring over Rodman. He also outrebounded Dennis, 15-12.

Where Rodman had been able to set off Alonzo Mourning in the earlier series with the Miami Heat, he wasn't getting to Malone. The two knew each other from the Dallas summer league early in their careers and had even played on the same team. Malone had brushed off Rodman's antics in the 1994 playoffs while Dennis was with the San Antonio Spurs. He seemed to know where Dennis was coming from and it didn't seem to bother him. But something else would.

With 9.2 seconds left in the game, Malone found himself at the free-throw line with the score tied at 82. The Mailman had hit nine of his last 12 shots, but still the Bulls had rallied to tie the score. Now Malone had a chance to move the Jazz back into the lead. Scottie Pippen moved forward and whispered to Malone, "The Mailman doesn't deliver on Sunday." It was Sunday. Malone missed them both.

That set the stage for Jordan, who dribbled the ball to within 18 feet of the basket, then pulled up and calmly drained a jump shot. The Bulls escaped, 84-82. Besides coming up with one of the more memorable one-liners in league history, Scottie Pippen had played marvelously, scoring 27 points, with nine rebounds, four assists and three steals.

"What people don't realize," said Tex, "is Scottie Pippen played that series hurt. He was limping from a soft tissue injury to his left foot that would require surgery in the off-season. It was a tremendous effort."


The Bulls seemed to have the measure of the Jazz in Game Two, winning 97-85. The tone was set early when Karl Malone missed his first two free throws, to the delight of the United Center crowd. The Bulls stopped Utah's trademark pick-and-roll, forcing John Stockton out of the middle and thereby limiting his options.

"The Jazz run one of the most disciplined offenses in the league," said Tex, "but they're predictable."

"We would run our patterns," said Jeff Hornacek of the Jazz, "and they would call out to each other where the pick was going to be or where the cutter was going. They were right."

Jordan's 38 points had Bulls fans chanting "MVP" both as a tribute and to goad the struggling Malone. Afterward, Jordan spoke of having "figured out" the Jazz offense. It was probably true, but it was also the wrong thing to say.

"We are who we are and we do what we do," said Jazz coach Jerry Sloan before the start of the series. "We don't make a lot of drastic changes, we don't try to be geniuses and outsmart anybody. If what we do isn't working, we don't usually look to do something different, we just try to do it better."

The operative word was "usually."

In Game Three, played at the Delta Center, the Jazz ran an offense that looked a lot like Tex Winter's triangle. Gone was the old pick-and-roll the Bulls had defended so easily. In its place was a motion offense, complemented by quick passes and better spacing. By the time the Bulls broke the code, they found themselves down 24 points in the third quarter. The Jazz hung on to win, 104-93, behind a rejuvenated Karl Malone, who scored 37 points.

"They changed things up on us," said Tex, "and they shot well. We might have been a bit over-confident."

Worse, there was an incident on the bus. Jerry Krause, the general manager, was aboard and Jordan had made fun of his weight as the bus struggled to get up one of the mountains between the Delta Center and the hotel. Jordan suggested the bus moved a lot faster without Jerry aboard. It made for an awkward situation; Jordan had been drinking and he carried on against Krause while the players snickered or laughed out loud. Jordan routinely teased his teammates, but he especially liked to work on Krause.

The spectacle of a player working over "the boss" was unique. The Chicago Bulls were indeed unique in that sense — Jordan's superstar status made him bigger than the boss and Phil Jackson, who didn't want Krause on the bus in the first place and who had his own problems with Krause, was more than willing to let it go on. So on it went, Jordan riding Krause to the delight of a captive audience. Jordan ran down the list of stupid draft choices Krause had made over the years. Most of Krause's maneuvers had been brilliant, but Michael liked to keep him humble.

Tex saw the situation as symptomatic of the widening rift between Krause and Jordan and was uncomfortable about the message being sent to the team. Krause was the vice-president and general manager of the Bulls and despite Michael's exalted position, Krause still had the power to hire and fire everyone on the bus. Tex had talked to Phil about reining in Jordan, feeling Phil should talk to Michael about the situation. Apparently they had talked, but without much result.

Tex was also concerned about the team's use of alcohol. It was normal for the players to have a beer or two after a game to unwind, but increasingly it was leading to situations that were counterproductive to the effort. How long would it be before a player went too far and said or did things that could not be undone?

His concerns would prove to be well-founded.

Tex was wearing earplugs before Game Four, having learned a lesson before Game Three. "The Delta Center is the loudest arena in the NBA," said Tex. "The pregame introductions are literally deafening. My hearing is amazingly good considering what it has been subjected to over the years. But I'd like to keep what hearing I have left. The Delta Center is the one to watch out for."

There were other things to watch out for. As the game wound down, the Bulls seemed to be running out of gas. Jordan and Pippen both complained of stomach cramps; Jordan asked out of the game, a rarity. Pippen made a special run to the bathroom and needed to lie down during timeouts.

Team trainer Chip Schaefer discovered the problem — the Bulls were drinking Gator Lode instead of Gatorade. Gator Lode is a post-performance drink, containing the equivalent of 20 potatoes worth of carbohydrates. The Bulls' own ball boy had been serving up the wrong stuff.

By the time Schaefer deduced what was happening, the damage had been done. The Bulls had dominated the game but were sinking fast. They were still up, 71-66, with 2:42 left when Stockton canned a three-pointer. He then stole the ball from the ailing Jordan and dribbled the length of the floor before being fouled. He made a free throw. Thirty seconds later, he made two more. When Jordan missed from 17 feet, Stockton snagged the rebound. He then hurled it 80 feet down the floor, barely eluding the leaping defensive effort of Michael Jordan, into the hands of Karl Malone, who laid it in for the lead. Malone sealed it with two free throws, exorcising the demons of Game One. The Jazz had executed a 12-2 run to win, 78-73. The series was tied, 2-2.

Michael Jordan awoke at 3 a.m. with a stomach virus. He took something to make him drowsy, but the vomiting was so severe he never got back to sleep. By the time he arrived at the Delta Center, he was drinking coffee, trying to stay awake. He spent the last few minutes before tip-off curled up in a small room adjacent to the visitors' locker room with a vomit bucket. Not the way one would choose to report to Game Five of an NBA Championship series.

By halftime, he was dehydrated from the fever, caffeine and the rigors of playing the game. He played on, leaning on Pippen during timeouts, near collapse. With 46 seconds left, he missed a free throw that would have tied the game, but got his own rebound. Twenty-one seconds later, with John Stockton on his wrist, he buried a three-pointer. The Bulls hung on to win, 90-88. Jordan scored 38 points, 15 of them in the fourth quarter. Many Jordanologists consider it his best game ever.

Tex was less effusive. "It was a great game," he said, "but I wasn't as concerned about Michael's condition as some were. Knowing Michael, I knew he would play. I thought his physical discomfort would just create better concentration for him. He has ways of compensating."

Somewhat lost in Jordan's heroics was the play of his teammates, including Steve Kerr, who held John Stockton to a single fourth quarter basket in Game Five. Kerr was in his fourth season with the Bulls and had averaged a consistent eight-plus points per game in each of them. Known primarily as a three-point shooter, Kerr was effectively filling the shooting guard niche as John Paxson had before him. He hit 110 three-pointers during the regular season, shooting at a .464 clip — good enough for second in the league.

"A tough player who responds when challenged," said the *Pro Basketball Handbook* of Steve Kerr. Born in Beirut, Lebanon, Kerr lost his father to an assassin's bullet during the conflict there. A player with only average physical ability, he had taught himself to be a consistent jump shooter — a key component in the triangle offense. His blonde hair and innocent good looks belied a fierce competitor who did not back down. Though an ardent Jordan admirer, he and Jordan had rough moments on the practice floor, including an outbreak of fisticuffs during Jordan's first season back from baseball. The two became good friends, with Jordan appreciating Kerr's sense of humor and his tenacious play. Jordan depended on Kerr to bail him out when he was double-teamed and the shot clock wound down. More often then not, Kerr would come through.

He came through in Game Six before a home crowd at the United Center. Despite Jordan's 39 points, it had not been a pretty game — the Bulls led for less than five minutes of the 48 minutes played. As the game clock wound down with the score knotted at 86, Jordan found Kerr open at the top of the arc. Without hesitating, he passed the ball. Kerr drained it and the Bulls had their fifth championship — the one that's sometimes forgotten.

*They say this and they say that.*

*They make me wonder where I'm at.*

*Identify those who are known as they,*

*And I'll have more respect for what they say.*

—Anonymous poem, The *Triple-Post Offense,*
1962

# CHAPTER FOURTEEN
# MUD ON THE HORNS

For the casual Bulls' fan, it was difficult to understand the incessant problems the Bulls were having over the course of the 1997-98 season. There was talk of breaking up the team, of this being Phil Jackson's last year, of Jordan leaving with him and hence Pippen and the rest. The Bulls were on their way to a sixth championship and they had sold-out 500 consecutive home games. Why did things seem so wrong?

Roland Lazenby's *Blood on the Horns: The Long Strange Ride of Michael Jordan's Chicago Bulls* provided many of the answers. The book picked up on the team's well known logo, which features a mean-looking Bull with blood on its horns. With the intense media interest that followed every nuance of the mud-slinging of the season, it might just as well have been "mud" on the horns. The book was a well-researched chronicle that laid out in meticulous detail the myriads of internal battles between coaches, players, management and media. It was not a pretty picture and it placed Tex Winter "square in the middle."

With the personal relationship between Jerry Krause and Phil Jackson virtually destroyed, it was Tex who arbitrated and held together the tenuous professional relationship that often hung by a thread between the two men. Tex loved them both, though at times it appeared they hated each other. Tex found the situation frustrating, but he understood as few others did, the heavy burden of success the Bulls carried. He remained dedicated to the organization and the team. While he was hired for his basketball expertise, he increasingly found himself engaging his diplomatic skills. "What I tried to do," said Tex, "was to help each of them understand what the other was doing and the reasoning for it. I tried to be a buffer. "

The 300-pound gorilla in the situation was Michael Jordan. Revered by fans and possessing public relations skills beyond the reach of Krause and Reinsdorf, he, too, played a role in the power struggle for the soul of the franchise. Jordan clearly wanted Jackson back as coach and when Krause commented to the effect that Jackson would not return, Jordan trumped him by stating that if Jackson didn't return, he wouldn't, either.

That got to the heart of the problem for Jerry Krause — how best to transition from the Jordan era, which obviously could not go on forever. Krause believed he had been fair to Jackson, offering him a long-term contract that would take him through the transition years — including after Jordan retired. Jackson balked at the offer, not sure he had the desire or energy to soldier through what would certainly be a difficult period.

Neither Reinsdorf nor Krause wanted a high-payroll, low-performance team and aging players. They'd seen that happen to the Boston Celtics. The Celtics, they thought, held onto their players too long without a plan for the future. When those players left — for the most part, as a group — the team spent the following years mired in losing seasons. Krause's long-range plan was to keep that transition period to a minimum, by phasing new players in and aging players out gradually while retaining the coaching staff to keep the team functioning.

He also wanted a coaching staff and players who would continue running the triangle, thinking an equal-opportunity offense would help cover some of the talent shortcomings they would undoubtedly experience. They might not win the championship every year, but they could spike to win it and at least be competitive. Most of all, he wanted to avoid the total collapse the Celtics had experienced. If Phil wanted the long-term job it was his, but Jerry wanted someone who would commit to the long haul — beyond the Jordan years.

Also in the mix was the money. The Bulls had generated lots of it and were one of a declining number of NBA franchises reaping huge profits.

The growing trend was for teams to commit big bucks to untested rookies, a problem that would come to a head in the lockout prior to the 1998-99 season. The Bulls' organization had been fortunate, avoiding overpaid rookies and paying most of their players, including Jordan and Pippen, well under their market value. But with Jordan, Pippen, Rodman and Longley set to become free agents before the 1998-99 season, the handwriting was on the wall. It would take megabucks to keep the team together. At a time when players' advancing ages cast increasing doubt on their ability to continue winning, logic dictated it would be better to begin restructuring before the 1997-98 season and phase it in.

There was another item on the agenda — Jerry Krause wanted very much to win the title without Michael Jordan and for that matter, without Phil Jackson. Krause had been in a power struggle with both men for years and by most criteria, he had been losing. Jackson and Jordan clearly held the hearts and minds of the team, while Krause was largely reviled. Much the same was true with the fans and media. Jordan and Jackson simply had too much media savvy, as well as the advantage of being on the front line of the team's efforts where the spotlight ranges.

Krause had too often assumed the role of "big, bad management," often finding himself at odds with his star performers. Jordan usually went around him on issues, directly to Krause's boss — Jerry Reinsdorf. Krause would like nothing more than to win a championship with another team of his own making — without Jackson or Jordan.

Much of the debate centered around who got the credit. Jordan and Jackson got plenty; Krause didn't feel he got enough. He was the one who put the whole thing together, finding just the right ingredients to make it all work. He found Jackson, Winter, Pippen, Kukoc and the rest — had made intricate trades to make just the right things happen. His eye for talent was unassailable. Only Michael Jordan had been there before Krause and Michael Jordan had become a problem. He challenged Krause at every turn, made fun of him and tried to humiliate him in front of the players. Krause had something to prove to Michael Jordan.

---

**"It's hard for some people to see why it couldn't last. But even success can't heal all wounds. Sometimes there isn't enough credit to go around, or it seems to go only to certain people. There's an awful lot of ego in an organization like the Bulls."**

---

Krause felt Jordan had forced his hand with his comments about "bringing the team back" after the '97 championship. It was the last thing Krause wanted to hear, so naturally, that's what he got. Jerry wanted his options kept open. Instead, Jordan used the '97 championship as a platform to appeal directly to a rabid fan base to keep the team together. It was symbolic of a classic power struggle, with Jerry Krause continually being cast as the bad guy. It was effective. "Michael's comments after the championship were probably out of school," said Tex. "But they put enough pressure on Jerry Krause that he was forced to keep the team together."

Jordan held powerful cards in the situation. If he announced his retirement after July 1, his salary would be applied to the Bulls salary cap, thereby effectively precluding the signing of any significant new talent. Since Jordan insisted the team return intact, including a contract for Phil Jackson, it was essentially an all-or-nothing proposition. The public was very much on the side of returning the team intact. Jerry Reinsdorf finally agreed to pay nearly $70 million in players' and coaches' salaries to keep the team together for the 1997-98 season. While it gave the Bulls a legitimate chance to compete for the championship, it did not heal the wounds.

Reinsdorf and Krause made it clear to Jackson it would be his last year. From Jackson's point of view, Krause seemed to glory in the situation. Krause's comments to the media further cast him as the heavy. The situation was exacerbated when the Krause's selective guest list to their daughter's wedding was revealed. The Winters were invited — the Jacksons and other assistant coaches were not. Also invited were Tim Floyd and his wife. Floyd, the basketball coach at Iowa State, was widely rumored to be Jackson's replacement with the Bulls.

Jackson was furious. It became obvious to the staff that an even deeper iciness had developed between the two men, with Jackson at times ignoring a summons to Krause's office. Behind the scenes, the two clashed on several occasions, with Krause reminding Jackson it was his last year and he expected Jackson to make that clear to the media.

With rumors swirling about the Bulls and Dennis Rodman still unsigned, the Bulls' media day at the start of training camp was especially well attended. Krause held court for awhile, doing his best to explain the status of Phil Jackson and management's approach to the transition years ahead. Late in the give and take, Phil Jackson arrived, distracting many of the newscasters and reporters, just as Krause was explaining how he saw the relationship between management and the players. The distraction resulted in a misquote. Krause was widely quoted as having said, "coaches and players don't win championships, organizations do." What he in fact said was, "coaches and players *alone* don't win championships, organizations do."

The misquote was immediately taken to Jackson and Jordan for comment, further cementing the new controversy in the public mind. "He would say that," Jackson replied, later confirming that this would indeed be his last year. Jordan was more expansive, noting management had not played sick last year, or stepped on the court in Game Five. He saw the basketball team winning championships, with management in a support role — paying for planes and providing infrastructure.

Tex realized the majority of the emotion being generated was a result of the apparent decision to make this Phil's last year. The rest was due to the ongoing battle for credit sharing. Tex sympathized with Phil. Phil was an excellent coach and associate and had been a big part of the Bulls' success. Phil had earned the respect and admiration of Michael Jordan, repeatedly turned distractions into pluses and recognized the gold mine of the triangle.

Phil was family and Tex loved him like a brother. Nine years was a long time to coach in the NBA, even with the success Phil had enjoyed. Tex could understand why Phil would balk at a long-term contract and coaching through the inevitable post-Jordan transition. Winning was tough enough, what would losing be like? Jackson and Krause essentially agreed on the team's future, but the pressure of the situation and the personal slights had made it impossible for the two to function together.

The "who gets the credit thing" was a shame too, Tex thought. Here, he believed Krause and Reinsdorf deserved more than they got. The players and to some degree, the coaches received notoriety and the adoring cheers of the fans. Staff and management received less immediate feedback and were often underappreciated. To a certain extent, that went with the territory. What wasn't fair was the villainization of management to the point where Krause and Reinsdorf were booed whenever they were introduced. For many, the implication was that the Bulls had succeeded in spite of management and that certainly wasn't the case.

*"Jerry surrounds himself with capable people. As an evaluator of talent he's not bad. But he lacks the ability to relate in a positive manner. He's paranoid, suspicious, and negative — a real pain. That's the image he projects. Not many see his depth, compassion, or the goodness of his heart. You've got to work to get there."*

The fact of the matter, in Tex's view, was the Bulls had the best of everything. They had the best player in the history of the game in Michael Jordan. For the last two years at least, they were the dominant team in the NBA. As the championships piled up, it was also clear the Bulls had built the best basketball organization in the game — including players, coaches, support staff and facilities. There was only one man who deserved credit for that — Jerry Krause.

Krause had the foresight to shape and reshape the team as the situation warranted. Not only did he have the conceptual skills to visualize what was needed, but he also had the action skills to make things happen. Tex Winter was Jerry Krause's idea. So was Phil Jackson, Scottie Pippen, Dennis Rodman and most of the rest of the quality players and staff that made the Bulls the dominant team of an era. Tex didn't buy the theory that Michael Jordan had been there when Krause arrived and that the winning had been inevitable. It was a ubiquitous theory — even Nancy would tease him that they were all just "riding Michael Jordan's coat-tails." Tex knew better. Many other teams had fallen short of championships with a superstar on the roster.

Winning in the NBA took a team effort and that included management. It was ludicrous to suggest otherwise. Why was it so difficult to share the credit? If there was one thing that bothered him about the Bulls, it was the underlying power struggles that a little credit-sharing might have cured. It was Jerry Reinsdorf's organization and he had brought in Jerry Krause to run it. The organization was an unmitigated success, thanks in large part to the vision and hard work of Jerry Krause. Just as there were few who could equal Michael Jordan prowess on a basketball court, there were few who could match Jerry Krause in running a basketball franchise. They were different skills and should be appreciated in their own right. Why was that so hard?

Part of the problem was Jerry Krause's Achilles' heel — public relations. It wasn't an area he was good at and it was an area where Jackson and Jordan excelled. They also had the advantage of being in the public eye. Jerry wasn't a people person. He expected people to be professionals and had difficulty with the nuances of interpersonal relationships. It was also the nature of his job to see players and staff as commodities, inter-changeable cogs that could be bartered or let go. That was the toughest part of the business anyway, Tex thought, the dealing with people as human beings in a business that rewarded achievement and tended to overlook intangibles. A G.M. had to be tough; it was a business. Obviously, Jerry took the heat pretty well — a prerequisite for being a G.M. in Chicago. Jerry had the business piece down, but he needed to work on the interpersonal side.

When Dennis Rodman joined the team a couple days into training camp, Tex saw it as another triumph of Krausian diplomacy. Not only had Dennis been Jerry's idea two years ago, with all of the dangers inherent of bringing in someone so risky, but now he was re-signing Dennis to a one-year contract. The contract was loaded with incentives, giving Rodman some responsibility for his performance while allowing management some influence on his behavior.

While Tex normally didn't care for incentive clauses because he thought they distracted players from the intangibles of team play, he thought the incentives would be helpful with Dennis. He would be make between $4.5 and $10 million, depending on his performance. Not bad for someone who had initially said he'd play for free. It was several weeks before Rodman actually signed the contract; he was rumored to be concerned about the number of performance incentives he could actually meet.

While Tex and Phil would again have their hands full coaching Dennis, with the strong influences of Jordan and Pippen and the incentives of his contract, Tex felt they could succeed. He credited Krause with the overall concept. Jerry had the type of contract that would keep Rodman focused; Winter, Jackson, Jordan and Pippen would be the environment to keep him from straying too far over the line.

Krause and Jordan continued feuding throughout the season, with players either choosing sides or struggling to remain neutral. Jackson, Jordan and Pippen made a strong triumvirate, but Jerry Krause would do next year's hiring. Paranoia was rampant. Jackson opined to the press that Krause had certain players who kept him informed of Jackson's maneuverings. Players were seen as "Jerry's guy" or "Phil's guy." Chip Schaefer, the team trainer, described his situation in *Blood on the Horns*. "I'm trying to remain neutral, like Switzerland, but I just can't. I'm being pulled to one side or the other and it's really difficult."

Tex tried to downplay the situation, noting Jackson was a "players' coach," popular with players as evidenced by Jordan's willingness to risk his career to bring him back. It was natural that Phil would be closer to some players and as a result, he would experience varying levels of loyalty. Tex saw the situation as a great opportunity to study human nature.

While he frequently tired of the pettiness and marveled that success could create frequent unhappiness, he felt he had an important role to play. He was still the fundamentals and concepts guy. At age 75, he was still running the first part of practice, still teaching the triangle. On the court, they could still make magic and for the period of the game at least, the distractions were relegated to the sidelines. At times, the players and staff seemed to withdraw into the game itself, using the game and its success to get away from it all. In that sense, Tex wondered if the controversies might stoke the competitive fire in the team.

---

*"I'm probably made fun of by some of the players who maybe find my frugality a bit excessive. But once you've gone without and seen others go with even less, you never again see the logic of wasting things."*

---

Tex felt tremendous loyalty to Phil and Jerry. He worked to bridge the chasm between them, to calm the situation where he could. He always liked Jerry, who had done a lot for him. Tex accepted Jerry's lack of people skills and viewed his shortcomings with a sense of humor. Of course, he worked with Phil every day and they had grown especially close. Tex usually drove Phil to the United Center on game days. Ironically, even with Phil's mastery of people skills, he had such difficulty getting along with his own boss, Jerry Krause. But it was a bad situation and the two men were not going to be on the same page anytime soon. Both men respected Tex and kept him out of the fray as much as possible.

Tex was struggling with arthritis and wasn't sure how much longer he could keep working. Unlike many of his contemporaries, Tex still loved to travel. He loved everything about it — the anticipation, the packing, the accommodations and the opportunity to feel the world changing around him. Tex had it down to a science. On the road, the per diem rate was $89.00 a day, with the hotel room paid for by the team. He was always amazed that players and media people spent time and money in restaurants when there was free food right in front of them.

It was akin to buying a newspaper. Tex seldom bought a newspaper or shampoo. Why would you buy a newspaper when there were always copies to be found in hotel lobbies or airports? Why would you buy shampoo when it was provided by the hotels? He and Nancy had hundreds of those little soaps and shampoo bottles at home. Conditioner, too. Why would you need to buy the stuff? You could get a dozen washes from a one-ounce shampoo sample, maybe even eke out one more by filling the bottle with water and shaking loose the residue. When you've worked all day for leftover vegetables, the amenities of traveling as a world champion are not taken lightly.

The Bulls got off to a 4-4 start for the 1997-98 season, not the kind of play expected from world champions. They clearly missed Scottie Pippen, who had foot surgery a few days into training camp. Tex was peeved, because Scottie had hurt the foot in May. Why had it taken until October to figure out he would need surgery? Now Jordan would be shouldering more of the load at a point in his career that it would be more difficult. Tex respected Michael's motivation to take on a task, but he was equally chagrined that the organization had allowed Scottie's medical situation to languish. It would certainly stretch the team.

Rodman was becoming a real pain, obviously more focused on the trappings of fame than playing basketball. His pronouncements were getting more play in the media and were only exacerbating the situation. There was Dennis on the future of the Bulls; Dennis on the merits of professional wrestling. Then, after a miserable defeat in Atlanta, there was Dennis on personal motivation. He told reporters, "The interest level is just not there. I'm all right physically, but mentally I'm just not into it. I'm going through the motions right now. If I can't get into it mentally, maybe I need to do something else."

Jordan, himself struggling to play with nagging injuries, was quick to respond through the media. "If that's the case, go home. If you're not into it, you don't need to be out there. Step aside and let someone else get in there and get the rhythm."

Michael pretty much summed up how Tex felt about the situation. In the old school, Rodman would have been due for a good benching. But Tex knew Dennis couldn't ignore Michael Jordan. That was the way things worked with the Chicago Bulls. You didn't mess with Michael and when he had words for you, you listened. Rodman had a good thing going with the Bulls. Part of the good thing was playing alongside Jordan, who provided sufficient spotlight for both of them. Dennis enjoyed following Michael onto the floor before games, both to bask in the glow and affirm a leadership position in the player hierarchy. For the moment at least, Jordan's comments had the desired effect on Rodman. The following night against New Jersey, he seemed his former self.

But the Rodman distractions continued. Prior to the team's western road trip, he flew to Oakland for a Rolling Stones concert, followed by a gambling spree in Las Vegas. During most of his career, Dennis had an uncanny ability to cover his excesses, but this time he came up short. He missed a wide open layup at the end of a game with the Phoenix Suns, costing the Bulls the game. It came at a bad time. In addition to the absence of Scottie Pippen, the Bulls were without Steve Kerr, who was also out with an injury. Jordan was struggling with his shooting and the Bulls offense was sputtering.

Despite the advice of Jackson, Jerry Krause had chosen to accompany the team on its western swing, further adding to the pressure the team was feeling. Each year, Krause used an extended road trip to evaluate the team and complete a strategy before the February trading deadline. Tex could see the stress building in Phil as Jerry extended himself into the coach's domain. Phil had asked Scottie Pippen to accompany the team in the hopes of working him in during practice time. Tex could see the handwriting on the wall, bracing himself for what he now knew would be a miserable trip. The signs were all there — an opening loss, a lame-duck coach, Rodman, Krause, a struggling Jordan and an unhappy Pippen — and the West Coast media lying in wait.

Pippen used the media to vent his anger and send a message to management — attention Jerry Krause. Pippen was hurt that the Bulls had reportedly shopped him around during the off-season, adding to his sense of being under-appreciated. He was further annoyed that Krause sent him a letter over the summer threatening to fine him if he played in his charity basketball game. Pippen told reporters he wanted to be traded, that he was tired of how he'd been treated and he didn't want to represent

Jerry Krause. He further intimated he might be healthy enough to play, but wouldn't come back to the Bulls.

Pippen was in a strong position tactically because the Bulls were obviously struggling without him. Such talk would surely bug Krause; Pippen's market value would not be re-established until he returned to the lineup and demonstrated he was his old self. If he refused, the Bulls would be stuck. The story was soon reported nationwide.

Tex saw the pot coming to a boil. There was an argument in the training room prior to the Sacramento game. Somehow Jordan, Pippen and Krause had been talking about draft choices and wound up yelling at each other. Tex was always amazed at how these rows started. This time it had been something about Jerry's drafting of Earl Monroe 20 years ago. The discussion had moved to Krause's drafting of Pippen, another event for which credit had naturally been attributed to him. Then the shouting started. It was becoming increasingly obvious how deeply the ill will was running.

Alcohol joined the mix on the flight to Seattle, setting the stage for the ugliest scene in Tex's tenure with the Bulls. Tex had always lobbied for personal discipline on the team and he viewed alcohol use as job one. He knew the players' room at Berto Center was always well stocked and he questioned why alcohol was necessary at a practice facility. Its overuse led to tired players. In addition, players said some truly ignorant things while under its influence. Being the players' coach that he was, Jackson maintained the players were adults and moderate drinking was a way to relax and blow off steam.

After the flight to Seattle, the entourage split onto two buses to head for the hotel; one for players and coaches, the other for media and staff. Jerry Krause opted for the team bus. Few NBA general managers traveled with their teams; it was more of a tradition in baseball, where Krause spent his formative years. He felt it was his right to be with the team when he chose to be and he resented inferences that he was not welcome. As he did on a bus ride in Utah in 1997, Jordan used the opportunity to belittle Krause — few were better at it. Jordan had plenty of experience jawing with opponents and teammates and Krause was no match for Jordan's taunting — especially with his teammates egging him on and enjoying the show.

Tex found such behavior embarrassing and he sometimes signaled Phil to put an end to it. Phil usually let it go, in hopes Jerry would take the hint and allow the players more privacy. Tex was impressed with Jerry's ability to take a verbal jab, along with his gallant, though often ineffective attempts to counterpunch.

"Bus Ride in Seattle" was all Scottie Pippen, all the time. Emboldened by drink, Pippen unloaded on Krause, mercilessly riding the G.M. and venting his pent-up anger. He demanded to be traded.

At one point, Jackson held up a beer bottle to signal Pippen that he was letting the alcohol do his talking. To some, he appeared to be toasting Pippen's efforts.

Tex was sickened by the scene. How had the world champions sunk so low?

Again, affirming Tex's accolade that Jackson was a master of handling distractions, Phil was at his best in controlling the damage from the incident. Admitting Pippen's behavior was "over the edge," he was nonetheless determined to bring Pippen back into the fold. He arranged for the team psychologist to work with Pippen on his anger. When his personal discussions with Scottie failed to bring him around, he publicly expressed his feelings about the situation. He told the press neither he nor Jordan would have returned for the season without Scottie and they were both feeling betrayed. After all, it was Scottie who asked Michael to come back in '95 to help him carry the load. Now it seemed Scottie was unfairly leaving Michael to shoulder the burden.

Immediately after his 500th coaching win, Jackson chose to share the credit with the entire Bulls' organization. "It's a great success story. A lot happened in this organization that clicked: the players, ownership, general manager. Motivation isn't something you teach players. They have to bring that themselves. This organization, Jerry Krause and this staff, have found players who have that kind of motivation."

Jackson went on to downplay his feud with management, saying his leaving after the season was a mutual decision. Tex was proud of his boss, feeling he had chosen the high road in a situation that had been careening out of control.

Jordan, noting Jackson's 500th win had come faster to him than to any other coach in the NBA, was less conciliatory and continued to lobby for Jackson's return. "It's too obvious to see the guy's success in such a short amount of time to say, 'Now we need a change.' It's something deeper than what you see on the basketball court."

Tex thought it was both. To be successful in the NBA, an organization had to be effective both on and off the court. Both pieces had to fit. Tex found Phil's remarks about basketball to be right on the mark. Jackson said of the team, "The only thing they don't like is monotony and constancy. But we still make one thing constant and that's fundamentals. The one thing we always strive for is to make fundamentals and execution part of our game."

The focus on fundamentals was a unique characteristic of the Bulls. Lost amidst the hoopla and personality discussions was a simple truth — the Bulls were a team that fixated, more than any other team in the NBA, on fundamentals. Too many teams simply assumed their players to be fundamentally sound, or considered fundamentals to be an individual responsibility. Not so with the Bulls, where fundamental development was primary. Players were assessed and individual training plans maintained. If there was something you couldn't do, you were expected to learn. Fundamentals were largely Tex Winters' domain and he saw it as his job to keep the "fun" in fundamentals.

Fundamentals kept the Bulls winning, even on an emotional roller coaster. Sound fundamentals were the glue that kept the team executing even when the wheels seemed to be coming off the organization. With the prospect of Pippen's return, they were 24-10. A humiliating defeat to Pat Riley's Miami Heat reminded them that they were still a vulnerable team without Pippen. After a first quarter lead, the Bulls were routed, losing 99-72. Jackson never liked losing to Riley.

A couple days later, with the Bulls in New York to play the Knicks, Jackson mentioned he would take a year off before coaching again. His comment was quickly combined with Jordan's offering that he would "love to play in New York."

With Jackson's New York Knick roots and Jordan's affection for Madison Square Garden, the comments fanned the flames of speculation that the two could be reunited in the Big Apple. A real possibility, or just a ploy to keep Jerry Krause on his toes?

The issue was overshadowed when Scottie Pippen returned to the lineup the following evening to an enthusiastic welcome from the hometown crowd. He played over half of the game and scored 14 points. It was obvious his presence gave the team a needed boost as they rolled over Golden State, 87-72. Pippen answered a barrage of questions after the game, the upshot of which was that he had decided to play out the season regardless of his problems with management. But with the trade deadline still more than a month away, his immediate future with the Bulls remained in doubt.

The following week, Dennis Rodman decided to steal the limelight. Seen partying til the wee hours at a New York strip club, Dennis was absent from a pregame practice the following day. Jackson immediately sent him back to Chicago with a one-game suspension. He would rejoin the team for its big home game against the Utah Jazz, when the Bulls would be defending a 17-game home winning streak.

Even with Rodman, Pippen and home-court advantage, the Bulls didn't have enough for the Jazz, who pulled away with a 101-94 win. The Jazz looked like a team on a mission — the Bulls had the feel of ancient Rome, in the process of falling. With their tails between their legs, they headed out on a six-game road trip to the West Coast, a trip that would include a rematch with the Utah Jazz.


With a very odd sense of timing, Krause used the opportunity to unburden himself to *Chicago Tribune* reporter Fred Mitchell. Many of the issues discussed could have waited until the end of the season for resolution. It had always been part of the Krause-Reinsdorf philosophy to leave doors open and make decisions when the time was right. Krause's comments, therefore, seemed to imply the decisions already had been made. Michael Jordan, for one, would assume the comments had the approval of Jerry Reinsdorf. Reinsdorf, angry with Krause for creating another controversy, would later indicate they did not.

Krause made it clear Phil Jackson would not return. Jackson had not wanted to be part of a rebuilding process, which it appeared the Bulls were heading for. If Michael would play for no one except Phil, that was his choice. No one was driving him out. On the other hand, it would be difficult to rebuild under the salary cap with the salary Jordan was making. "It was complicated," Krause said.

The comments created a media frenzy around the Bulls as they prepared to meet the Jazz at the Delta Center, in a game they would lose after building a 24-point lead early on. The team headed home for the All-Star break while Jordan headed to New York for the game and a highly-stoked media.

Jordan used the occasion to respond to Krause's comments. He made it clear he would love to return to the Bulls for another season with Jackson at the helm, but it appeared management had already made up its mind. It made no sense to dump Jackson while he was still having success; it made no sense from a business standpoint, either. Even with a high payroll, the Bulls' value was maintained by the quality of its players, releasing them would simply reduce the value of the franchise. "I think it's more personal than anything," Jordan concluded about the situation. "They're willing to take the risk at this stage."

Tex continued to hope the situation could be resolved, counseling Phil not to close any doors. As the trading deadline neared, tensions mounted. Pippen's status remained in doubt, although it appeared he would remain — absent a serious offer from another team.

The status of other players remained questionable. Krause wanted to trade Jason Caffey to Golden State for David Vaughn and two second-round draft picks. Tex lobbied against the move, arguing the Bulls needed Caffey's rebounding abilities. To the players, the Bulls apparently were already focusing on next season. As it turned out, the Bulls waived Vaughn, then picked up Dickey Simpkins, whose ability to guard other big men was a welcome addition to the team. Again, Krause made a brilliant move. But once again, it was the way the move went down that was bothersome — with Krause and Jackson arguing about everything.

At 35-15, the team was performing well; however, Tex saw signs he thought unhealthy. Particularly irksome was a loss to the lowly Dallas Mavericks. With the Bulls up 18 points with only five minutes remaining in the game, they suffered a total meltdown. "I've seen a couple of other collapses, but none like that," Tex said of his 13 years with the Bulls. "We've had games where I've felt we've given up, where we were down and really didn't come back, more so this year than in the past."

The normally even-keeled Winter was unusually bitter about the loss — he clipped newspaper articles of the debacle, producing them whenever the Bulls' heads got too big. Trying to put the best face on the situation, Tex concluded, "In the long term, it'll be good for us."

Dennis Rodman put his own spin on the situation. "What can we learn that we don't already know?"

*The coaches who enjoy life are those who have remained young at heart, have faith in God, have cultivated a sense of humor, have learned to like people and to get along harmoniously and pleasantly with them.*

*— Tex Winter, The Triple-Post Offense, 1962*

# Chapter Fifteen
# Last Tango in Utah

By the spring of 1998, Tex Winter was getting a reputation as a worrier and he didn't like it. There was a difference between worrying and having a realistic view of yourself and your opponents. A worrier is fearful, sees only the negatives and is anxious about the future. Tex wasn't any of those things; he slept like a rock at night and shared plenty of laughs during the day. But he did find the Bulls a bit enamored of themselves, a bit proud of their achievements. Therein lay the seeds of their demise. If they weren't careful, Tex thought, they would be ambushed in the playoffs.

The collapse against the Dallas Mavericks and Dennis Rodman's smart-aleck comments afterward still bothered Tex. The Bulls had also failed to close out the Utah Jazz for home-court advantage, losing their last two regular-season games of the 1997-98 season. Both losses further rankled Tex. Larry Bird's Indiana Pacers had upset them at the United Center, giving the Pacers a jolt of confidence as they headed into the playoffs. Then the Bulls lost their final game of the season in Detroit. The loss put them in a regular season tie with the Jazz, who would carry home-court advantage throughout the playoffs, since Utah defeated the Bulls twice during the year.

Tex saw the Bulls playing in spurts, often losing discipline in offensive execution, then being forced to score their way out of holes. Part of this inconsistency could be contributed to aging players whose energy was more finite. But part of it was just plain brinkmanship. A "high-wire act," he called it — a dangerous way to play basketball. Ever the systems man, Tex could not find the logic of unnecessarily flirting with danger when disciplined play would more surely carry the day.

He saw the problem played out in the Bulls' opening playoff series with the New Jersey Nets. The Nets were a young, inexperienced team, yet they overcame a large deficit in Game One to take the Bulls to overtime. Only Jordan's heroics at the end of overtime secured the win. Though the Bulls went on to win the series in three games, their play was spotty throughout and they almost lost Game Two in a fourth-quarter lapse.

The distractions continued. Not only had the Bulls' difficulties with the Nets raised the issue of their stamina and focus in the news media, but Phil Jackson's diary had wound up there as well. Jackson had kept the diary throughout the season, chronicling his problems with management. The insights were personal; the intent was to edit them later for a book. Instead, the diary was published in *ESPN Magazine*, essentially raw, showing an egotistical side of Phil Jackson the public had not seen previously. Jackson seemed to be gunning for a coaching job with either the Knicks or Lakers; his negative comments about Jerry Krause further exacerbated the lack of trust between the two men.

Jackson was skewered in the media. He was accused of holding Jordan hostage to his own career in Chicago and seeking the demise of the Bulls' organization by counseling Jordan to retire.

Once again, Tex found himself caught in the middle between two friends. Krause was justifiably angry, Jackson despondent — and Tex was the only conduit between the two. It called for high-order damage control and a limited objective — keeping the team on a winning track and not derailing all the hard work that had gone before. Tex agreed with Jerry that Phil's diary had been a terrible mistake; he suggested that Phil had never wanted his inner thoughts published in unedited form. It was obvious the two would not be able to reconcile. With Phil, he tried to keep the focus on basketball. After all, running a basketball team was what they did best. The best solace would be winning.

The Bulls split the first two games in their series with the Charlotte

Hornets, winning the first game easily. However, they appeared unfocused and over-confident in losing the second. B.J. Armstrong, whom the Bulls had let go in the '95 expansion draft, had a big fourth quarter and appeared to delight in defeating his former teammates. Tex agreed with Jackson's assessment of the situation — the Bulls were just going through the motions.

Following the loss, team owner Jerry Reinsdorf was interviewed for *The Chicago Tribune* and indicated he wanted to bring the team back if they won the championship. That was the good news. The bad news was Reinsdorf put responsibility for the probability of a break-up squarely on Phil Jackson's shoulders. The comments created a flurry of responses from Jackson and his agent, as well as Jordan and Pippen — the upshot was that with the Bulls struggling, the comments were poorly timed.

For Reinsdorf's part, he defended the remarks and their timing because he feared "the world was getting the wrong impression." Indeed the world, particularly the world in Chicago, was dealing with myriads of impressions. Accounts of circumstances and forecasts for the future varied widely as a blood-hungry media searched for answers. Fortunately, as if on cue, the team responded to the mayhem, taking out its frustrations on the basketball court and sweeping the remainder of the series. It was the Hornets who cracked. The sight of the Hornets Anthony Mason jawing with his coach, Dave Cowens, was a not-too-subtle reminder that losing brings its own special tribulations.

Indiana was a difficult opponent. They were younger than the Bulls and the team had more depth. With Larry Bird as their coach, they had added an intangible. As a player, Bird had been the ultimate competitor — stalwart, determined and tricky. Slow of foot and with mediocre jumping ability, Bird had great hands and eyes and a knack for finding a way to win. His game looked very much like a throwback to an earlier era, but it had merged brilliantly with the high-flying routines of the contemporary NBA.

Bird was a disciplinarian. He imposed heavy fines for tardiness and insisted his players maintain themselves in peak physical condition. He also had an eye for talent. For instance, he was developing the skills of

Jalen Rose, who had been little more than a cast-off in previous regimes, but whose play was now reaping huge dividends. The Pacers had an excellent point guard in Mark Jackson, a solid big man in the Dutchman Rik Smits and a big scoring threat in Reggie Miller — the emotional leader and heart and soul of the team.

> **"Bird was one of the smartest players ever. He didn't let his ego get in the way. He made his teammates better."**

The Bulls' defense was the deciding factor in Games 1 and 2 of the series, played at home at the United Center. The Bulls shot pathetically in the first half of Game One, with Jordan, Pippen and Kukoc combining for a measly three for 25 shooting. It was defense that kept them in the game, with Pippen swarming all over Mark Jackson and Harper methodically limiting Reggie Miller. Jackson, who normally maintained a four-to-one assist to turnover ratio, had seven turnovers and only six assists. The Bulls prevailed in an ugly one, 85-79.

Pippen's defensive heroics continued in Game Two with five steals. But this time, the offense was in sync with both Jordan and Kukoc finding the range. Jordan was awarded the league MVP title just prior to game time and he played up to it, scoring 41 points and hitting key baskets down the stretch.

In spite of the two wins, all was not well in Camelot. Dennis Rodman was sulking, peeved that he had not started in the two games. He took to riding an exercise bike when not on the floor, ostensibly to stay loose. The new hobby bothered Phil Jackson, who had to send someone to fetch his star rebounder when his services were requested. Rodman played about half of Game Two, netting only two points and six rebounds.

Jerry Krause and Michael Jordan had words after the game, reportedly about statements attributed to Michael in *New Yorker* magazine. The quotes were over a year old, but they still carried the power to create tension between the two men.

Larry Bird used the media to suggest Pippen was getting away with too much in his continued harassment of Mark Jackson, suggesting such tactics would never be tolerated were the ball handler the great Michael Jordan.

Finally, on the team flight to Indianapolis for Game Three, Krause lit into Phil Jackson for allowing the team to skip a mandatory media event before leaving town. The absence cost the Bulls $50,000. Krause took it as a direct slap at the organization from a coach who was on his way out. The incident began in front of the entire team and continued down the steps of the plane and onto the tarmac.

Despite the pair of wins, the series of incidents made for bad karma. Early in Game Three, it became apparent Bird's carping would pay dividends when Pippen was called for ticky-tacky fouls while blanketing Mark Jackson. When Pippen backed off, the Pacer offense began to jell. Further, Bird began calling on his bench, giving his younger and quicker backups a chance to strut their stuff. Jalen Rose in particular gave the Bulls trouble. At 6'8", he was an oversize guard who matched up well with Jordan. Bird used a combination of defenders to wear Jordan down and the Pacer defense became more physical. The Pacers won by a basket, 107-105.

Tex thought it important that the Bulls run the triangle in more disciplined fashion. The Pacers were running more and younger players at the Bulls, so it was essential that Michael and Scottie conserve energy for crunch time when their winning experience would be critical. The Pacers were capitalizing at the end of quarters, taking advantage of the Bulls' fatigue. The end of quarters had traditionally belonged to the Bulls, when they would bury their opponents. Now the tables were turned. In a rare moment of pessimism, Phil Jackson told the press he thought the Bulls' dynasty had run its course, that it was the end of a basketball team that "had a great run."

Game Four was a memorable battle, the signature game of the series. Tex spent much of the game pointing out to the refs the illegal screens the

Pacers were setting on Ron Harper to free up Reggie Miller. Ironically, it was an illegal screen call on Dennis Rodman with 33 seconds left in the game that was decisive. It was the only illegal pick call of the game and it gave the Pacers the ball only a point down.

The Bulls defense stiffened. Scottie Pippen intercepted a pass and was fouled with 4.7 seconds left. Tempers flared and it appeared the Pacers' Reggie Miller took a swing at Ron Harper, an incident the refs chose to overlook. Pippen missed both free throws. After the second shot, the ball was tipped out of bounds. One ref signaled jump ball, but was overruled and the possession went to the Pacers.

The Pacers in-bounded the ball at half-court with 2.9 seconds remaining. Reggie Miller came off yet another down screen, gave Jordan a hard shove to get open, caught the ball and cleanly drilled a three-pointer. When Jordan's desperation heave with .7 seconds rolled out, the Pacers had evened the series.

Feeling that Bird's whining about the officiating was obviously paying off, Jackson did some whining of his own, likening the Game Four officiating to the U.S.-Soviet game in the '72 Olympics. He was fined by the league. As bad as the officiating seemed to be, it couldn't mask the fact that Pippen shot two for seven from the free-throw line and that the Bulls were playing tired basketball.

The teams split games five and six; the Bulls winning in a blow-out at the United Center and falling just short in Indianapolis, 92-89.

The Bulls quickly fell 13 points behind in Game Seven at the United Center. It certainly looked like the end of an era. Then Jackson went to his bench — something he had done sparingly throughout the series. First it was Rodman for Kukoc and the lead was soon halved on Dennis' energy. Then Kerr and the journeyman Buechler were added and by half-time, the Bulls owned a three-point lead.

In the third quarter, Kukoc picked up the scoring slack from an ineffective Jordan, whose shots were not falling. Kukoc had a perfect third quarter, including three three-pointers.

The Bulls struggled through the fourth period. Jordan continued missing shots, despite a lengthy rest. The Pacers were hammering him every time he drove to the basket, hoping to wear him down with punishment. The Bulls clung to the slimmest of leads throughout the final quarter. With four minutes left, Bird reinserted his starters, who appeared rested and ready for the final push. The Bulls' starters appeared spent. The championship was there for the taking.

The Bulls simply took it. The Pacers looked as if they didn't know how. After almost seven games of contesting, it was as if they forgot how to play. The Bulls beat them at every critical juncture down the stretch, despite their obvious fatigue. Jordan, his shot ineffective, drove to the basket again and again, hitting his free throws when fouled. The teams performed like two spent fighters — playing on instinct; trying to survive. In the end, the Bulls' instincts were sounder and they did what they had to do to win.

The final minutes of the battle with the Pacers made a powerful film clip for Phil Jackson to show the team as they prepared for the 1998 Finals with the Utah Jazz. The Bulls were underdogs and would play the final series without their traditional home-court advantage. Beating the Jazz would take the same kind of effort that had beaten the Pacers.

---

**"We played to win. The Pacers played to keep from losing."**

---

Tex saw in the Jazz a mature team that made few mental mistakes and would not beat itself. The Jazz had breezed through the Western Conference Championship, humbling the younger, more physically gifted Los Angeles Lakers in four games. They enjoyed a well-deserved 10-day rest leading up to the Finals with the Bulls.

The key to the Jazz, Tex correctly surmised, was the discipline in their offense, which featured the two-man attack of Stockton and Malone.

Stockton was an excellent point guard, blessed with huge hands and an uncanny ability to feed the ball to Malone. At 6'9", 256 pounds, Malone was a physical presence with great inside moves and a soft shooting touch. The discipline in their offense, while a plus, also made them somewhat predictable. Tex looked for illegal screens, especially back picks, with Stockton hitting people from behind. "The Baby-faced Assassin" Tex called him, because he looked so innocent while his court play was deadly. The key to containing Utah was pressuring and containing Stockton. Control Stockton and you controlled Malone.

Tex predicted Longley would have difficulty containing Malone without getting into foul trouble and recommended Dennis Rodman be given the defensive task. When Rodman bridled at the job of guarding someone with a 40-pound weight advantage, Tex gently reminded Dennis that it was his unique ability to handle the big guys that made him so valuable.

The Bulls hoped to steal Game One from the well-rested Jazz and they almost succeeded. The defensive tandems the Bulls threw at Malone seemed to throw off his game, although Stockton's individual heroics more than made up for it. Time and again, Stockton beat the Bulls' defenders to the basket. The Bulls seemed to struggle against both the fatigue of the Indiana series and the thin air of the Rockies, yet finally managed to tie the game on two Pippen free throws and a cool Longley jumper with seconds remaining in the game. They lost in the final moments of overtime, with John Stockton again carrying the load, hitting a pull-up jumper after putting a move on Steve Kerr.

The Bulls came back to the triangle in Game Two, spreading the offense and cutting to the basket for easy shots. "The first half was fine," Tex recalled. "We followed through on our principles a lot better. We got a lot of cutting to the basket and Michael gave up the ball, he was looking to feed cutters."

The second half was not so pretty. "We abandoned it," Tex said. "We tried to go one-on-one. Michael forced a lot of things."

Jordan had indeed begun driving to the basket, but unlike the final game against Indiana where he got the home-court calls, at the Delta Center he found the calls going the other way. With less than two minutes to go, the Jazz took the lead, 86-85.

With the score knotted at 88, Steve Kerr missed a transition three-pointer, got his own rebound and flipped the ball inside to Jordan who made the basket and was fouled. The Bulls went on to win, 93-88. Despite Jordan's less than Jordanesque play, in the fourth quarter he made four field goals and five of six free throws. Malone shot five of 16 on the game and did not make a basket in the second half.

It appeared the entire team caught the confidence in Game Three, when the Bulls went on a rampage at the United Center. Though Malone got off to a hot start, hitting his first six shots, the Bulls took over the game in the second quarter and never looked back. The final score, 96-54, was the largest margin of victory in the history of the NBA Finals. Utah's 54 points was the lowest ever scored by an NBA team since the advent of the shot clock.

Tex's minor criticism about the Jazz offense being predictable had proven prophetic. The Bulls seemed to know where the ball was going before the Jazz did. Pippen and Harper were all over the Jazz guards — harassing, trapping and denying the passing lanes. The Jazz committed 26 turnovers and were soundly outhustled and beaten on the boards. Jazz coach Jerry Sloan said he was "embarrassed" for the NBA.

It was unexpected from a Jerry Sloan team — and therein lay what Tex saw as a problem for the Bulls. "Basketball history is replete with teams coming back from blow-outs with renewed energy," Tex said. "There was a classic example in the old Laker-Celtic rivalry. Good teams will respond to a shellacking in a big way and human nature usually causes a bit of a let-up in the team that feels it has already proven itself."

Tex was especially peeved that Dennis Rodman skipped practice between games to appear as "Rodzilla" in an out-of-town professional wrestling event. When Tex questioned the off-the-wall forward about the logic of missing practice and risking injury, Dennis explained it was a business decision. Though he was fined $10,000 for his absence, he netted a quarter-million for the appearance.

As usual, Phil Jackson took the absence in stride and Tex was relieved Dennis at least got in some free-throw practice. He felt that Dennis would be the logical target to be fouled with the game on the line.

Sure enough, Game Four saw a different Jazz than the patsies of Game Three. The game came down to Rodman free throws. In the timeout called to ice the unpredictable Rodman, Tex told him, "Shoot the way we shoot 'em in practice. You know how to shoot in practice. Shoot the same shot."

A lot rode on those free throws for Dennis Rodman and the Chicago Bulls. Miss them and Rodman would have been the goat of the game and possibly the series. His wrestling indiscretion would have been touted as the reason for the Bulls' loss, sinking them to two and two in the series. As it was, Dennis canned all four of his free throws in the last two minutes of the game, providing the Bulls' margin of victory in an 86-82 win. Dennis was a hero.

The letdown Tex feared came in Game Five. The distractions leading up to the game were legion and Tex didn't see the team handling them particularly well. There was too much talk of champagne and early celebrating and laughs about their luck in the series to date. Chicago was gearing up for riots after the game; it took most of the team an extra 90 minutes just to get to the United Center. Plus, Tex reasoned, it was harder than anyone thought to beat a team like the Jazz in four straight games. Sloan would have them ready. He would make the adjustments.

Tex's thinking proved prophetic — the Bulls weren't focused on doing what they had to do to win. Jordan and Pippen had horrendous shooting problems. And worse, Karl Malone finally broke out of his slump, scoring 39 as the Jazz pulled out a squeaker, 83-81.

The city suffered a tremendous letdown; the momentum shift was palpable. Whereas the Bulls had the Jazz on the ropes on their home court, now the series shifted to the Delta Center for the deciding game or games. Commentators who had written off the Jazz now saw the series in a whole new light. One more loss and it would be the Bulls who were on the ropes.

The situation was not helped when Harper and Pippen missed the game day shoot-around; Harper because of a stomach virus and Pippen with back spasms. A lesser team might have folded.

Tex, like everyone else associated with the organization, fought to keep his emotions in check, wondering if the best shot at the championship might have already passed the team by. He saw a lot of leadership in Jackson and Jordan, both of whom remained calm and in control. They even put on a little show for Pippen, Phil asking Michael if he could go the full 48 minutes while Scottie was being worked on the training table. Normally, a player in Pippen's condition would not be expected to play. Pippen played anyway; certainly not as well as he would have in perfect health, but his mere presence would inspire others.

As it turned out, he gave just enough. Pippen ran the offense in the second half, assisting Jordan, who scored 45 points, including the picturesque game-winning jump shot. The Bulls triumphed, 87-86.

It had been a near thing, Tex thought on the plane ride home. The game turned on a trifle as he had seen so many times before. Despite the merrymaking, Tex Winter sensed he was experiencing the end of an era.

*Often we are inclined to blame our environment or our particular situation for our failures and unhappiness when actually we should be pointing the finger at ourselves. Chances are that we would be just as unhappy in any environment, for, as has often been said, happiness is a state of mind.*

**Tex Winter, *The Triple-Post Offense*, 1962**

# CHAPTER SIXTEEN
# ESCAPE TO L.A.

There almost was no 1999 NBA season. The players were locked-out from July of 1998; an ugly spate of collective bargaining rounds took place throughout the summer and fall months. As late as December, NBA Commissioner David Stern said it was "more likely than not there won't be an NBA season." Only the last minute impetus of a winter without basketball brought the two sides together in the first week of January.

The agreement spans seven years, with the players' salaries to account for 55 percent of annual revenues in the fourth through sixth years. Essentially, the league got what it wanted — salary caps. Maximum salaries were limited to $9 million for players with up to five years experience; salaries cap-out at $14 million for players with ten or more years experience. Performance incentives were limited to 25 percent of a contract's value. Provisions were made for longer suspensions and higher fines for player misconduct. All players would be drug-tested once per season, and marijuana and steroids were added to the list of banned substances.

With only ten days between the signing of the agreement and the start of training camp, teams had little time to sign players and plot strategy. Central to the effort was a single question — "What would Michael Jordan do?"

He was out of the country. He would turn 36 in February. But the collective-bargaining agreement grandfathered current players, allowing teams to pay 105 percent of a previous year's salary. In Jordan's case that would be $34.7 million for a full season, or about $22 million for the shortened season of 50 games. Of course Michael Jordan hardly needed the money. But then maybe he could be enticed to play the shortened season, maybe that was what he wanted all along.

The Bulls offered Phil Jackson his coaching job back. He declined.

On January 13, 1999, at a press conference at Berto Center, Michael Jordan announced his retirement. He paid tribute to Tex Winter, attributing the development of his mental skills to Tex's critiques of his "game" in a way that became a driving force in his quest for excellence. The cameras caught Tex and Michael embracing after the announcement.

On January 16, the Bulls announced Tim Floyd as their new head coach. He would be the fourth Bulls coach of the Winter era. Tim Floyd grew up around basketball, his father coached at Southern Mississippi for 14 years; Tim was a walk-on player there before taking a scholarship at Louisiana Tech. He coached 12 years in the college ranks, compiling a respectable 243-130 record. There was one problem—Tim Floyd had never coached or played in the NBA. He would rely on Tex Winter to "help him with his knowledge of the league and the players in the league."

With the loss of Jordan, the players were changing rapidly. Pippen went to the Houston Rockets; Rodman to the Los Angeles Lakers; Longley to the Phoenix Suns; Kerr to the San Antonio Spurs; Buechler to the Detroit Pistons. There wasn't a whole lot left. The Bulls were faced with what amounted to an 80 percent turnover rate.

The only returning starter was Harper, a role player with bad knees who would celebrate his 35th birthday three days into training camp. Kukoc was back, the lone hope for a scoring capability. Randy Brown, Bill Wennington and Dickey Simpkins had worked with the triangle before and knew what was going on. Much of the rest of the roster did not — and it was Tex's job to teach them, as well as help identify those who could — and couldn't — quickly master the triangle. "We exposed them to an awful lot of basketball in a very short period of time," said Tex. "We did that purposely because we want to see who can respond to an over-load, who learns quickly and picks things up fast. That's very important to us. We're not going to adjust too much to take care of individual abil-ities. We don't feel we have to do that. The system itself gives them that opportunity once they learn it."

Time was not on their side. There was only two weeks from the start of training camp to the start of the regular season. Floyd was determined to keep the triangle despite the difficulty of learning it in so short a period. He had visited Chicago while a college coach at Iowa State to discuss the basics with Tex. He continued the Bulls tradition of allowing Tex to teach the triangle, taping many of the sessions for future reference. "It's one thing to see it on the chalkboard," said Floyd, "but it's something entirely different to hear Coach Winter talk about the key teaching points as they develop on the floor."

Tex focused on the four basic passes of the triangle, realizing the option specialties would not come until the players learned the basic concepts and had internalized the principles. "It's a question of going over things — repeat, repeat, repeat." Tex said, "It's a matter of repetition until it becomes an instinctive reaction. The learning process sets its own pace. Some of the guys pick it up rapidly; others never will. I'm patient with them. At the same time, I point out mistakes because that's the only way they learn. They have to realize what they're doing wrong and make cor-rections. Those bad habits a lot of them got playing individual basketball are hard to break."

Few players had the quick learning ability Tex had enjoyed with Jordan and Pippen. In addition to Hall of Fame skills, they were both quick stud-ies of the triangle, mastering nuances with relative ease. Selling them on the unselfishness of the triangle may have been challenging, but they were fast learners. The new crop of Bulls had less time, less talent, and in most cases — less learning ability.

There were exceptions. Rusty LaRue was one of them. Like Paxson and Kerr before him, LaRue was a good shooter who had difficulty creating his own shots in the NBA. The triangle was the perfect platform for his game. In addition to incentive, LaRue had an advantage — as a college quarterback at Wake Forest, he had been able to learn what each of 11 players were doing on any particular play. That kind of thinking made picking up the triangle a lot easier. LaRue understood intuitively that it wasn't about what the individual was doing — but what the entire offense was trying to achieve.

Early in the abbreviated 1999 season, with the Bulls at 4-10, *Sports Illustrated* ran a sidebar entitled — "Old Man Winter: The architect of Chicago's triangle offense is weathering a harsh season." Citing the Bulls NBA low points scored per game, the article quoted Tex — "We knew it was going to be rough, and it has been."

Noting that the players "were honored to have Winter around," it went on to explain that when they failed to run the triangle well, "they feel as bad for Winter as they do for themselves."

It wasn't easy going from the top of the league to bottom in a matter of months. "It's got to be frustrating for him," said new team member Bret Barry in the article. "For years he's seen it run to perfection. Now he's got a bunch of guys learning it on the fly."

Tex stayed patient, enjoying his new relationship with Tim Floyd, whom he found to be a consummate professional who understood and was committed to the triangle. Losing in a town sated with winning was tough on the new coach, and Tex thought Floyd handled the situation better than most. "He came in with the reputation as a screamer," said Tex. "I think the fact he came in with that reputation has made it more important than ever to control his emotions." Tex enjoyed Floyd's sense of humor, and the two shared a lot of laughs together. It was better to laugh than cry.

As if the basketball gods were determined to completely humble the Bulls, in the second half of the season their meager talent pool was further depleted by injury. Writer Terrence Armour called the Bulls a MASH unit. Harper, Barry, Kukoc and Randy Brown hobbled in and out of the lineup. The losses piled up. In early April *Sports Illustrated* ran a sidebar called "The Gore Campaign," citing the team's "marks for futility." It was a long list. The Bucks snapped their 12-game losing streak against the Bulls. The Pistons ended a streak of 18 straight losses to the Bulls. The Raptors beat the Bulls for the first time ever. The list went on.

And the beatings continued.

On April 2, the Bulls took a 115-68 hammering from the Orlando Magic at the United Center. The 47-point loss was the largest margin of defeat in franchise history. "We had no effort and no intensity. It was a poor effort. There are no excuses," said Floyd, who immediately cancelled a scheduled day off, replacing it with practice.

Worse was to come.

A week later the Miami Heat raced to a 15-0 lead at the United Center, the Bulls missing their first 14 shots. They trailed 45-23 at halftime, and finished the game with just 49 points — the lowest point production of any team since the introduction of the shot clock. Ironically, the previous low was set by the Utah Jazz last year in their playoff loss to the Bulls. They had mustered 54 points.

As if to create even more irony, three days later the Bulls rallied to beat the Heat in Miami. Go figure.

The Bulls finished the 1999 season 13-37, the worst finish in franchise history. They averaged an NBA-worst 81.9 points per game and shot an NBA-worst 40 percent from the field.

There were bright spots.

Randy Brown, a bench warmer in years past, showed he was a bona fide NBA guard averaging nearly 10 points a game and demonstrating the kind of defensive energy the team needed.

Journeyman Mark Bryant played through injuries, leading the team in shooting percentage at 48 percent.

Ron Harper showed he could step up and lead.

Randy LaRue hit all his free throws on the season — 17 in a row.

The Bulls crappy record put them in contention for a decent draft pick.

◆  ◆  ◆

Former Bulls struggled as well.

Michael Jordan flirted with team ownership, attempting to buy 50 percent of the Charlotte Hornets from team founder George Shinn. NBA Commissioner David Stern was clearly supporting the move, both as a means of keeping Jordan involved in the league and shoring up Shinn's financial situation with the team. The Fox News Network reported Jordan would play one full year for the Hornets while his ownership shares were held in trust. Shinn was willing to give Jordan control of basketball operations, but balked when Jordan wanted more involvement on the business end. The talks broke down when Jordan pulled out of the negotiations.

Scottie Pippen signed a $67.5 million, five-year deal with the Houston Rockets. While his money numbers were up, his performance numbers were down — almost eight points a game below his career mark. "It's been a pretty tough adjustment," Pippen said. "In this offensive system it's hard to find your rhythm. I catch myself standing around more than I've done in the past." Late in the season, after a Rocket loss in which he scored only four points and was beaten repeatedly on defense, Pippen was arrested on suspicion of drunken driving. Although he upped his game for the playoffs, the Rockets lost in their first round series with the Lakers.

Dennis Rodman was waived by the Los Angeles Lakers after a seven-week experiment that began with the resignation of head coach Del Harris and ended when interim coach Kurt Rambis sent him home from practice after he showed up late and was "still searching for his shoes and socks." The incident was the last in a series of incidents in which Rodman either showed up late or failed to show at all. He frequently declined to return to games in which bench time had caused his body to stiffen. Early in the season he missed four games because of personal problems resulting from his November marriage to actress Carmen Electra. In March the couple announced they were filing for divorce. Dennis' waiver made him ineligible for the playoffs when NBA chief legal counsel Jeffrey Mishkin revealed a little-known NBA rule approved during lockout negotiations, stipulating that players waived after midnight on March 17 would be ineligible. Dennis celebrated his 38th birthday in May, 1999.

Luc Longley signed a five-year $30 million contract with the Phoenix Suns. His play was inconsistent and he struggled in the first round of the playoffs during which the Suns lost to the Portland Trailblazers.

Jud Buechler experienced increased playing time and point production after signing with the Detroit Pistons. The Pistons lost their first-round playoff series to the Atlanta Hawks.

Steve Kerr signed a five-year $11 million contract with the San Antonio Spurs, but suffered through a difficult season which saw his role marginalized as his production numbers dwindled. His primary job was to dump the ball into the big guys and make his defender illegal. He missed the triangle and the scoring opportunities it opened up for him. At least Steve was sitting on the right bench — he picked up his fourth NBA championship ring with the Spurs.

Phil Jackson returned to the United Center for the final game of the Bulls 1999 season and a halftime ceremony during which a banner commemorating his nine years with the Bulls was unveiled. Jackson was frequently mentioned throughout the year as the heir apparent to New York Knicks coach Jeff Van Gundy — a possibility that became increasingly remote as the Knicks continued their unlikely success in the NBA playoffs.

Despite the Bulls' woes, the 1998-99 season was one of accolades for Tex Winter. In September he was named the 25th winner of the John Bunn Award, presented by the Naismith Memorial Basketball Hall of Fame. The Bunn award is the highest honor outside of enshrinement. Tex was honored at the Hall of Fame Dinner as part of enshrinement activities in Springfield, Massachusetts, the birthplace of basketball. Previous winners of the Bunn Award include John Wooden, Henry Iba, Red Auerbach and Bob Cousy.

In March, Tex was honored at the annual National Association of Basketball Coaches awards ceremony at the Tampa Bay Performing Arts Center in conjunction with the NCAA Final Four. He was the lone recipient of the Hillyard Golden Anniversary Award for 50 years of outstanding service to the game of basketball. In his 52nd year of coaching, the association recognized Tex's coaching career as the longest tenure of any active coach in college or professional basketball.

He received his sixth NBA championship ring at pregame ceremonies at the United Center.

In May the Bulls announced that Tex would be asked back for another year. He was noncommittal when asked about it, saying it would depend on what kind of players the Bulls were able to pick up in the off-season. Though he had been patient with the 13-37 crop of Bulls, he made it clear throughout the year that he was frustrated with the situation. It was tough to lose after winning for so long. And next season would be of the 82-game variety.

On the other hand, he felt needed and had enjoyed coaching the triangle to a group that depended on his wisdom and technical know-how. He felt great chemistry with Tim Floyd and his fellow assistants Frank Hamblen, Bill Cartwright and Jim Woolridge. So it would depend on players.

**"I never coached high school ball. I regret that in a way."**

On May 22, 1999, the Bulls overcame the odds and drew the number one draft pick in the NBA lottery, a one in seven possibility. There was Jerry Krause, shirt collar askew, receiving congratulations from the Deputy Commissioner while the other G.M.s looked on in stunned silence. The Chicago Bulls were going to be picking up at least one quality player, perhaps another serendipitous inducement for the continued career of Tex Winter.

The Bulls had a month in which to decide how to use their number one pick. It was a grueling time for Floyd and Winter, with endless splicing and dicing as they analyzed the possibilities with Krause. Meanwhile the nation yawned through a five-game playoff series between the unlikely coupling of the New York Knicks and San Antonio Spurs. The series' TV rating fell to the lowest rating in eighteen years, down 40 percent from the year before. The Knicks arrival in the NBA Finals eliminated any chance Phil Jackson had of taking over the team.

He went instead to the Los Angeles Lakers. Speculation was immediate. Would Jordan come out of retirement to play for the Lakers? Could the Lakers trade for Pippen? Would Rodman return? Kerr? Buechler? B.J. Armstrong?

Meanwhile, the Bulls made Duke University's Elton Brand their number one pick. Tex supported the choice. Not only was Brand coming out of a great program, he had the physical tools to be an impact player. At 6'9" he had the wingspan and hands of a seven-footer. He ran the forty in 4.6 seconds. In a dunking drill he dunked 20 times from a standstill position. Most big men are pooped after 10. The Bulls used their second pick to strengthen their frontcourt with a forward, Ron Artest of St. John's. They were well under the salary cap, with money to burn for the free agent market. Unfortunately for the Bulls, there wasn't the kind of talent Jerry Krause had counted on. Most of the top players who might have been available had already signed long-term contracts in response to the lockout.

Tex remained under contract with the Bulls until July, 1999, technically prohibited from discussing other job opportunities with other teams. He had a friendly conversation with Phil Jackson, but the two carefully avoided the subject of Tex's future. Kobe Bryant called, asking about the triangle. He seemed genuinely interested, having fallen in love with the concept while running it in practice while preparing for the Bulls. He and fellow superstar Shaquille O'Neal had spent much of the season try-ing unsuccessfully to share the basketball, in the process relegating the Lakers to the season's most conspicuous underachievers. Shaquille O'Neal was rumored to be leaving the team — at least up until the Jackson announcement. On June 25 O'Neal announced he would stay. With O'Neal and Bryant returning, the Lakers could be a force.

Three days later Jeff Hartwig broke the U.S. pole vault record, clearing

19'9". It was a long way from Tex's best of 14'4", achieved with a bamboo pole over fifty years ago. Tex said he could still do 10 feet.

July 1st was vacation day. No longer under contract, Tex was free to talk to Phil Jackson and the Lakers. He discussed things with Jerry Krause and took off with Nancy for ten days in Greece, where Nancy went sight-seeing, while Tex — what else? — conducted basketball clinics. The two hoped to arrive at a decision while out of the country. The choices were clear: go to the Lakers, stay with the Bulls, or retire.

"Tex Winter is in a quandary," wrote Terry Armour of *The Chicago Tribune*. "Does the longtime Bulls assistant remain a part of the team's rebuilding process, which could take a number of years? Or does he pack his bags and head for Hollywood, joining Phil Jackson's Los Angeles Lakers for a shot at a seventh championship ring?"

Tex found himself in the middle of an NBA bidding war. "I feel very fortunate and very flattered to have two great franchises interested in my services," Tex told the *Trib* upon his return, "but at my age, I probably should be looking at the nursing home next door."

Tex weighed the alternatives. He told the *Sun-Times* — "The big attraction with the Lakers is that they've got the personnel who have a chance to win it all. The better the talent, the better they can execute the system. That would be an awful nice way to go out. If I didn't feel like the system could help that group, I wouldn't even be interested."

On the other hand Tex enjoyed working with Tim Floyd and was pleased with the Bulls off-season acquisitions. "The attraction with the Bulls is that I'm situated," he said. "I've been here 14 years. I feel like a Bull and I don't know whether I'm ready for a change or not. I like Chicago. But I'm not crazy about the weather. That's a plus for the other side."

Krause played his cards carefully. The Bulls were offering substantially more money and he assumed Tex would stay. He was peeved upon learning of Jackson's earlier phone call to Tex. Finally, he was pressed into a statement. "Tex and I have talked," he said, "and we'll just leave it at that until we have an announcement. There's no reason for me to go into a public thing with this. I will say that, without question, Tex is an outstanding basketball coach, a great person and a pioneer of the game who should be in the Hall of Fame. Obviously, he would be a very major loss for us."

Tex agonized. "This is the hardest basketball decision that I've ever had to make," he said, noting, "and I've made a number of difficult decisions." Like Washington, Northwestern and Long Beach State?

In mid-July, 1999, after returning from Greece and taking a few days to recover from jet lag, Tex reached a decision. It must have been a close one; Nancy wasn't sure what he would do until she found a note on the kitchen table saying he had gone to the office to tell Tim and Jerry he was leaving the Bulls. Despite their less lucrative offer, he opted to join Phil Jackson and the Los Angeles Lakers.

Tim Floyd was very understanding but there was a stormy scene with Jerry Krause, who vented his bitterness. After Tim calmed him down the two men parted as friends, though Tex felt a new, uncomfortable distance in the relationship. This was one of the difficulties of the decision; Tex clearly values his friendship with Jerry Krause.

By the same token Tex was weary — as were many of the those who had worked through the long seasons of the Bulls. Tensions had developed; perhaps a change would be healthy.

The deciding factor was the Lakers "good crack at winning the championship." Tex said he wanted to "finish up my career on a winning note if possible." It helped that Kobe Bryant had called with his questions about the triangle and Tex's philosophy of the sport. It was flattering, but it also made Tex feel like he might be welcome with the team.

Leaving the Bulls was difficult, but Tex rationalized his leaving. Tim Floyd was capable, had able assistants in Bill Cartwright and Jim Wooldridge, and had a young team that Tex felt "would be back on top soon." There was no reason they couldn't continue with the triangle if they chose to do so. "Plus," noted Lacy Banks at *The Chicago Sun-Times*, "Winter will leave his personal library. He taped many practices and some presentations on the offense, a valuable resource for Floyd."

A week later the NBA released its 1999-2000 schedule, with the Bulls and Lakers to meet on November 19 in Los Angeles. On February 15 Phil Jackson and Tex Winter would return to the United Center for a game against the Bulls.

Things happened fast in September. Tex and Nancy put their Deerfield home on the market — and Tex moved into an apartment in Los Angeles. "Tex always enjoys moving," Nancy noted gamely. The Lakers acquired A.C. Green, a Rodman-style player without the Rodman-like problems. At 36, Green had been 12 years in the league, playing in 1,028 consecutive games — a league record. He plans to become a minister upon retirement.

The Lakers also signed 35-year-old John Salley, out of the league for some three years since playing for the Bulls in 1996. Another Rodman-like player, Salley was a teammate of Dennis' with the Pistons and, along with Bill Laimbeer, one of his mentors.

As if the Lakers might not be glamorous enough already, on September 26, Laker Rick Fox and singer/actress Vanessa Williams were wed.

As for Tex, he was happy to be re-joining Phil Jackson and former Bulls assistants Jim Cleamons and Frank Hamblen, who had also signed on.

In late September the NBA's Board of Governors voted to implement several rules changes for the 1999-2000 season. Among them is a five-second rule limiting the amount of time an offensive player with his back to the basket can control the ball below the free-throw line before he must pass, shoot, or pick up his dribble. The rule will impact play of the Lakers' Shaquille O'Neal, who has made a career of butting his way to the basket. With his penchant for big men, Tex should have fun acclimating Shaq to the center-oriented triangle as well as assisting with his free-throw shooting. At a time when Ted St. Martin's web page lists his consecutive free throw mark at 5,221, O'Neal struggles to make half his attempts. Phil Jackson has not been silent on O'Neal's potential, suggesting he "ought to be the league's MVP," but that he needs to know "that Wilt won his only two titles playing the triangle, first with Alex Hannum and the 76ers and then with Bill Sharman and the Lakers. Both these coaches were teammates of Tex Winter ..."

In an October exhibition game Kobe Bryant broke his hand. Within a week the Lakers had Ron Harper, acquired from the Bulls, ready to go. With his superior knowledge of the triangle, his impact was immediate. After helping the Lakers to a first period lead against the Golden State Warriors, he re-entered the game with 4:49 left in the game and the Lakers down by 16 points. By the half, they were down only two. When Harper sat down again in the third quarter, the Lakers were up by 10. "I know the offense," Harper said later. "I know where I'm supposed to go and what I'm going to do."

Meanwhile the Bulls took on a retro look, having acquired Will Perdue and B.J. Armstrong, both veterans of the first three championships. Perdue and Armstrong brought triangle knowledge and experience. Another acquisition, 12-year veteran Hersey Hawkins was not so fortunate. "I don't know any of this stuff, " he said. "I'm still learning the system and all the plays just like the younger guys are." System yes, but plays?

Former Bulls who might have made a real difference were doing other things. Michael Jordan was getting out of the restaurant business. In October, 1999, Michael Jordan's Restaurant in Chicago became Sammy Sosa's Restaurant. Sales had slipped.

Scottie Pippen unloaded on teammate Charles Barkley who said he had been disappointed in Pippen's play. Calling Barkley "selfish" and "fat" and questioning his desire to win an NBA Championship, Pippen said he wanted to play for Jackson and get back to the system that won six championships. He was traded to Portland instead.

In an odd twist, it was reported in October that NBA Commissioner David Stern missed Dennis Rodman and that "having Rodman back wouldn't be so bad." After commenting on his hair colors, Stern acknowledged, "He added a little intrigue." In the same week Phil Jackson indicated a possible Rodman role with the Lakers, "... once we get our roles established and players get comfortable with playing under this system." He mentioned "January or February or some time in April." The idea was not welcome news to Laker players who made guarded comments or declined them altogether.

Tex Winter also made the news. *The Kansas City Star's* Kent Pulliam reported Tex had been working with Kansas State basketball coach Tom

Asbury on the triangle offense. Asbury was spotted taking in Laker work-outs in Los Angeles. "Tex doesn't think we should run it," said Asbury. "He says, 'You can't understand it; you'll never understand all the nuances unless you spend a long, long time.'" Still, it was nice to see Tex playing an advisory role with his favorite school.

The Lakers, meanwhile, struggled through the 1999 exhibition season, focusing on coming to grips with the triangle. They lost their final pre-season game, 92-76, to the Utah Jazz — with whom they were scheduled to start the season on November 2.

They needn't have worried.

Even without Kobe Bryant the Lakers dominated the Jazz, winning the opener, 91-84.

Two weeks later they hosted the Chicago Bulls, who had struggled to a 1-7 start. Tim Floyd broke the ice by presenting Tex with a shoebox full of food — Tex's time-worn method of carting home team leftovers after a ball game. The two had a nice visit, but Tex had no regrets about his decision. The Bulls were in trouble and they would be 2-25 by the end of December, and Tex was enjoying working with a team that had a chance to win. The weather in Los Angeles was a pleasant change as well.

The game itself was emblematic in the difference between the two teams. Bulls rookie Elton Brand pulled down 17 rebounds and scored 29; but Shaquille O'Neal matched his rebounds and scored 41. The Bulls kept it close, but, like the year before, lacked the firepower to compete down the stretch. The Lakers triumphed, 103-95, moving their record to 8-3.

They were 11-4 when Kobe Bryant returned, wearing a special glove to protect his right hand. He had used the time to work on his left-hand game and learn the triangle. He was a welcome addition. The Lakers took off, pushing their record to 29-5 by the middle of January. Phil Jackson was the NBA coach of the month for December. *Sports Illustrated* joined in the coronation, showcasing the red-hot Lakers in their feature article, with an action shot of Shaquille O'Neal on the cover. Suggesting the "true era of O'Neal's dominance might just be starting," Phil Taylor reeled off an impressive array of the star center's achievements as the sea-son neared the half-way point: he was leading the league in rebounds, second in scoring, and second in shooting percentage. Even his assists were up, as the triangle provided him teammates cutting to the basket. The article also quoted Philadelphia 76er coach Larry Brown calling the Lakers "the favorites to win the championship."

Tex had a much different view of the situation. While it was nice to be dominating so early in the season, the Lakers were now the victims of rising expectations. The 82-game season had not even reached the mid-way point; talk of championships was premature. Besides, the Lakers had a history of successful regular season play; this year they would be judged by their playoff performance.

He also saw the hoopla about O'Neal's play as hyperbole. Tex saw Shaq's 57.6% shooting percentage largely a result of his taking 70%-style shots. While Shaq was doing well with the triangle and was fun to be around, he could also be stubborn and self-satisfied. He did not take instruction particularly well, and seemed to resent even constructive criticism. Unlike the rest of the world, Tex saw in O'Neal a player who was only scratching the surface of his potential. It was similar to his thoughts on superstars past like Elvin Hayes and Michael Jordan, echoing the biblical advisory, "to whom much is given, much will be required."

Case in point was Shaq's free-throw shooting, which hovered around a career low 45%. Phil Jackson saw his practice regimen as a case of "reinforcing failure." While Tex saw his practice more favorably, he saw him "tensing up" in games, losing his arc, and releasing the ball off his knuckles instead of his finger tips. Knowing some of the problem was psychological, Tex devised a ritual for O'Neal, designed to keep his mind off distractions and focused on the basket. It has yet to pay dividends, and O'Neal may be the only MVP candidate who finds himself on the bench in the closing minutes of ball games — when other teams look for someone to foul.

Despite what the media widely perceived as a better relationship between O'Neal and Kobe Bryant, Tex saw the Lakers as having more fragile personality and interpersonal relationships than the Bulls of the championship years. When things got crazy in Chicago, Michael Jordan was always there to keep things under control. The Lakers lacked that kind of presence; what they had were all of the distractions that go with success in tinseltown. Kobe Bryant was launching a singing career, teaming with super model Tyra Banks for a debut song on the NBA *TeamUp Celebration 2000* TV special. His first album, "Visions," was set for release in March, 2000.

Rumors of Dennis Rodman continued to surface. He appeared on Jay Leno in January with normal hair color, sans earrings, indicating he was again ready to play basketball — for the Los Angeles Lakers. That was the plus side. The down side were his recent arrests for drunken driving and fighting with wife Carmen Electra. Tex doubted whether the Lakers fragile personality infrastructure could handle the addition of the Menace.

In mid-January Toni Kukoc surfaced as a Laker wannabe. His return to the Bulls lineup after an extended injury absence sparked a three-game winning streak — a remarkable occurrence for a team that was 2-26 at the time. Phil Jackson apparently started the speculation with remarks to *The Los Angeles Times* that "Toni could really contribute to this team, yeah. That's a legitimate-type addition to this team."

Kukoc seemed interested, intrigued by the possibility of playing for a contender. In somewhat convoluted English, Kukoc explained to *The Chicago Tribune* — "If it happens, I've got to go. It is a system that I played pretty much my whole NBA career, so I think I know — as Tex Winter would say — almost everything about it."

For the record, Tex Winter would not say that, but he appreciated what Kukoc, with his unique talents, could accomplish for the triangle in spreading the floor.

For several days there was speculation that Bulls G.M. Jerry Krause would initiate action against Phil Jackson for "attempting to entice" a player under contract.

The story was quickly overtaken by bigger news: on January 19 Michael Jordan was announced as a full partner and President of Basketball Operations for the Washington Wizards. While His Airness would not return as a player, he would be doing the hiring and firing. He also planned to practice with the team. "The best evaluation of a basketball player I can get is to look into his eyes," said Jordan, "and see how scared he is."

Phil Jackson was quick to discount scenarios where he and Tex would coach for the new executive, then highlighted the very qualities for which the two were famous. "He's going to want a system," said Jackson, "he's going to want discipline."

Tex paid a left-handed compliment to the player he coached for 13 years. "He's confident and decisive," said Tex, "once he makes up his mind he won't get confused by the facts."

Meanwhile, the Lakers soared to 31-5, on target to challenge the Bulls' record season of 72-10 in 1995.

Tex is modest about the Lakers' prospects, surprised by their accomplishments, and leery of comparisons and predictions. He tires at times, and knows the team will too. "It's a marathon," he says, "and there are a lot of hills up ahead."

Tex has gone about his business quietly, as is his manner. He has no regrets about this latest move in the nomadic saga of his life.

"It's a great opportunity," he says, "but a heck of a challenge."

He's been there before.

*Extraordinary people display calling most evidently. Perhaps that's why they fascinate. Perhaps, too, they are extraordinary because their calling comes through so clearly and they are so loyal to it. They serve as exemplars of calling and its strength, and also of keeping faith with its signals.*

*— James Hillman, from The Soul's Code — In Search of Character and Calling*

# EPILOGUE

Basketball is a trial. It's Saturday night at the Los Angeles Staples Center and the stars are out. Chris Rock, Dustin Hoffman, Jack Nicholson, Denzel Washington, Penny Marshall and 18,992 others are on hand to witness what they hope will be a successful Laker attempt to stop the bleeding.

An NBA season can sour quickly. A week ago the Lakers were the toast of the town, featured on the cover of *Sports Illustrated*. Now it appears they are simply victims of the *SI* Cover Curse.

It's been a rough week.

At 31-5 on January 14, 2000, the Lakers had their 16-game winning streak snapped by the Indiana Pacers, 111-102.

Three nights later their 14-game home win streak falls to the Seattle SuperSonics, 82-81, at the Staples Center.

Now they face Scottie Pippen and the Portland Trail Blazers, their primary division rivals for home-court advantage in the playoffs. The Blazers are loaded.

Things begin well. Shaquille O'Neal finds Ron Harper cutting to the basket for the Lakers first score, in a perfect execution of the triangle. O'Neal will have five assists in the first half alone. Harper looks remarkably fluid for a man who turned 36 two days before. Harper and Shaq co-captain the team, and they have set the tone in the opening moments. Shaq has re-dubbed himself "Dingy-Don-DaDa" before game time, a pleasant change from "Big Stock Exchange" of the week before. It is unclear to what the new moniker refers, but the previous nickname came as a result of the "big numbers" he's been putting up.

The Lakers have a big first half and lead by ten. Tex is mostly concerned with his clipboard, and providing a running commentary into the ear of Phil Jackson at his left. Kobe is dominating Pippen; he will score 28 on the game to Scottie's 15. Shaq already has 16 rebounds and is one for four from the line—his sole success a bullet line drive that defies the odds and goes in. Everything is according to plan.

The Lakers give back most of their lead at the start of the third quarter in an 11-2 Portland run. Tex is off the bench and yelling. The Lakers have abandoned the triangle. They steady themselves and begin to build a lead again.

With nine minutes left in the fourth quarter, Tex and Shaq share a laugh during a Portland timeout. It is the last time a smile will crack the Laker bench.

Shaq runs out of gas. He's dead out there. He looks like George Foreman in the fifth round of his fight with Ali. Still they leave him in. John Salley, his back-up, remains on the bench, a bemused look on his puss.

The Lakers tank, 95-91. They shoot six of 24 in the fourth quarter; Shaq scores two points with nary a rebound. Even the Laker Girls look stale.

"Sometimes we outsmart ourselves," Tex says afterwards.

Basketball is a trial.


Perhaps we are all merely products of heredity and environment. Certainly these two things account for much of who we are. But perhaps there is something else.

James Hillman, borrowing from the ancient Greeks, calls this something *daemon*. Like an acorn that foretells the oak tree, daemon is the catalyst that synthesizes our character, calls forth our genius, and makes clear our calling. According to Hillman, a biography that "sticks to the facts as closely as it can" finds "ever clearer traces of the invisible, those symptoms, serendipities, and intrusive inventions that have led, or pursued, the life the biography recounts."

We at American Biography have discussed these matters at some length. Why did Tex Winter leave Kansas State when he had the makings of a dynasty there? Why would he head for Washington University at a time when Wooden and UCLA were so dominant? And why to Northwestern where academic standards made it near impossible to compete in the Big Ten? The answer that includes the "serendipitous invisible," or fate, is that the difficult, circuitous road Tex chose led him to Chicago where he renewed acquaintance with that most difficult of personalities — Jerry Krause — who held the key to Michael Jordan and the Chicago Bulls. Life is sometimes wacky that way.

A question that particularly troubled me was — "What is the theme of the book?" I took that to mean — "What is the theme to Tex Winter's life?" Since we at American Biography look for interesting, successful lives that will inspire us, it was probably a legitimate question. Still, it made me uncomfortable. The best I could ever do with it was run down the litany of Tex's distinguishing characteristics — his frugality, technical genius, ability to put team ahead of self, and, because we had a man still performing into his late seventies — his incredible longevity.

And of course there is basketball, which led to the recurring criticism that the book has too much basketball, too much Jordan, and too much Chicago Bulls. Did the work focus enough on Tex Winter's contributions? Here too, Hillman was helpful. He reminded us of W. H. Auden's response to biographers — "The reason you want a biography of me is because of my work, so the 'I' you are searching for is in my work."

We also looked for symbolism in the triangle. The cover of Phil Jackson's book, *Sacred Hoops*, featured a basketball goal in a western setting with a superimposed circle and the subtitle— "spiritual lessons of a hardwood warrior." Certainly we could do something with the triangle. There were triangles in the pyramids; the YMCA uses a triangle to represent the connectivity of mind, spirit and body. There is the holy trinity. We were dismayed to learn Tinky-Winky sported a triangle atop his head.

In the end we found both solace and humility in another of Hillman's observations — "Maybe it takes genius to see genius."

Two days after the Lakers lose to Portland, they lose again to the Utah Jazz, this time in double overtime, 105-101. After winning 16 straight, they have now lost four of six. I ask Tex if he'll be back for another year. "Basketball has been my life," he says. "There are trials and tribulations, it's time-consuming. But there's glory and the thrill of competition. I've never emphasized winning or losing. It's giving your best and the glory of competition — that's what keeps me in it."

Reflecting on Tex's career got me thinking about longevity, both in terms of life span and career. I was continually astounded with the fact that Tex was willing and able to cope with the rigors of the NBA at the age of 77. My military career had ended in the Army's youth movement when I was 47. Yet Tex was still relevant. And there are few places on the planet more unforgiving of irrelevancy than the NBA.

I was reminded of Jimmy Carter's comments on *Hardball* at Tex and Nancy's house back in the fall of '98. I borrowed a copy of *The Virtues of Aging* from a local library. It was full of interesting statistics about the ever-extending vigor of the human species. We're increasing life expectancy by seven hours with each passing day. For every week we live, we get an extra two days as an added bonus.

And when are we old?

The surveys say age 73.

But Carter makes a compelling case that we're only old when we think we are — "when we accept an attitude of dormancy, dependence on others, a substantial limitation on our physical and mental activity, and restrictions on the number of people with whom we interact."

The Lakers have finished what seems an endless regimen of stretches in preparation for today's practice. I suppose when you consider what a muscle pull could cost the franchise, they figure the time spent is a worthwhile investment. Glen Rice, the Lakers' hot shooting forward, is reportedly making $14 million this year. Lord knows what Shaq and Kobe are making.

The players grab jump ropes and begin skipping. They are supremely conditioned athletes, gifted, taller and more muscular than the rest of us, and they execute the task with grace and aplomb. Some of them could have been prize fighters.

Tex picks up a rope and joins in. He begins slowly, then quickly climbs to warp speed. The players ignore him at first, but he keeps jumping, changing steps now, revving the tempo with apparent ease. "Show off!" Phil Jackson yells from across the gym.

Tex slows to a Texas two-step, then revs her up again, whipping the rope while he shifts through a medley of jigs. It's an absurd sight, and the players stop to take it in, not sure how to respond. Shaq smiles, and the team erupts in amusement and laughter.

A minute later, Coach Winter is pitching them a lesson on footwork.